Praise for *Leveling the Learning Curve*

"The connection between digital education and international development is crucial but often overlooked. This book explores key ways universities can make an impact beyond their gates."

> —Jendayi Frazer, Former US Assistant Secretary of State for African Affairs

"By focusing on connectivity and inclusivity, *Leveling the Learning Curve* shows us how universities can dramatically extend their contributions across what previously were considered barriers"

> —Stephen Goldsmith, Professor, Harvard University, Former Mayor, Indianapolis, and Former Deputy Mayor, NYC

"Fantastic examination of real-world examples of how innovative universities are using digital tools. Explores the key role that digital can play in increasing learning equity."

> —Joshua Kim, Dartmouth, Co-Author, *Learning Innovation and the Future of Higher Education*

"*Leveling the Learning Curve* provides a comprehensive assessment of how technology and innovative teaching techniques can reinvent the university classroom, providing better learning for more students in more places at a lower cost."

> —David Osborne, Author, *Reinventing Government*

LEVELING THE LEARNING CURVE

CREATING A MORE INCLUSIVE
AND CONNECTED UNIVERSITY

**WILLIAM B. EIMICKE,
SOULAYMANE KACHANI,
AND ADAM STEPAN**

COLUMBIA UNIVERSITY PRESS
NEW YORK

Columbia University Press
Publishers Since 1893
New York   Chichester, West Sussex
cup.columbia.edu

Library of Congress Cataloging-in-Publication Data
Names: Eimicke, William B., author. | Kachani, S. (Soulaymane), author. |
Stepan, Adam, author.
Title: Leveling the learning curve : creating a more inclusive
and connected university / William B. Eimicke, Soulaymane Kachani,
and Adam Stepan.
Description: New York : Columbia University Press, 2023. |
Includes bibliographical references and index.
Identifiers: LCCN 2022062012 | ISBN 9780231203845 (hardback) |
ISBN 9780231555258 (ebook)
Subjects: LCSH: Internet in higher education. | Web-based Instruction—
Design. | Education, Higher—Aims and objectives. | Instructional
systems—Technological innovations.
Classification: LCC LB2395.7 .E43 2023 | DDC 378.1/7344678—
dc23/eng/20230221
LC record available at https://lccn.loc.gov/2022062012

Printed in the United States of America

Cover design: Noah Arlow
Cover image: Shutterstock

CONTENTS

LEVELING THE LEARNING CURVE

1

LEVELING THE CURVE

Higher education is at a crucial crossroads. After two years of forced emergency remote and HyFlex learning due to the COVID-19 pandemic, many universities returned to mostly in-person classes, while others embraced a new world of blended learning in which the traditional boundaries between in-person and online learning have been blurred or erased. A generation of students and faculty had a glimpse of the opportunities digital tools could provide—as well as their limitations.

The successes and failures of higher education led many to question the value of a traditional degree. Overall college enrollment in the United States from 2019 to 2022 was down 6.6 percent, or more than one million students. Enrollment in community colleges fell even more, with 16 percent fewer students today than in 2019. We believe digital tools can improve the on campus in-person educational experience and help make learning richer and more accessible. These tools can connect students and universities to the wider world and level the learning curve for students both on and off campus. These tools are not meant to substitute or replace in-person learning but to enhance it.

Digital tools can make education more equitable, and they can better support learners from underserved communities. They can also play a key role in helping universities achieve financial sustainability. To do this, university leaders must effectively navigate between the organizational structures needed to design and run fully online programs (traditional online education) and blended learning innovations designed to improve learning on campus. They must also understand how to invest wisely in different forms of digital learning while choosing which tasks to perform in-house and which services to contract to outside firms and partners.

The biggest obstacles to success are management challenges. The shift to digital learning and its integration into a new connected university creates substantial stress for faculty leaders and administrators. Most university infrastructure was created in a very different era of teaching and learning. The successful mainstreaming of digital tools into a new networked university will require strong and visionary leadership, shifts in budgeting and staffing, new incentives and support systems for content creation, new forms of delivery, and new forms of student services.

The potential payoffs for universities making these investments are huge. We can create more inspiring and effective learning experiences for students on and off campus. In the following chapters, we illustrate how investing in "digitally enhancing" on campus teaching can significantly improve student outcomes, especially for those who come to our campuses from underserved communities. These innovations can also help build new hybrid programs for nontraditional learners, creating new revenue streams for universities.

Universities around the world that had not invested in educational technologies and teaching and learning infrastructure before the pandemic are emerging from a traumatic period of "emergency Zoom teaching." Returning to in-person classroom instruction, their teachers, students, and administrators are trying to make sense of the complex and often conflicting messages from the global pandemic teaching experiment. So far, the messages are mixed. On one hand, the experiment was a failure. Students and instructors alike found Zoom teaching underwhelming. Survey after survey at these universities show widespread frustration with online learning as delivered during the pandemic. On the other hand, studies show that well-designed and well-planned digital programs received high marks. Despite the failures of Zoom University, surveys also show that students do not want to go back to the prepandemic normal (Burt 2021).

Predictions about the postpandemic university vary widely. Some see a new reality in which digital tools replace traditional classroom teaching (Govindarajan and Srivastava 2020). Others predict that frustration with poor Zoom teaching will result in a return to old-school in-person lectures and multiple-choice examinations. Based on our experiences of teaching and learning throughout the twenty-first century, we believe the pandemic supercharged what had been slow but steady progress toward a HyFlex active learning system with flipped classrooms, video case studies, team-based projects, student research and discovery, and a dramatic expansion of a wide range of guest speakers from all over the world via Zoom and other platforms.

The stakes are high. Poorly executed online and hybrid teaching programs can lead to subpar results and student disengagement. Done well, the intentional integration of digital tools provides richer and more rewarding learning experiences for both professors and students, and it can level the learning curve for both traditional and nontraditional learners alike.

The author team for this book is directly involved in teaching and learning innovations. Soulaymane Kachani, Columbia's senior vice provost, led the development and practice of our innovations before COVID and the creation of our HyFlex model, enabling us to provide the best possible education, live and online, throughout the crisis. William B. Eimicke, founding director of both the Executive Master of Public Administration (EMPA) and the executive education program at Columbia's School of International and Public Affairs (SIPA), taught nine fully online and live courses, as well as HyFlex courses, from March 2020 through the return to predominantly live teaching in the fall of 2021. Adam Stepan, director of the Picker Center Digital Education Group (PCDEG), oversees many of the projects and programs described in the following chapters, including SIPA's video and written case study collection and Columbia's exciting collaboration with the Open Society University Network (OSUN) and other international partners.

Our work for this book grew out of the groundbreaking work of Arizona State University president Michael Crow (formerly our colleague here at Columbia University), who helped advance the debate on digital tools and expanded access to high-quality education to countless students over the past two decades (Crow and Dabars 2015, 2020). We also learned from Harvard's Clayton Christensen, who helped begin mapping how digital tools affect the DNA of universities (Christensen and Eyring 2011), and the work of Northeastern University president Joseph Aoun (2017), who helped us understand the importance of connecting learning to jobs and real-life challenges. We also draw on the postpandemic work and analysis of colleagues, such as Justin Reich's (2020) study of edX and the challenges of learning at scale, Edward Maloney and Joshua Kim's (2019) study of learning innovation, and the works of NYU dean emeritus Robert Ubell (2017, 2021).

We also draw extensively from a collection of more than fifty interviews conducted in 2021 and 2022 with leaders from the worlds of higher education, EdTech, and philanthropy. These include CEOs and senior leaders from all major massive open online course (MOOC) and online program management (OPM) providers, along with directors of digital education programs at Stanford, Brown, Cornell, UPenn, Dartmouth, UC Berkeley, UCLA, UC Irvine, Georgia Tech, Rice, Arizona State University, University of Michigan, University of Washington, Purdue Global, and international organizations such as the World Bank and the United Nations. We also benefited from an extensive series of hands-on demos, in which colleagues from across a wide variety of institutions shared challenges and approaches as well as actual course websites, video classes, and collaborative online projects.

In our surveys and reviews of programs, we cast a wide net in our search for digital teaching and learning excellence. Fantastic advances and cautionary tales are to be found both in for-profit companies and nonprofit university research groups. This is to be expected. We are sharing reports from the front lines of a new type of learning that is being invented as we write. We are convinced that the future of learning will involve a new sort of mixed modality structure—with in-person seminars, prerecorded video cases, readings, and planned peer-to-peer interactions all contributing to the learning experience. Some of these will happen live, others asynchronously.

Neither of the current modalities—in-person or online—is as good yet as they can or will be. Blending in-person and remote learning is not just a question of technology and logistics; it involves the creation of new pedagogies. Different combinations of these modalities will benefit different types of learners. In this book, we attempt to present what has been proven and shown to work, both in the classroom and in the management of programs. We begin with an overview of what has happened in the past two years during the COVID pandemic and the ten years of innovation, debate, and controversy over digital tools and online learning that preceded it.

CRISIS MANAGEMENT

We begin with the forced experiment in Zoom teaching (chapter 2) during the COVID-19 pandemic and place it in the context of the ten years of digital education innovation that preceded it, which is often ignored in discussions on pandemic teaching. No time to plan . . . just Zoom! Most universities did not build on knowledge about how to teach using technology; instead they simply used Zoom to move old and outdated forms of teaching online. Many students did not like the change, mocking it as Zoom University (Blackwell 2020; Lederman 2021). Many faculty members were also suspicious of online tools (Watermeyer et al. 2020).

Yet this low level of approval contrasts with high levels of student and instructor approval for *designed digital courses*. In one study, nearly three-quarters of students reported wanting to take some of their courses fully online after the pandemic (Kelly 2021). Many other studies conclude that digital tools often deliver a richer learning experience if implemented correctly. One of the key findings of learning science is that people learn by doing. Digital tools— including well-built course websites, offline discussion forums, prerecorded content, and digital case studies—can make active and project based learning possible, both for classes that meet in person and for online/hybrid courses.

Initial reports on the benefits and shortcomings of online learning during the first months of COVID, both in K–12 and higher education, focused on how the move online was especially hard for students from less affluent backgrounds and for first-generation college-goers. This was true across the nation and around the world, and the impact of this lost learning will be felt for years to come. However, a deeper look revealed that along with this "digital divide" was a "digital dividend" that could be realized through well-developed and well-supported digital tools, which can play a crucial role in leveling the learning curve for our most vulnerable learners. By providing needed scaffolding and support, digital tools can help learners compensate for gaps in K–12 education and help students understand and master concepts needed to succeed and advance in college.

Massive open online courses (MOOCs) play a crucial role in this story. They promised to transform education during the Year of the MOOC in 2012, but they fell short. MOOCs did enable U.S. universities to apply digital tools and led to the establishment and growth of centers for teaching and learning (CTLs). One of the key findings in our review of this recent history is that these early MOOCs failed largely because they underestimated the importance of student engagement. By not investing in tools for rich peer-to-peer learning, MOOCs failed to take advantage of an important moment. This is a shortcoming that digital learning platforms are only now beginning to address.

In the immediate post-MOOC era, few schools made significant new investments in digital tools or programs, with the notable exceptions of digital programs of major public universities and executive education programs. For many others, online program management (OPM) companies such as 2U, Noodle Partners, Wiley, Pearson, and Emeritus filled the gap, providing expertise in content creation and online program marketing that schools themselves chose not to develop in-house. Some universities outsourced at an enormous cost—deals often took more than 50 percent of program revenues—while keeping the core digital know-how outside of the university.

As we survey the current landscape and the road ahead, it is clear that the core challenges are much more managerial than technical. Data on the benefits of well-designed blended courses are clear. We outline some of the key issues and decisions that managers face in implementing these programs, and we share our playbook for creating digital content based on what has worked for leading OPMs, Columbia University, and our peer institutions.

THE NEW CONNECTED UNIVERSITY

In chapter 3, we explore the potential for the new "connected university," which is being built at universities across the world as we write. We are all online learners in our normal lives. We use Google, email, and Zoom all the time for personal and professional endeavors. Until the pandemic hit, these tools were seldom used in the typical college classroom. Learning management systems (LMSs) were often used only for grading and displaying old-fashioned syllabi and PDFs. Yet students share videos constantly on TikTok, Instagram, and YouTube and visit sophisticated, content-rich, and user-friendly websites in every other area of their lives.

Studies show that students embrace blended learning models when they are offered. Residential students at institutions that range from Stanford University to the University of Central Florida and Arizona State University chose a blend of face-to-face, hybrid, and online courses when they were offered. Postpandemic surveys of students' desires show a pent-up demand for flexible course offerings and delivery methods (Burt 2021).

Digitizing content, creating flipped lectures, and producing digital cases promote content sharing. Faculty from different disciplines have much to learn from each other; creating digital assets facilitates this sharing. New tools also allow for novel forms of online collaboration between students, including the so-called social annotation of documents. When used as part of a well-designed program, these tools can enable new forms of interaction and engagement and open the door to contributions from learners who might be lost in conventional classrooms.

One of the most important discoveries of the pandemic teaching experiment is the power of guest speakers. *Appearances* by the busiest and most influential academics, government, and industry leaders are easy and virtually free from anywhere in the world via Zoom. Similarly, creating short, sharable TED talk-style video lectures is another way to enrich the classroom with professors and practitioners across different areas of study, geographies, and time zones. For the study of issues such as climate change—which requires diverse perspectives and cross-disciplinary approaches—these tools can make a major contribution to insight and innovation.

VISIONARY LEADERSHIP

Creating this new connected university is possible, but it requires strong leadership (chapter 4). One of the biggest challenges these leaders face is how to articulate the need for digital innovations and to dispel misconceptions about them. Investments in digital learning will pay huge dividends through improved student outcomes, increased student satisfaction, increased enrollment, and alumni giving. Communicating these facts to all stakeholders is key.

Resistance to digital education has historically been connected to the reduction of full-time faculty, which declined from 78 percent of all instructors at U.S. universities in 1969 to only 22 percent by 2013 (Kezar and Maxey 2013; Ubell 2021). Most of this dramatic decrease in full-time faculty positions preceded the introduction of digital tools, but these events are still connected in many people's minds. In fact, the coming digital revolution in higher education will open many new employment opportunities for faculty and academic support staff, both for creating new content and for managing new learning experiences. Leaders must also address the widespread perception that digital tools are the "lower quality" and "cheaper" alternative, a misconception connected to the history of for-profit online degree players.

Another misperception is that digital learning is purely a technical challenge of finding the best LMSs and video conference tools. These tools are necessary, but the key investment must be in professional development and creating institutional incentives for faculty to use digital tools effectively. During the pandemic, many universities focused on IT infrastructure but did not prepare faculty on how to use technology to improve learning. Leaders must also work to help their university communities understand the difference between digital enhancements for core classes on campus and the work needed to create entirely new online and hybrid programs for off campus students and lifelong learners. Both are connected, with investments in online digital enhancements for on campus learning helping to create online courses as well. Improved course design and pedagogy, better course websites, flipped course lectures, and digital case studies all support the creation of fully online versions of these courses.

Investing in the digital enhancement of courses must be seen as an investment in core university infrastructure. Leaders must encourage and incentivize participation by leading faculty in this crucial investment in higher education for the twenty-first century.

PROGRAM BUILDING

Once you have high-level buy-in and funding, the connected university must address significant questions of program management and implementation (chapters 5 and 6). Should digital transformation be managed centrally or decentralized to the school, degree, or even program level? What existing on campus units might be best positioned to lead these efforts?

The "MOOC Moment" led to the creation and growth of centers for teaching and learning (CTLs) at many leading universities (Maloney and Kim 2019). But these CTLs often focused on requested services and research rather than on designing and leading major projects. Some are now moving to become more pro-active operations, focused on the creation and delivery of digital learning experiences at scale. In the following chapters, we explore whether CTLs can evolve into in-house OPMs and discuss the skills and tools they will need to do so.

Universities need a strategic plan to go digital. Developing a state-of-the-art learning management environment is a critical first step. Core courses should be given priority for digital investments and enhancements. Financial incentives are important. And students must be involved in the process.

THE BLENDED LEARNING TOOLKIT

In chapters 7 and 8, we provide a playbook of some of the specific actions and techniques necessary to create the new connected university, including a set of tools to design courses and create content. We present this as part of a series of self-paced online courses in our "Blended Learning Toolkit" and the "Digital Case Method" MOOCs, available on edX, Coursera, and Canvas Commons platforms. These courses cover active learning by design, creating and maintaining a well-functioning LMS, making flipped lecture capture easy (including self-recording with Panopto and other green screen capture software), making "live sessions" lively, and involving students in content creation. They also provide the core training and content needed for the creation of a digital case creation unit at your university.

CREATING THE NEW CONNECTED UNIVERSITY

We conclude with examples of the connected university becoming a reality (chapter 9) and the future of digital learning going forward (chapter 10). Examples include content partnerships, networked courses, and a new role for MOOCs. The recent COVID crisis has both created the necessary conditions to realize this vision and made it imperative that we put in the work needed to see it through. The COVID pandemic, and the poorly delivered remote learning it brought to most high schools and universities around the world, has left us with a generation of learners in dire need of catching up. This moment has also opened the minds of many students and faculty to what is possible. We must reconsider the bundle of educational services each university can provide well and what services should be provided by others. Throughout, we must push for digital inclusion to provide the highest quality of education to all.

If we do all of these things, it will help make the world a much better place. That is why we wrote this book.

REFERENCES

Aoun, Joseph. 2017. *Robot-Proof: Higher Education in the Age of Artificial Intelligence*. Cambridge, MA: MIT Press.

Blackwell, Ashleigh. 2020. "Opinion: Zoom University Is Not Worth $56,000." *The Gettysburgian*, April 22, 2020. https://gettysburgian.com/2020/04/opinion -zoom-university-is-not-worth-56000/.

Burt, Chris. 2021. "College 2030: A Conversation on the Future of Higher Ed." *University Business*, April 19, 2021. https://universitybusiness.com/college -2030-a-conversation-on-the-future-of-higher-education/.

Christensen, Clayton M., and Henry J. Eyring. 2011. *The Innovative University: Changing the DNA of Higher Education from the Inside Out*. Hoboken, NJ: Wiley.

Crow, Michael M., and William B. Dabars. 2015. *Designing the New American University*. Baltimore, MD: JHU Press.

——. 2020. *The Fifth Wave: The Evolution of American Higher Education*. Baltimore, MD: JHU Press.

Govindarajan, Vijay, and Anup Srivastava. 2020. "What the Shift to Virtual Learning Could Mean for the Future of Higher Ed." *Harvard Business Review*, March 31, 2020. https://hbr.org/2020/03/what-the-shift-to-virtual-learning -could-mean-for-the-future-of-higher-ed.

Kelly, Rhea. 2021. "73 Percent of Students Prefer Some Courses Be Fully Online Post-Pandemic." *Campus Technology*, May 13, 2021. https://campustechnology .com/articles/2021/05/13/73-percent-of-students-prefer-some-courses-be -fully-online-post-pandemic.aspx.

Kezar, Adrianna, and Daniel Maxey. 2013. "The Changing Academic Workforce." *Trusteeship* 21 (3): 15–21.

Lederman, Doug. 2021. "Courts View COVID-19 Tuition Refund Lawsuits Skeptically." *Inside Higher Ed*, May 6, 2021. https://www.insidehighered.com /news/2021/05/06/courts-view-covid-19-tuition-refund-lawsuits-skeptically.

Maloney, Edward J., and Joshua Kim. 2019. "Why We Will Not Use the Term 'Internal OPM' in 2020." *Inside Higher Ed*, November 27, 2019. https://www .insidehighered.com/digital-learning/blogs/technology-and-learning /why-we-will-not-use-term-internal-opm-2020.

Reich, Justin. 2020. *Failure to Disrupt: Why Technology Alone Can't Transform Education*. Cambridge, MA: Harvard University Press.

Ubell, Robert. 2017. Going Online: Perspectives on Digital Learning. New York: Taylor & Francis.

Ubell, Robert. 2021. "Lacking Online Programs, Many Colleges Are Rushing to Partner with OPMs. Should They?" *EdSurge*, June 7, 2021. https://www .edsurge.com/news/2021-06-07-lacking-online-programs-many-colleges -are-rushing-to-partner-with-opms-should-they.

Watermeyer, Richard, Tom Crick, Cathryn Knight, and Janet Goodall. 2020. "Forced Shift to Online Teaching in Pandemic Unleashes Educators' Deepest Job Fears." *Nature Index*, April 9, 2020. https://www.natureindex.com/news -blog/forceshift-to-online-teaching-in-coronavirus-pandemic-unleashes -educators-deepest-job-fears-.

2

THE COVID MOMENT IN CONTEXT

THE CALM BEFORE THE STORM

When the first mention of an unusual and deadly virus in the Wuhan province of China appeared on international newswires in December 2019, most U.S. universities were busy wrapping up their fall semester and looking forward to a calm holiday break. Digital education and online learning, which had dominated the agendas of many university leaders between 2012 and 2014, were a much lower priority (Kim and Maloney 2020). Digital tool use continued to expand in executive education programs and in a limited number of innovative schools and programs. But at most universities and colleges, the classroom learning experience for most students remained largely unchanged from nineteenth-century models—large lecture hall teaching, with students passively listening (Lederman 2020a; Ubell 2021). In these institutions, professors used a learning management system (LMS) to track class attendance and record grades. In most classes, the LMS was used principally as a place to store PDFs of syllabi and readings, with little use of discussion boards, prerecorded videos, or other digital tools. Except for the use of laptops for notes and emails for communication, teaching and learning largely stuck to traditional methods.

Although hidden from most university students, innovative teaching and learning experiments were underway. Active

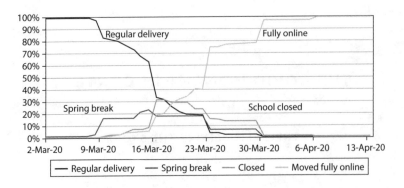

Figure 2.1 Percentage of U.S. higher education institutions moving to fully online delivery of traditional face-to-face courses during COVID-19 crisis (not including institutions already fully online)

learning, recorded video lectures, and digital case studies were being used effectively in experimental classes and programs, as well as in online education courses. These innovations were often created and run by for-profit online program management (OPM) contractors or by executive education programs, but generally they were not found in university core offerings (Pelletier 2018).

As the COVID-19 pandemic spread around the world during the first three months of 2020, most universities were just beginning their spring semester. As infections rose rapidly, universities began to contemplate a previously unthinkable scenario. By March 23, 2020, more than 25 percent of universities had closed. Another 40 percent of students transferred to "emergency Zoom teaching" courses (Hill 2020; Kim and Maloney 2020). By summer 2020, nearly 100 percent of courses were being taught online (figure 2.1).

ZOOM UNIVERSITY

Most universities and schools in the United States had some core digital infrastructure in place when the pandemic hit. Although

Figure 2.2 Zoom gallery

generally used in rudimentary ways, almost all universities had LMSs such as Canvas, Brightspace, or Blackboard to provide the foundation for digital connectivity and communications. Zoom had been little used by most courses but was available and integrated into the LMSs. Many universities responded to the pandemic by simply moving classroom lectures to Zoom. Professors lectured to "gallery views" of students instead of in traditional lecture halls (figure 2.2).

PowerPoint slides, if used, were shared on Zoom. Professors and students learned their way around basic Zoom tools such as "Zoom chat" and "raising hands." Eventually, more tech-savvy instructors added more exotic Zoom tools including "breakout rooms" and "polling." Professors purchased better webcams, bought ring lights, and perhaps thought a bit more about how their home offices looked on screen.

"When the pandemic happened," explained Paul Krause, vice provost for external education at Cornell University, "the school had two weeks to figure out how to migrate online and support 2,000 faculty, many of whom had little experience with online learning, so it was triage. There was not enough time to implement best practices; rather the focus was on teaching the basics of Zoom with audio and video and some simple approaches to migrate online" (Krause 2021).

In taking these steps, most professors entered a new world of digital communication that was already familiar territory to most of their students. Most of today's students are digital natives raised in the age of Snapchat and TikTok. Many young "vloggers" already record themselves and share ideas on everything from climate change to the latest shoes on platforms such as YouTube and Instagram.

The Zoom University experiment transmitted the classic nineteenth-century course lecture model online. It was often not thrilling, and most professors and students soon tired of the endless hours of Zoom lectures. During the summer of 2020, many colleges and universities focused on the logistics of some sort of limited "return to school" rather than on curricular changes. To protect against the spread of the virus, these universities adopted rules for masks, distancing, and testing. To make it possible for professors to deliver HyFlex classes—hybrid flexible classes in which professors teach face-to-face classes in a classroom as other students watch online—schools set up cutting-edge A/V equipment.

Lecture capture technology providers such as Panopto were suddenly much more relevant than they ever had been before. "If schools already had Panopto," said Panopto CEO Eric Burns (2021), "overnight, they quadrupled their usage." Those who did not scrambled to catch up. "There were organizations that were caught flat-footed because they had been observing what for them was an experiment and sitting on the sidelines," Burns explained. "The laggards had to really hurry up . . . there was a flurry of activity."

These investments in cameras and monitors provided some long-term benefits in terms of improved digital infrastructure but did little to adjust the traditional teaching style to the new realities. Because of the continued spread of the virus, 33 percent of university courses met fully, or primarily, online in the fall of 2020 (Nelson 2021a). Unfortunately, many students returned to classes at Zoom University, which had made little improvement in course design or delivery.

"Online learning is a very front-loaded investment," explained Joshua Kim (2021) of Dartmouth's Center for Advancement of Learning. "You don't just sort of go and do it. You've actually got to design effective online learning. So none of us experienced online learning (during the pandemic); we experienced academic continuity. Remote learning, as we say."

For Ben Nelson, president of Minerva Project, an innovative "digital first" university, the pandemic exposed long-hidden deficiencies in the ways most universities approached teaching and learning. "The pandemic, beamed into half-a-billion living rooms around the world, was an 'Emperor Has No Clothes' moment," Nelson (2021b) explained. "It was an opportunity for a large swath of humanity to see that no education was happening at universities. . . . It was horrific . . . people remembered, 'Oh My God, I loved university despite the classes, not because of them!'"

But despite its shortcomings, emergency Zoom teaching enabled many colleges and universities to remain open and avoid financial disaster. Administrators were thrilled to be able to continue operating. A significant number of incoming first-year undergraduate students chose to defer enrollment for a year, but 75 percent reported their intention to continue their studies (Top Hat 2020).

For many students and university faculty members, the pandemic represented their first experience with online learning. Most of them found the experience a poor substitute for in-person classes. For many professors, the shift confirmed their negative views of digital tools. For them, online education was an inferior product. In August 2020, only 49 percent of professors saw online learning,

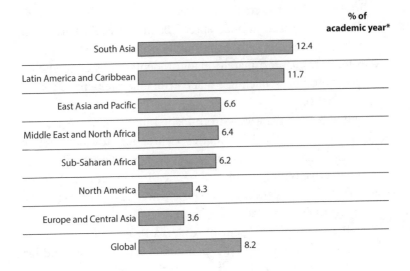

% of academic year*

South Asia	12.4
Latin America and Caribbean	11.7
East Asia and Pacific	6.6
Middle East and North Africa	6.4
Sub-Saharan Africa	6.2
North America	4.3
Europe and Central Asia	3.6
Global	8.2

Figure 2.3 Estimated months of learning delay by region during the pandemic, February 16, 2020 through January 31, 2022 (Chen et al., 2021)

as delivered during the pandemic, as an effective method of teaching (Lederman 2020b).

For K–12 students in the United States and beyond, the pandemic had dire consequences, especially for poorer students and students in school districts with insufficient online teaching support. A Brookings report showed that less than 25 percent of low-income countries provided any sort of online education at all, and that much of what was provided came via TV and radio (Olsen 2021). A McKinsey study found that students across the world lost months of learning due to poor remote teaching, with students in North America losing on average four months—or almost a semester—of education. Students in poorer areas of South Asia and Latin America lost up to twelve months of instruction, the equivalent of almost a year and a half of schooling (Chen et al. 2021; figure 2.3).

In the United States, similar disparities can be seen across schools, with students in underfunded historically Black schools

Learning gap	By race schools that are majority...		By income household average, per school		By location school site	
Math 5 months behind	Black	6	<$25K	7	City	5
	Hispanic	6	$25K–$75K	5	Suburb[1]	5
	White	4	>$75K	4	Rural	4
Reading 4 months behind	Black	6	<$25K	6	City	4
	Hispanic	5	$25K–$75K	4	Suburb[1]	4
	White	3	>$75K	3	Rural	3

Figure 2.4 Pandemic learning loss for U.S. children in grades 1–6 by race and income by end of school year 2020–21 (Dorn et al. 2021)

suffering up to six months of learning loss, and those in majority-white schools, who generally had access to higher quality online education, suffering an average of four months of learning loss (Dorn et al. 2021; figure 2.4). These impacts worsened preexisting income-based disparities in learning outcomes (figure 2.5).

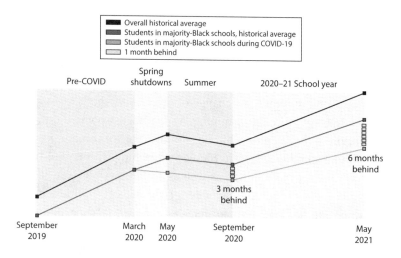

Figure 2.5 Race and cumulative pandemic learning loss in the United States, grades 1–6 (Dorn et al. 2021)

THE PATH NOT TAKEN

It did not have to be this way. Although Zoom lectures got low marks from most professors and students, studies show that rigorous and well-designed online learning experiences in which digital tools are used to create active learning experiences for students rate highly. A meta-analysis by the U.S. Department of Education found online learning outcomes to be comparable to face-to-face learning. A study by Frontiers in Science found that online educational media led to learning outcomes statistically indistinguishable from face-to-face instruction, all while providing the greater lifestyle flexibility preferred by many students (Paul and Jefferson 2019).

Major providers of online education solutions took this argument a step further. Chip Paucek, the founder and CEO of the OPM 2U, noted the difference between "emergency remote instruction and intentional high-quality online education" (Schwartz 2020). Anant Agarwal (2020) of edX made the same point. In a virtual talk at Columbia University in April 2020, he explained that "Zoom teaching is not online learning." Some universities, especially those that already had robust digital education programs in place, fared better. "When the pandemic came along, many of our edX partners will tell you they were very well prepared because they already had strong digital learning portfolios on campus" explained Agarwal. "They were able to use the same content for the on campus students."

Going online requires a change of delivery methods *and* different course structure and planning. As Ian Bogost pointed out, the invention of the telephone did not simply improve communication but fundamentally altered it. Similarly, teaching with digital tools requires a shift in paradigm as well as technology (Bogost 2017). Effective online teaching includes a rich mix of activities, many of which can be done asynchronously according to each student's schedule. These online courses require students to be active learners, use course materials on their own, work with partners in peer-to-peer learning, and then use the live course time (on Zoom or face-to-face) for debate and discussion (Linder 2017).

Schools that already offered a rich mix of in-person and online instruction had the digital infrastructure in place to deliver well-designed course websites for students and had training programs in place to help instructors teach effectively on the new medium (Jeffe 2021). Professor Armando Fox of UC Berkeley was part of a team of professors and support staff who already had deep remote learning experience. "When the lockdown happened, there were a lot of terrible things about having to go 100 percent remote, and having to do it in a hurry," explained Fox (2021). But Berkeley was able to pivot quite easily to blended and remote delivery "because we were already doing some of these things."

The data from the pandemic support these arguments in various ways. For K–12 students in private schools, where resources were available to create higher-quality online education experiences, student outcomes with online learning were 41 percent better than the public school averages (Chen et al. 2021; figure 2.6).

At schools with a rich mix of in-person and online options, courses were already using discussion boards, videos, and digital case studies (Mintz 2020). At Columbia's School of International and Public Affairs (SIPA), content originally created for massive open online courses (MOOCs) and online executive education

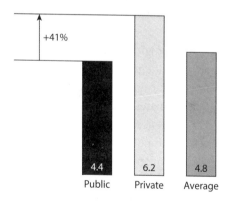

Figure 2.6 Effectiveness of remote learning: Private versus public school pandemic online outcomes (Chen et al. 2021)

classes—including prerecorded video lectures and digital cases—became a core element of many regular degree program courses. SIPA professor Glenn Denning had long used digital case studies on issues ranging from conservation agriculture to postconflict investment programs. "Especially when teaching online during the pandemic, having rich materials that students could engage with offline—like our digital case studies—made a huge difference," said Denning (2021). "We could use class time on Zoom for discussion and debate—rather than a passive one-way communication."

For other professors, moving online was harder, in part due to resistance to the use of digital tools long viewed with suspicion by many senior faculty and administrators (Figaredo 2017; Mintz 2021). For many, fighting online tools had been a cause célèbre. These ingrained views continued to play a major role in discussions on digital learning, and it is worth exploring their history and origins.

PREQUEL—THE HOUR OF MOOC

To understand the fear and confusion that gripped higher education in the summer of 2020, it's helpful to consider the "Hour of MOOC," from about 2012 to 2014. MOOCs were launched with much fanfare but failed to live up to expectations. But the MOOC experience produced important and far-reaching consequences for the current landscape of digital education.

MOOCs gained prominence when Peter Norvig and Sebastian Thrun first streamed their classes at Stanford University in 2011. In an email to 1,000 affiliates of the Association for the Advancement of Artificial Intelligence, Norvig and Thrun announced a free open online course on computer coding. People from 190 countries enrolled, and 23,000 completed the course (Reich 2020). Venture capitalists from Silicon Valley joined the movement, providing funding for companies that would become Coursera and Udacity. Meanwhile, Harvard and MIT invested $60 million in the nonprofit that would become edX.

Anant Agarwal, an MIT professor who would go on to serve as the founder and CEO of edX, began by offering open classes as part of MIT's OpenCourseWare. He took inspiration from the success of one of his former students at MIT, Sal Khan, from Khan Academy, which utilizes simple videos and exercises to teach lessons to a broad audience. "Khan Academy showed that you could teach online and do video distribution at scale. . . . Many technologies came together in what I call the 'Perfect Technological Storm' for education, and these included cloud computing, video distribution at scale, social networking, and mobile computing" (Agarwal 2020). He realized that the tools were now available to "enable new classes of experiences" for online learning. "It was not a matter of technology, but a matter of will to go and do it. And that's how we got into it . . . we said, let's go do it!"

Coursera cofounder Daphne Koller followed a similar path, motivated by the success of her open Stanford computing course that also quickly attracted thousands of online students. "None of us really knew what was going to happen," explained Koller (2021). "It was amazing to see that in a period of a few weeks each of the courses had an enrollment of 100,000 learners or more! . . . It wasn't just the numbers. It was people from every country, every age group, every walk of life. That led us to the realization that there was this incredible hunger out there for the kind of quality education that very few people have the fortune to access in their lifetime."

For tech watchers, these MOOCs offered the disruptive technology that people had long predicted would upend higher education. As Clayton Christensen of Harvard Business School explained, disruption occurs when new technologies offer new ways of producing or delivering products or services—lowering costs, improving convenience, and offering new features and benefits (Christensen and Eyring 2011). Once people could click a link on their computers to order books, clothes, and other consumer products, Amazon transformed retailing. Likewise, once people started to use smartphones to book and pay drivers, Uber, Lyft, and other services upended the entrenched taxi industry. Was education ripe for disruption? Christensen and others thought so. Ryan Craig (2015)

Figure 2.7 Headlines during the "Year of the MOOC" (Shah 2020)

predicted that MOOCs would usher in a great "unbundling" of higher education.

By the summer of 2012, MOOC fever was underway, with the *New York Times* declaring it "The Year of the MOOC" (Pappano 2012). Many experts predicted that MOOCs, with their recorded lectures by "rock star" professors, would soon put most small colleges out of business (figure 2.7). "In 50 years, there will only be 10 institutions in the world delivering higher education and Udacity has a shot at being one of them," Udacity founder Sebastian Thrun famously exclaimed to *Wired* magazine in 2012 (Watters 2013).

"Suddenly, within a year, MOOCs are going to disrupt higher education," explained Dhawal Shah (2021) of Class Central, a MOOC-focused research website. Some even went so far as to suggest that MOOCs should be named *Time*'s 2012 "Person of the Year," creating parody covers like the one in figure 2.8 (Shimabukuro 2012).

University boards put huge pressure on presidents and provosts to join the MOOC bandwagon, pressuring the University of Virginia president Teresa Sullivan to resign for inaction on the MOOC front, although she was later rehired (Rice 2012). By the spring of 2013, leading MOOC providers edX (figure 2.9), a nonprofit consortium

Figure 2.8 *TIME* "Person of the Year"? (Shimabukuro 2012)

led by Harvard and MIT, and the for-profit Coursera (figure 2.10), founded by the former Stanford professor Andrew Ng and Daphne Koller, had signed content deals with the "Who's Who" of top universities, including Columbia, Yale, Brown, Duke, UC Berkeley, University of Michigan, and hundreds of others (Korn 2013).

Figure 2.9 edX MOOC platform

Figure 2.10 Coursera MOOC platform

Koller believed that schools were driven by the fear that higher education would be upended by digitalization and suffer the same massive layoffs and closings that had destroyed the value of most traditional print media companies. Commenting on the mass closures of paper-based magazines and newspapers, Koller (2021) said, "People were looking at that and saying 'This could happen to us unless we do something different'—I think it really created a sense of urgency." Nevertheless, the fact that so many universities moved quickly was remarkable. Koller explained, "This was them saying 'We are going to let our content be made available for free. We're going to let our brand be used.' It was a very big step for them to take in terms of intellectual property rights . . . it was impressive." Almost overnight, the company's popularity skyrocketed, and "EdTech suddenly became Cool Tech" (Branon 2021).

MOOCs proposed to offer courses free of charge. Investors and entrepreneurs skirted the question of how this work would be financed. They also left unaddressed the long-term impact of MOOCs on university revenue and enrollments. The MOOC fever of 2012 to 2014 created an immediate backlash. Many professors teaching introductory courses at smaller institutions saw the MOOC movement as an existential threat to their livelihood. San Jose State philosophy professors fought back against a plan to use a Harvard MOOC in their classes, denouncing it in an open letter and describing MOOCs as "cultural monocropping," explaining that they opened the door to "intellectual colonialism" in which elite institution professors create content to be consumed by mostly poorer students at community colleges (*Chronicle of Higher Education* 2013).

But MOOCs proved to be far less effective teaching tools than hoped. The courses originally created by Agarwal, Koller, and others all had extensive "synchronous" elements—TA or peer-to-peer discussion sessions or labs—but these elements were soon dropped due to costs. Koller (2021) explained that digital learning needs to have elements of "Content" and "Engagement." In her words, "The product we ended up creating was really much more focused on the former rather than the latter." The MOOC creator and provider Gary Matkin (2021) of the University of California Irvine explained: "Frankly, we had to actually design the instructor out of the process almost entirely because we couldn't afford to have instructors coming in and serving the students because there was no way of getting them paid."

"To really scale MOOCs, they had to remove the instructor from the day-to-day operations of a course," explained Dhawal Shah (2021) of Class Central. To make matters worse, MOOC providers failed to compensate for this with a new investment in other tools, such as rich forums designed to encourage peer-to-peer interactions. Such "user-generated content" had been at the heart of the success of other scalable digital platforms such as Facebook and Twitter, but early MOOCs failed to make these investments in "social learning" a key part of their platforms. Slowly, the rich online community of learners, who had grown up around early MOOC experiments, began to fade away.

Without users who could help "contribute to the topic" by sharing their own experiences and knowledge, MOOC discussion forums became places for answering technical questions only

(Shah 2021). For professors such as Bard's Erica Kaufman, the lack of rich interaction with others meant that MOOCs, which had begun with the promise of facilitating human interaction, became sterile and uninviting. Writing notes or comments seemed a waste of effort. "You feel like you're posting into a void," she explained. "It made me not feel particularly motivated to continue to do it" (Kaufman 2022).

By 2014, the MOOC frenzy was over. Research showed that only a small percentage of students who signed up for a MOOC actually completed the online course. Other studies found that MOOCs worked well for highly motivated self-starters, especially educated users with previous university degrees, but they were not effective in engaging new students who needed more support and guidance. The MOOCs themselves—many featuring videos produced by university AV teams filming this sort of content for the first time—often suffered from subpar production quality. Recognizing these limitations, in 2013 Udacity's founder Sebastian Thrun famously did an about-face on his bold predictions for massive disruption, stating that "we had a lousy product" (Chafkin 2013).

The MOOCs' spectacular fizzle made an interesting boom and bust story for the media. Many senior faculty and administrators breathed a collective sigh of relief when the feared "disruption" of the higher education sector failed to materialize. By joining MOOC consortiums and producing a few courses, "early mover" professors and universities gained valuable experience in digital education and appeased forward-thinking donors without actually having to enact far-reaching changes to business as usual. Most MOOC programs continued as minor experimental ventures at their host universities.

But despite these limitations, the impact of the MOOC experience was significant and long-lasting. Most universities joined MOOC consortiums like edX and Coursera, spurring the creation of centers for teaching and learning (CTLs) at major colleges and universities. As Kim and Maloney (2020) note in *Learning Innovation and the Future of Higher Education*, one of the key MOOC legacies was the creation of new communities of teaching and learning professionals across most universities. The new units included the Michigan Office of Academic Innovation, Berkeley's Center for Teaching Innovation, Boston University's Digital Learning and Innovation Center, Duke's Center for Instructional Technology, and Columbia's Center for Teaching and Learning.

These centers became part of a growing network of EdTech innovators around the world. The annual edX Global Forum became the "go-to" meeting place for digital education innovators. But despite their important experimentation and research, most CTLs lacked the mandate to lead change or create new programs. Instead, they were positioned as support centers for professors who were innovating on their own in their pedagogy, or use of technology, or both. Without a central administrative mandate to make digital tools and active learning central to their teaching methods, most faculty did not seek out their school's CTL services. By 2020, more than eight years after the MOOC revolution, most top universities continued to have a very uneven level of educational technology training among their faculty, and they made little use of innovative educational technologies in their mainstream courses (Gallagher and Palmer 2020).

THE DIGITAL PUBLIC UNIVERSITY

While elite universities flirted with MOOCs and conducted their own small-scale digital experiments, many large public universities put the MOOC concept into action at scale as massive private online courses. They did this by building on the tools and techniques of the MOOC as well as the pre-MOOC online education programs developed by for-profit outfits such as the University of Phoenix, which had enrolled thousands of adult learners in the early 2000s.

A number of these early for-profit online programs used predatory recruitment practices and relied on students who took out huge amounts of government-supported loans. When the Obama administration made moves to regulate the for-profit educational market in the late 2000s, many of the worst actors closed, and a set of new nonprofit "mega universities" set out to fill the unmet demand for training and increasing the skills of adult learners.

Typical were the innovative programs developed by the University of California Irvine (UCI), led by Gary Matkin, who would later coin the term the "60 Year Curriculum" to describe courses designed for lifelong learning. Matkin (2021) explained that UCI had used online tools before and that the MOOC moment gave them a new impetus: "We got with Coursera early in January 2013," he explained, "so we developed our video program partly as a result of that." UCI's program pivoted to offering fee-paying short certificate programs for adult learners that soon far surpassed their MOOC offerings in volume. By 2019, the UCI direct enrollment program offered more than six hundred short online courses to over 35,000 learners and had total revenues of more than $40 million.

At the University of Washington, a similar digital revolution was underway. The University of Washington also focused on adult learners, and online tools and asynchronous content were key to their success. The University of Washington had offered online courses since the late 1990s, but due to constraints with internet bandwidth, they were mostly text-based affairs. "Thumbnail videos were acceptable if they were under two minutes," said Rovy Branon (2021), vice provost for Continuum College at the University of Washington, "but you still had to have a transcript (for) people who didn't have the bandwidth to download those videos."

These new executive education and adult certificate programs used online tools to reach beyond traditional students. Of prime interest were older students already in the workforce who could not attend in-person classes (King and Alperstein 2017). To meet the needs of mid-career-executive education and other nontraditional students, these universities developed impressive in-house content production capacities. With a central mandate and funding to create quality content, they invested in sophisticated media production centers. By 2019, the Branon group at the University of Washington had grown to more than two hundred professionals and managed full-time video production facilities. "There was a huge unmet need in adult and continuing education," explained Branon (2021). "We served 55,000 learners out of my office last year."

Other public universities went even further and integrated digital learning into on campus instruction. A theoretical framework for this was provided by Michael Crow, who led Fathom, an early Columbia precursor to MOOCs. In 2002, Crow became president of Arizona State University (ASU; Palladino 2002). His vision was and is of a public university conducting world-class research and simultaneously providing high-quality education to a large number of students, especially poor, working-class, and minority communities in Arizona and surrounding states. Online tools would play a key role in making this a reality.

Crow shared his vision in a series of talks and articles that culminated in his highly influential book *Designing the New American University* (Crow and Dabars 2015). By 2019, ASU had become an online education juggernaut, with 60,000 on campus students and 80,000 online learners. ASU is a "digital-first" campus, and all courses—both in-person and online—share the same curriculum and faculty (Crow and Dabars 2020). ASU also invested heavily in course creation and production techniques and workflows, taking models first developed for MOOC platforms and expanding them to deliver massive classes that met both in-person (Campus Immersion) and online (iCourse) needs.

Other nonprofit mega universities soon followed ASU's lead, creating large in-house production and management teams using online learning to drive huge enrollment numbers. Many of these universities match and surpass the enrollments of the for-profit online universities they replaced, including Western Governors University, which had 136,139 students in 2019, and Southern New

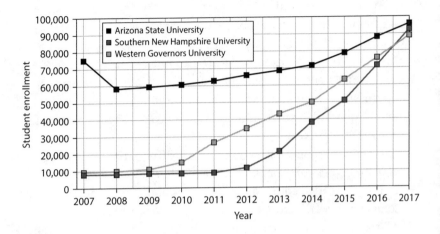

Figure 2.11 Growth of the digital public university (*Chronicle of Higher Education* 2019)

Hampshire University, which has 135,000 students in 2021 (Data USA 2021; Southern New Hampshire University 2021). The impressive growth of these universities can be seen in figure 2.11. Overall, it is in these digital public universities, rather than private universities, where the significant growth in online learning took place before the pandemic (figure 2.12).

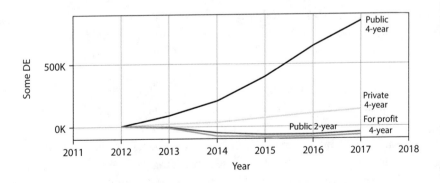

Figure 2.12 U.S. growth in public versus private online enrollments (Shirky 2019)

THE COVID MOMENT IN CONTEXT

ENTER THE OPMs

For universities seeking revenue from online programs but unwilling to make the investments required, online program management (OPM) companies became the solution. The OPM 2U and the traditional educational publisher Wiley developed sophisticated teams devoted to all aspects of program creation and management. Backed by venture capital, many of the for-profit OPMs also served as investors, offering cash-strapped universities and colleges an attractive option in which the OPM would typically pay for all costs of creating, filming, and launching online degree programs in exchange for long-term contracts in which they would receive 50 percent or 60 percent of program revenues (Povejsil 2021).

Many universities embraced these offers because they lacked the in-house skills needed to run effective online programs. OPMs developed deep know-how in online program creation. They also invested heavily in online marketing and recruitment, using data analytics to develop carefully targeted online advertising and recruitment campaigns, which were often spectacularly successful in recruiting students (Pelletier 2018).

OPMs also developed sophisticated workflows for designing and creating online course content. Renowned faculty were recruited to teach in-demand courses, and they were well compensated to work with experienced instructional designers to transform courses into evergreen online content. Content creation teams made Power-Point presentations and filmed and edited lectures, demonstrations, and other course content.

OPMs such as 2U developed a sophisticated course design and production system based on their work with more than eighty university partners, and 250,000 students have graduated from 2U-managed courses. With a team of more than six hundred in its course design, production, and delivery unit, it is the mega-studio of online course creation. "We produced twice as much original video content as Netflix did in 2020, just to give you a sense of scale. It's massive," explained Luyen Chou (2021), 2U chief learning officer. "My challenge today is how can we build online learning experiences that are better than what you could do in a campus classroom?" 2U has educational film studios in Virginia, Los Angeles, London, and South Africa and invests heavily in reimagining learning in the online environment.

According to its leadership, 2U understands that its role is to be the expert in online and digital pedagogy, acknowledging that its university partners are the experts in the curriculum. As Chou (2021) states, "It's taken a while, because most universities did not think of pedagogy and curriculum as different." Now they understand that 2U is much more than an "operational" partner. "We have gotten really good at the science and art of teaching online." All 2U courses are built following its official guidelines, a document called the "Learning Experience Framework," which is built around the ideas of "feel," "do," and "think." "It's all about getting the right cadence and the right cycle and iteration of these modalities. How do we appeal to people's hearts and make them feel the emotional connection with what they're learning? How do we make them actually do, rather than sit back and passively receive?"

Beyond course design, OPMs also offered services in the areas of marketing, research, and delivery. OPM teams create websites—branded as their university partners—and send emails and make calls to prospective learners and students, supply support staff, and at times even help identify potential adjunct instructors to manage courses.

In the pandemic summer of 2020, the OPM business was booming. Many universities and colleges with no in-house digital capacity looked to quickly put programs in place (Acosta and McCann 2020). 2U also developed workflows for remote production of "flipped class" lectures by professors at home, using a set of gear known as the "studio-in-a-box." This delivered the gear needed for home recording—including webcam, lights, and microphone, along with remote guidance instructions—directly to the homes of professors at partner institutions (Chou 2021). OPMs pushed the envelope in course design and production in ways that most in-house shops could not manage. The results were impressive and generally much more successful with students than most MOOC content, which was often produced without the benefits of streamlined production processes and techniques the larger OPM operations were able to marshal.

The EdTech industry and venture capital markets saw the huge potential of the OPM model, and groups such as 2U received large new investments during the pandemic, culminating in the purchase of nonprofit MOOC providers edX by for-profit OPM 2U in July 2021 for $800 million (Wan 2021). OPMs such as 2U, Wiley, and Noodle Partners were joined in this success by two other groups who bet big on the market for professionally produced educational content: MasterClass and Outlier.

MasterClass offered a subscription service of professionally produced classes on a wide range of topics, delivered with Hollywood production values by A-List celebrities such as Martin Scorsese and Serena Williams. Topics ranged from novel writing to space travel. With per-course production costs in the hundreds of thousands of dollars for each class, MasterClass blurred the lines between education and entertainment. The service proved to be a huge hit during the pandemic, and subscriptions increased tenfold over the average in 2019 (Chocano 2020). After paying MasterClass a $180 annual subscription fee, subscribers gained access to its library of eighty-five classes. A headline in the *New York Times* captured the moment: "It's the Year 2120. MasterClass is the Only School Left" (Nevins 2020).

When MasterClass's cofounder Aaron Rasmussen created the website Outlier.org, he bet that the similar model might work for credit-bearing entry-level college courses (figure 2.13). Students, he reasoned, would happily pay $400 for a well-produced credit-bearing course that fulfilled their university's requirements. Classes were produced with the same highly polished production values used by MasterClass and filmed with media-friendly professors—the "rock star" professor that MOOCs had seemed to offer but in fact rarely delivered. Outlier also added a series of active learning activities and assessments, delivered on its own proprietary LMS. When Outlier signed a deal in which its courses would receive transferable University of Pittsburgh credit, the model began to gain traction,

Figure 2.13 Outlier.org

raising the bar for what would constitute a well-produced online learning experience (Ha 2021).

Despite these occasional forays into the world of Hollywood, the success of most OPMs lies in the consistent application of solid instructional design principles. By investing time and resources in the creation of dynamic and active online experiences, OPMs provided the necessary conditions for successful course creation, and most OPM-created online and digital courses rate highly with students, often achieving higher ratings than those created by less experienced in-house teams.

Although generally acknowledged for their expertise in course design and delivery, OPMs continued to generate controversy. In negotiations with often ill-informed and underfinanced colleges and universities, some OPMs negotiated exorbitant long-term contracts. The fact that OPMs handled online recruitment of students for their programs also caused concern. Aggressive recruiting techniques led to spectacular enrollment numbers, but in some instances the students recruited were poorly qualified, and many dropped out of these programs after one semester or less (Manoff 2019). With the emphasis on getting bodies in online programs, concerns were increasingly voiced about the quality of these programs and the qualifications of the students who were admitted (Donahue 2017).

Congressional committees began to investigate OPM contracts with public universities in 2020, which were prohibited by the Program Participation Agreement (PPA) to pay commissions for recruiting and enrolling new students (Warren 2020). Critics pointed out that some OPMs were staffed by professionals recruited from discredited "for-profit" private universities, such as Corinthian Group, DeVry Education Group, Career Education Corps, and 1,400 other programs that were closed during the Obama administration for luring "students with misleading promises, then (saddling) them with debts that they can't pay back with their newly minted degrees" (Grasgreen 2015).

In response to these criticisms, many OPM providers began to offer "unbundled" or "à la carte" services rather than the traditional tuition sharing models. These services allowed universities to pay for specific services, such as media production or recruitment analytics, while maintaining control over their own program management and revenues.

Another area in which most OPMs seemed to have fallen short was in designing new paths for faculty-to-student and student-to-student interaction. As for-profit ventures, OPMs naturally have a bias toward solutions that can scale—such as prerecorded videos—and invest less in areas that must be delivered with more faculty involvement, such as new forms of online discussion and engagement. This led them to overlook exciting digital tools and techniques that have emerged in these areas. It will be the job of university in-house teams to correct this imbalance.

Navigating the world of OPMs remains a major challenge for many university presidents, provosts, and other campus leaders. OPMs have developed valuable expertise in online and hybrid program development. The question is how to take advantage of these services without losing control of the university's valuable traditions, academic expertise, and integrity.

Despite their shortcomings, the autonomy of OPMs enables them to use project management systems that facilitate efficient content creation. They still have much to teach universities in this area. OPMs learned many of their techniques by studying and building on early university MOOCs and online programs. Now many universities are trying to complete the circle and bring this knowledge back inside the gates of the campus.

For Matthew Rascoff (2021), vice provost for digital education at Stanford, the debate over the role of OPMs is central. "I think there is risk in outsourcing something that really should be part of your core. I'm fine with outsourcing marketing. If that's what you are giving up . . . I don't view that as the core." Universities have a long history of outsourcing certain services, but they should be careful. "We outsource food services. We outsource the construction of buildings . . . those are things that are not core to an academic enterprise. Figuring out the future of teaching and learning is essential to what we do in higher education." For Rascoff, the key is to acknowledge that digital tools are not a passing fad but will be integral to learning going forward: "How much do we believe we should be doing this long-term? If you believe in it for the long term, then you have to get good at it. The way you get good at something is building up capacity over time and strengthening those muscles."

THE ROAD AHEAD—DIGITAL TOOLS
AND PROGRAM EQUITY

Students are sophisticated consumers of digital content, which they access every day on YouTube, Instagram, TikTok, and other platforms. The success of MasterClass and Outlier raises the bar for what constitutes professionally produced educational content. Top universities cannot afford to ignore these trends. Recent history indicates that previous boundaries between the world of online and in-person learning are blurring. The same digital tools used to make 100 percent online courses work well can also be used to improve on campus instruction. Although students were not impressed with the improvised Zoom University most schools offered during the pandemic, they do want the flexibility to study at their own time and pace and the experience of active learning that digital course content allows.

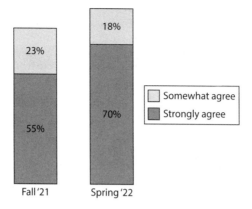

Figure 2.14 Percent of students who would want to continue to take some courses online (Cengage 2022)

A major pandemic survey in the spring of 2022 found that 70 percent of students would want to continue—postpandemic—to take at least some of their courses online, up 15 points from the previous fall (figure 2.14). The data also showed that from the spring of 2021 to the spring of 2022, overall student perception of the efficacy of their courses increased—both in-person (figure 2.15) and online (figure 2.16). This would seem to indicate that despite the

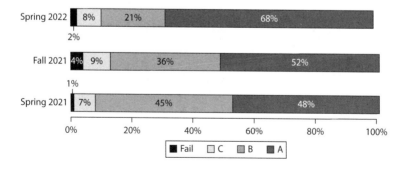

Figure 2.15 Perceived effectiveness of 100 percent in-person classes from spring 2021 to spring 2022 (Cengage 2022)

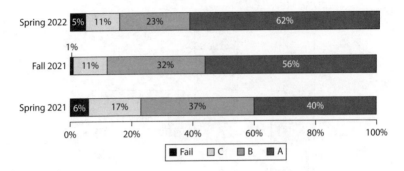

Figure 2.16 Perceived effectiveness of 100 percent online courses from spring 2021 to spring 2022 (Cengage 2022)

setbacks of the early years of the pandemic, longer-term results of the widespread introduction of technology in teaching have made for more effective courses, both in-person and online.

Postpandemic survey data from professors support these findings, with 69 percent agreeing with the statement that they would like to incorporate more technology in in-person courses, and 67 percent saying they would like to use more digital materials and digital resources in their courses (figure 2.17).

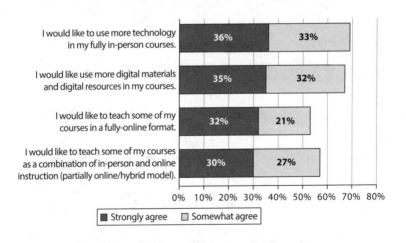

Figure 2.17 Faculty preferences for postpandemic teaching (Cengage 2022)

It is interesting to note that student demand for at least some online courses (70 percent) surpasses the 53 percent of professors who want to continue to teach online postpandemic. We suspect that this gap has to do with the fact that online teaching and the creation of digital assets and projects requires a great deal of pre-course prep work, which historically has not been compensated. We address these issues in more depth in chapters 4 and 6 and propose some potential solutions.

The postpandemic survey data show that students want digital tools and that these tools help improve learning outcomes. Professors are at least open to using them. The data on pandemic learning loss at the beginning of the chapter confirms that many students—especially students in grades 1–6 in underserved communities—emerged from the pandemic with major gaps in their knowledge, many up to a year behind their grade level (see figures 2.3–2.5). The combined data from these surveys, based on student demand alone, indicate that digital is here to stay, in one form or another. It also highlights the need for these tools to be directed toward addressing questions of equity and learning gaps of all kinds.

Sophisticated in-house OPMs demonstrated that it is possible to make engaging digital courses for use in both online and residential programs. The tools and techniques of many OPM providers hold many valuable lessons for residential programs. Their principal content creation innovations are in the area of management and project design. As we explain in the following chapters, these innovations are well within the capabilities of most medium-to-large institutions and could be implemented on campus using in-house teams.

Leading universities must make a conscious effort to incorporate what is good about digital learning into all aspects of teaching and learning. It will make on campus learning richer, and we believe it will open the door for connected learning experiences of all kinds.

REFERENCES

Acosta, Alejandra, and Clare McCann. 2020. "Considering an Online Program Management (OPM) Contract." *New America*, September 15, 2020. http://newamerica.org/education-policy/reports/considering-online-program-management-opm-contract/.

Agarwal, Anant. 2020. "PCoOL Anant Agarwal, edX CEO and MIT Professor, April 28, 2020." Presented at the Provost Conversations on Online Learning, Columbia University. https://www.youtube.com/watch?v=eOOxO456o7s.

——. 2021. Interview of CEO, edX, by Adam Stepan. October 19, 2021.

Bogost, Ian. 2017. "The Secret Lives of MOOCs." In *MOOCs and Their Afterlives*, ed. Elizabeth Losh, 271–286. Chicago: University of Chicago Press. https://doi.org/10.7208/chicago/9780226469591.003.0018.

Branon, Rovy. 2021. Interview of Vice Provost for Continuum College, University of Washington, by Adam Stepan. November 30, 2021.

Burns, Eric. 2021. Interview of Dean of Continuing Education and UCLA Extension, UCLA, by Adam Stepan. October 18, 2021.

Cengage. 2022. *Digital Learning Pulse Survey Results*. https://info.cengage.com/wrec_PulseSurveyResults_1470945.

Chafkin, Max. 2013. "Udacity's Sebastian Thrun, Godfather of Free Online Education, Changes Course." *Fast Company*, November 14, 2013. https://www.fastcompany.com/3021473/udacity-sebastian-thrun-uphill-climb.

Chen, Li-Kai, Emma Dorn, Jimmy Sarakatsannis, and Anna Wiesinger. 2021. "Teacher Survey: Learning Loss Is Global—and Significant." *McKinsey & Company*, March 1, 2021. https://www.mckinsey.com/industries/education/our-insights/teacher-survey-learning-loss-is-global-and-significant.

Chocano, Carina. 2020. "What Is MasterClass Actually Selling?" *Atlantic*, August 10, 2020. https://www.theatlantic.com/magazine/archive/2020/09/what-is-masterclass-actually-selling/614200/.

Chou, Luyen. 2021. Interview of Chief Learning Officer. 2U, by Adam Stepan. October 27, 2021.

Christensen, Clayton, and Henry J. Eyring. 2011. *The Innovative University: Changing the DNA of Higher Education from the Inside Out*. San Francisco, CA: Jossey-Bass.

Chronicle of Higher Education. 2013. "'An Open Letter to Professor Michael Sandel from the Philosophy Department at San Jose State U.'" May 2, 2013. https://www.chronicle.com/article/an-open-letter-to-professor-michael-sandel-from-the-philosophy-department-at-san-jose-state-u/.

——. 2019. "The Rise of the Mega-University." February 17, 2019. https://www.chronicle.com/article/mega-universities-are-on-the-rise-they-could-reshape-higher-ed-as-we-know-it/.

Craig, Ryan. 2015. "A Brief History (and Future) of Online Degrees." *Forbes*, June 23, 2015. https://www.forbes.com/sites/ryancraig/2015/06/23/a-brief-history-and-future-of-online-degrees/.

Crow, Michael M., and William B. Dabars. 2015. *Designing the New American University*. Baltimore, MD: JHU Press.

———. 2020. *The Fifth Wave: The Evolution of American Higher Education*. Baltimore, MD: JHU Press.

Data USA. 2021. "Western Governors University." November 29, 2021. https://datausa.io/profile/university/western-governors-university.

Denning, Glenn. 2021. Interview of Professor of Professional Practice in International and Public Affairs and Director of the Master of Public Administration in Development Practice, Columbia University, by Adam Stepan. December 1, 2021.

Donahue, John. 2017. "Understanding OPMs: A Reality-Based Analysis." *Synergis Education*, August 22, 2017. https://www.synergiseducation.com/understanding-opms-a-reality-based-analysis/.

Dorn, Emma, Bryan Hancock, Jimmy Sarakatsannis, and Emma Viruleg. 2021. "COVID-19 and Education: The Lingering Effects of Unfinished Learning." *McKinsey & Company*, July 27. 2021. https://www.mckinsey.com/industries/education/our-insights/covid-19-and-education-the-lingering-effects-of-unfinished-learning.

Figaredo, Daniel Domínguez. 2017. "Losh, E. (Ed.). (2017). *MOOCs and Their Afterlives: Experiments in Scale and Access in Higher Education*. University of Chicago Press." *Open Praxis* 9 (4): 483–84.

Fox, Armando. 2021. Interview of Associate Dean for Online Education, University of California, Berkeley, by Adam Stepan. October 19, 2021.

Gallagher, Sean, and Jason Palmer. 2020. "The Pandemic Pushed Universities Online. The Change Was Long Overdue." *Harvard Business Review*, September 29, 2020. https://hbr.org/2020/09/the-pandemic-pushed-universities-online-the-change-was-long-overdue.

Grasgreen, Allie. 2015. "Obama Pushes For-Profit Colleges to the Brink." *Politico*, July 1, 2015. https://www.politico.com/story/2015/07/barack-obama-pushes-for-profit-colleges-to-the-brink-119613.

Ha, Anthony. 2021. "MasterClass Co-Founder's Outlier.Org Raises $30M for Affordable, Virtual College Courses." *TechCrunch* (blog), April 22, 2021. https://social.techcrunch.com/2021/04/22/outlier-series-b/.

Hill, Phil. 2020. "US Higher Ed Set to Go Fully Online in Just Four Weeks Due to COVID-19." *PhilOnEdTech*, March 23, 2020. https://philonedtech.com/us-higher-ed-set-to-go-fully-online-in-just-four-weeks-due-to-covid-19/.

Jeffe, Scott. 2021. "What We Need to Know About Working with OPMs." *Ruffalo Noel Levitz* (blog), May 27, 2021. https://www.ruffalonl.com/blog//online-education-what-we-need-to-know-about-working-with-opms/.

Kaufman, Erica. 2022. Interview of Director of the Institute for Writing and Thinking, Bard College, by Adam Stepan. February 1, 2022.

Kim, Joshua. 2021. Interview of Director of Online Programs and Strategy at Dartmouth College Senior Scholar, Georgetown University, by Adam Stepan. October 21, 2021.

Kim, Joshua, and Edward J. Maloney. 2020. *Learning Innovation and the Future of Higher Education.* Baltimore, MD: JHU Press.

King, Elliot, and Neil Alperstein. 2017. *Best Practices in Planning Strategically for Online Educational Programs.* New York: Routledge. https://doi.org /10.4324/9781315677002.

Koller, Daphne. 2021. Interview of Founder of Coursera/Founder and CEO at Insitro, by Adam Stepan. October 19, 2021.

Korn, Melissa. 2013. "Online-Education Provider Coursera Signs 29 More Schools." *Wall Street Journal,* February 21, 2013. https://online.wsj.com /article/SB10001424127887323864304578316530544924000.html.

Krause, Paul. 2021. Interview of Vice Provost of External Education and Cornell University Executive Director, eCornell, by Adam Stepan. October 22, 2021.

Lederman, Doug. 2020a. "Survey Gauges the State of the Online Education Landscape Pre-Coronavirus." *Inside Higher Ed,* March 25, 2020. https://www .insidehighered.com/news/2020/03/25/survey-gauges-state-online -education-landscape-pre-coronavirus.

——. 2020b. "Faculty Confidence in Online Learning Grows." *Inside Higher Ed,* October 6, 2020. https://www.insidehighered.com/digital-learning/article /2020/10/06/covid-era-experience-strengthens-faculty-belief-value-online.

Linder, Kathryn E. 2017. *The Blended Course Design Workbook: A Practical Guide.* Sterling, VA: Stylus.

Manoff, Katerina. 2019. "How They (Online Graduate Programs) Get You." *Atlantic,* August 14, 2019. https://www.theatlantic.com/education/archive /2019/08/online-graduate-programs-recruitment/596077/.

Matkin, Gary. 2021. Interview of Dean of Continuing Education and Vice Provost for Career Pathways, University of California Irvine, by Adam Stepan. October 19, 2021.

Mintz, Steven. 2020. "Remote Learning Isn't Going Away." *Inside Higher Ed,* October 12, 2020. https://www.insidehighered.com/blogs/higher-ed-gamma /remote-learning-isn%E2%80%99t-going-away.

——. 2021. "Higher Education's Biggest Challenge: Rethinking Ingrained Assumptions." *Inside Higher Ed,* April 27, 2021. https://www.insidehighered .com/blogs/higher-ed-gamma/higher-education%E2%80%99s-biggest -challenge-rethinking-ingrained-assumptions.

Nelson, Ben. 2021a. "How Higher Education Can Do Better at Developing Skills for the Workplace." *Times Higher Education,* October 4, 2021. https:// www.timeshighereducation.com/campus/how-higher-education-can-do -better-developing-skills-workplace.

———. 2021b. Interview of CEO and Founder, Minerva Project, by Adam Stepan. October 14, 2021.

Nevins, Jake. 2020. "It's the Year 2120. MasterClass Is the Only School Left." *New York Times*, May 25, 2020. https://www.nytimes.com/2020/05/25/style /masterclass-secrets.html.

Olsen, Brad. 2021. "Adapting Education Innovations and Their 'Knock-on Effects' in the Time of COVID." *Brookings* (blog), November 8, 2021. https://www.brookings.edu/blog/education-plus-development/2021 /11/08/adapting-education-innovations-and-their-knock-on-effects-in -the-time-of-covid/.

Palladino, Lisa. 2002. "Crow Named President at Arizona State." *Columbia College Today*, May 2002. https://www.college.columbia.edu/cct_archive/may02 /may02_quads4.html.

Pappano, Laura. 2012. "The Year of the MOOC." *New York Times*, November 2, 2012. https://www.nytimes.com/2012/11/04/education/edlife/massive-open -online-courses-are-multiplying-at-a-rapid-pace.html.

Paul, Jasmine, and Felicia Jefferson. 2019. "A Comparative Analysis of Student Performance in an Online vs. Face-to-Face Environmental Science Course From 2009 to 2016." *Frontiers in Computer Science*, November 2019. https:// www.frontiersin.org/articles/10.3389/fcomp.2019.00007/full.

Pelletier, Stephen G. 2018. "The Evolution of Online Program Management." *Unbound*, 2018. https://unbound.upcea.edu/leadership-strategy/continuing -education/the-evolution-of-online-program-management/.

Povejsil, Elise. 2021. "The Hidden Secrets of an Online Program Management Company." *Collegis Education*, June 23, 2021. https://collegiseducation.com /news/online-learning/the-hidden-secrets-of-an-online-program-management -company/.

Rascoff, Matthew. 2021. Interview of Vice Provost for Digital Education, Stanford University, by Adam Stepan. October 29, 2021.

Reich, Justin. 2020. *Failure to Disrupt: Why Technology Alone Can't Transform Education*. Cambridge, MA: Harvard University Press.

Rice, Andrew. 2012. "Anatomy of a Campus Coup." *New York Times*, September 11, 2012. https://www.nytimes.com/2012/09/16/magazine/teresa-sullivan-uva -ouster.html.

Schwartz, Natalie. 2020. "2U Reports 'Unprecedented Demand,' but Challenges Lurk Ahead for OPMs." *Higher Ed Dive*, August 4, 2020. https://www .highereddive.com/news/2u-reports-unprecedented-demand-but-challenges -lurk-ahead-for-opms/582902/.

Shah, Dhawal. 2020. "Capturing the Hype: Year of the MOOC Timeline Explained." *Report by Class Central* (blog), February 4, 2020. https://www .classcentral.com/report/mooc-hype-year-1/.

———. 2021. Interview of Founder and CEO, Class Central, by Adam Stepan. October 22, 2021.

Shimabukuro. 2012. "TIME 2012 Person of the Year—MOOC." *Educational Technology and Change Journal* (blog), December 3, 2012. https://etcjournal .com/2012/12/03/time-2012-person-of-the-year-mooc/.

Shirky, Clay. 2019. "Clay Shirky on Mega-Universities and Scale." *PhilOnEdTech*, June 14, 2019. https://philonedtech.com/clay-shirky-on-mega-universities -and-scale/.

Southern New Hampshire University. 2021. "About SNHU." https://www.snhu .edu/about-us.

Top Hat. 2020. "Adrift in a Pandemic: Survey of 3,089 Students Finds Uncertainty About Returning to College." *Top Hat*, May 2020. https://tophat .com/teaching-resources/ebooks-and-guides/adrift-in-a-pandemic-survey -infographic/.

Ubell, Robert. 2021. "Lacking Online Programs, Many Colleges Are Rushing to Partner with OPMs. Should They?" *EdSurge*, June 7, 2021. https://www .edsurge.com/news/2021-06-07-lacking-online-programs-many-colleges -are-rushing-to-partner-with-opms-should-they.

Wan, Tony. 2021. "U.S Edtech Roars With Over $3.2 Billion Invested in First Half of 2021." *Medium* (blog), Reach Capital. July 1, 2021. https://medium. com/reach-capital/u-s-edtech-roars-with-over-3-2-billion-invested-in-first -half-of-2021-d69049dbce30.

Warren, Elizabeth. 2020. "Senators Warren and Brown Examine Questionable Business Practices of Largest Managers of Online Degree Programs." Official U.S. Senate Website of Senator Elizabeth Warren of Massachusetts, January 24, 2020. https://www.warren.senate.gov/oversight/letters/senators -warren-and-brown-examine-questionable-business-practices-of-largest -managers-of-online-degree-programs.

Watters, Audrey. 2013. "A Future with Only 10 Universities." *Hack Education*, October 15, 2013. http://hackeducation.com/2013/10/15/minding-the-future -openva.

3

THE NEW CONNECTED UNIVERSITY

The new connected university is being invented as we write at colleges and universities around the world. It is based on the belief that active learning and peer-to-peer engagement must play a central role in learning and that technology can enable these practices. It is also based on the idea that learning does not happen only during course meetings but through a continuum of activities ideally driven by students themselves. Finally, it is based on the understanding that a great deal of learning happens when students are connected to people from diverse backgrounds and are engaged with real-life issues and problems.

TWENTY-FIRST-CENTURY TOOLS

By integrating digital tools such as active discussion boards, prerecorded video lectures, video cases, collaborative projects, Zoom, and live chats into core teaching and learning offerings, higher education finally joined the twenty-first century. Robert Ubell (2021) states: "We are all online learners now. Every day that we use Google for research, send an email, or use Zoom, we use the tools of digital education."

The amazing amount of information available online has made us all "active learners." Today's incoming first-year college students have studied in a K–12 environment in which teachers used Google Classroom, Blackboard, or Canvas to create active learning environments. Today's students understand "googling it." They grew up learning how to find YouTube videos from educational digital content providers such as Crash Course or the Khan Academy, which explain how to solve basic science and math problems (figure 3.1), and then they applied these lessons to specific assignments.

In high school social studies, it's likely that teachers assign TED Talk videos, or clips from PBS shows such as *Nova, Nature,* and *Frontline* that PBS Learning Media makes available for easy downloading, along with teachers' notes and discussion subjects (figure 3.2).

In many high school classes, students complete project-based activities, applying academic concepts to real-world problems. This approach improves learning outcomes and makes learning relevant (Linder 2017). Why should this active learning end when students enter college? Deep reading of literature and academic works should remain a key part of the college experience, but

Figure 3.1 Khan Academy algebra class

Figure 3.2 PBS Learning Media website

readings should be complemented with the tools of twenty-first-century life and modern pedagogical practices. Techniques such as active learning, peer-to-peer engagement, and project-based teaching have been proven to improve student outcomes. Digital tools can help make them central to all classrooms. Finding the right balance between these different activities and modalities is the defining challenge of the twenty-first-century connected university.

ACTIVE LEARNING

The concept of active learning gained special prominence in the 1960s. It developed from constructivist learning ideas first advanced by theorists such as Jean Piaget (1896–1980), Lev Vygotsky (1896–1930), John Dewey (1859–1952), and others (Bain 2021; Reich 2020; Ubell 2021). Active learning was founded on the belief that people learn by doing, constructing their own knowledge by connecting it to their prior understanding and life experiences.

49

Digital tools can enhance active learning. Rather than only following lectures, students actively construct their own understanding of an issue. In *Super Courses: The Future of Teaching and Learning*, Ken Bain (2021) explores groundbreaking courses across a range of universities. One example of digital tools facilitating active learning can be found in physics courses at Harvard. In the 1990s, Eric Mazur gave his students videos and materials to read before class, and then used class time exploring "rich and inherently fascinating problems," which he called the ConcepTest. Other examples include research and project-based design courses at the Rhode Island School of Design, and a history course built on role-playing and simulations at Northwestern University (Bain 2021).

Active learning is the common denominator in all of these courses. Students work with peers and construct their knowledge through active research projects. Active learning can happen in both in-person and online settings, and digital tools and blended delivery can make the active learning process seamless. This is often surprising because the idea that digital tools *enable* active learning seems counterintuitive. Prerecorded content seems passive.

Poorly planned online courses fall into this trap. But the best online courses and digital content create active, multifaceted learning experiences. By watching prerecorded video lectures or digital case studies, students can come to class ready for discussion and debate. By allowing learning to be a flow of activities—rather than the read/lecture/test cycle typical of traditional instruction—students can become actively involved in the concepts and analysis of their subjects and learn by doing.

2U's Luyen Chou's (2021) interest in online learning began when he realized that he had learned little from the traditional lecture-based courses he took as a student. As a young high school teacher, he decided to create a digital archeology site for his class. In this virtual environment, students could find digital artifacts, conduct their own research, and work in teams to construct their own understanding of the issues. "They were doing what I had fallen in love with, which was true scholarship. . . . I looked at this and said, 'That's what I want to be doing.'" It was classic "active" learning concepts put into practice, and Chou realized that "digital technology allowed us to unlock that in a way that was much more robust than we could ever have done before."

In this paradigm shift, the instructor's role moves from "sage on a stage" to "guide by their side." At Columbia, Stanford, Arizona State University, and Georgia Tech, active learning drove course redesigns. For Stanford's Matthew Rascoff (2021), the key was to match the active learning strategy to the discipline, and physicists led the change. "Physics education, in most institutions now, is active, not passive," Rascoff said. "It's not lecture-driven anymore." This change was driven by the example of the physics innovators Eric Mazur of Harvard and Carl Weiman of Stanford, who realized that students could best understand certain key concepts through personal experience and peer-to-peer learning. "They led to a transformation of physics education," said Rascoff. Other fields soon followed their lead. The move online became a fantastic opportunity to rethink course design, turning a passive lecture-based learning experience into one that is built on the active construction of knowledge. "I think people within the discipline need to figure out the active learning strategy that is appropriate to their field. It's going to look different in a writing class than in a physics class," explained Rascoff.

Digital tools enable active learning activities that would pose logistical barriers or cost too much to run in traditional classrooms. These tools include digital labs and demonstrations, digital case studies, and simulations in subjects as varied as social work, engineering, and crisis negotiation. At Arizona State University, business management classes often include video scenarios based on common situations (Jhaj 2021; figure 3.3). At Purdue, students use 360-degree walkthroughs of boiler rooms and other heating plants, allowing them to virtually enter these spaces and interact with layouts and equipment (figure 3.4). At Columbia and the Open Society University Network, digital case studies present students with real-world problems in all their messy complexity.

At 2U, the instructional design team of a social work course filmed simulated clinical situations involving social workers and

Figure 3.3 Arizona State University WorkPlace simulation

their clients (figure 3.5). "We have actors and actresses who play the parts of patient, clients, and practitioners, and the students actually interact with them online," explained Luyen Chou (2021). The simulations and experiences are built into active learning experiences. Students interact with the digital activity or content, then build their own understanding of the issues.

Figure 3.4 Purdue/Wiley engineering 360

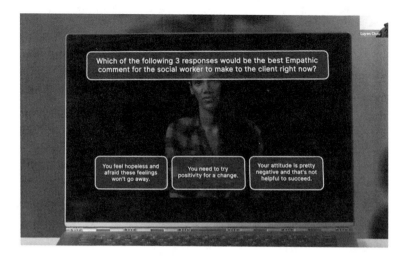

Figure 3.5 2U demo social work

PEER-TO-PEER LEARNING

Peer-to-peer learning is another core element of the new connected university that digital tools can support and enhance. Social
media platforms such as Instagram, Snapchat, and Twitter are part
of the daily routine of twenty-first-century digital natives. These
platforms are built on user-generated content, which can foster
peer-to-peer communication and sharing. Well-designed "digitally
enhanced" courses—be they fully online, blended, or in person—
also use these same concepts and techniques.

In networked courses at Columbia University, and with our partners at the Open Society University Network (OSUN), the most
exciting moments come when students engage with each other. In
live discussion or asynchronous debate, students share insights and
feedback from their readings, video lectures, classroom meetings,
professor conferences, and joint project conferences. The more
students share with their peers, the more they are invested in their
own learning. Being seen and heard is primal.

In OSUN collaborative courses, students from campuses around the world—in places such as Bangladesh, Kyrgystan, Russia, Germany, and the United States—meet online. Here peer-to-peer learning and collaboration are key. In countries that are transitioning to democracy or fighting growing authoritarianism, the OSUN courses focus on critical thinking and the exchange of ideas across cultural boundaries. "At its heart, liberal arts and sciences education is about the education of engaged citizens," explained OSUN Vice Chancellor Jonathan Becker (2021). "It is the antidote to rote learning if done properly." Digital tools such as video case studies, online discussion boards, and real-time brainstorming using tools like Padlet allow international project teams to connect and collaborate. "The assignments are meant to have students dialogue with each other," explained Becker, "because a view of citizenship . . . is radically different in Palestine than it is in the United States, and [than] it is in Russia." Despite the students' different life circumstances, online tools let them connect in ways impossible to imagine even ten or twenty years ago. "My view is that eighteen-year-olds, wherever they are from, tend to find much more in common than they do different," Becker said. "And that very fact of commonality gives a sense of normalcy that even people in incredibly difficult circumstances find comforting."

For eCornell's Paul Krause (2021), peer engagement can be more instructionally valuable than the production quality of prerecorded content. "We create a lot of highly produced videos with animations," Krause said. "The reality is students are more likely to remember how they engaged with other students, the projects they were able to apply, and the feedback from their instructor." These factors lead to high-impact courses that can "change the trajectory of someone's career."

Peer review sparks an exciting chain of activities: a virtuous cycle of student involvement and action that can drive learning in new directions. For Wiley's Bill Cochran (2021), peer engagement is the key to successful digital course design. "How are we weaving in those interactive touch points?" Cochran asked. "How are we creating opportunities for students to learn from each other?"

New educational conferencing platforms such as the Minerva Project's Forum and the new educational webinar tool Engageli make a strong argument that certain forms of peer-to-peer interaction can often be even better online than in person. Minerva University, a San Francisco-based educational startup founded in 2012, is dedicated to radically reimagining education around active and peer-to-peer learning concepts. It has no formal campuses or classrooms but runs student dorms in San Francisco, Buenos Aires, Hyderabad, Seoul, Berlin, London, and Taipei. All classes meet 100 percent online in digital seminars run on its proprietary Forum platform. Minerva founder Ben Nelson (2021) believes that the core role of all educational institutions is social learning. "It involves a group of individuals who are peers, who explore the black and the gray, not the black and the white . . . what is certainly true, and what could potentially be true . . . that is the core reason for being for a university," Nelson explained. "That entails active learning."

For the one thousand students in Minerva University's global cohorts, this active peer-to-peer learning happens on the Forum platform. "This is a technology that was built upon . . . decades of research into learning science about active, engaged, peer-based classroom environments," explained Minerva Project's Sharan Singh (2021). It allows professors to track participation by color coding each student's video feed based on how much the student has talked during the session, allowing the professor to know whom they need to call on (figure 3.6). Other tools for real-time polling and chat enable what many would argue is a richer experience online than can be found in a "normal" in-person classroom.

Engageli, another Zoom alternative, also promises richer real-time social interactions than traditional classes. Launched during the pandemic, Engageli was co-created by Dan Avida and Coursera cofounder Daphne Koller when their daughters found themselves in "Zoom School" in April 2020. Avida and Koller searched for alternatives. Avida (2021) remembers, "Much to our surprise, when we dug around, Zoom was the best game in town. To rephrase, it wasn't the best game in town; there was no real good game in town . . . so we set out to develop a platform that was built from the ground up for instruction."

Figure 3.6 The Minerva Forum platform

Although the Engageli platform began as a Zoom-like interface for video-conference-style classrooms, it soon moved into something that also offered tools for both asynchronous learning and live in-person classrooms (figure 3.7). Its real-time chat, document sharing, and polling features enable smooth transitions from general group discussion to smaller "breakout" rooms and back, and they can also be used to enhance and optimize in-person activities. Students in large classes can organize into smaller groups to meet online and synchronously "watch" a previously recorded lecture together, make notes, stop playback, and interact with the material in real-time in ways that are similar to the experience of a group video game (Avida and Spivak 2021).

The social aspects of online tools suggest the need to keep them in mind as classes return to campus. "A well-designed online course . . . helps you feel like you are part of a learning community," said Mathew Rascoff (2021) of Stanford University. Online tools and communities nurture learning "that is accountable, that is social, that is mind-expanding for our students." It is here that "transformative learning happens. . . . It's all about the interactivity among human beings that's enabled by technology."

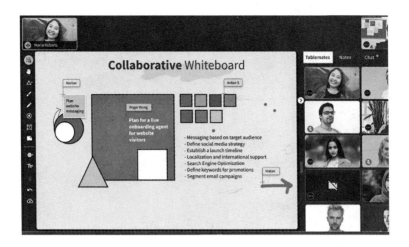

Figure 3.7 Engageli interface

EXPANDING INTERDISCIPLINARY TEACHING AND LEARNING CONNECTIONS

Another area in which digital tools can have a clear impact on both research and learning is interdisciplinary studies. If any one trend can define modern universities, it is embracing cross-disciplinary study and work. For most of the twentieth century, academic work was defined by ever-narrower areas of specialization, but crossing disciplinary boundaries is one of the core challenges of the twenty-first-century university (Heitzmann et al. 2021; Hesford 2021).

To encourage cross-disciplinary work, universities have funded courses co-taught by specialists from different departments. Faculty have searched widely in available literature for different voices and perspectives. In classes, they assign peer-reviewed articles from different disciplines and invite guest lecturers from other departments. As the president of Arizona State University (ASU), Michael Crow has made cross-disciplinary work the center of his vision for transforming higher education. He ties this vision to ASU's investment in digital technology (Crow 2021; Crow and

Figure 3.8 Arizona State University students in a virtual reality environment

Dabars 2020). Virtual reality–enhanced environments allow for immersive experiences that are, by their nature, multidisciplinary (figure 3.8). Crow (2021) explained that "this can be in the form of a virtual field trip, a mission to space, or a deep dive into human biology, but all these projects allow for cross-disciplinary collaboration, both by learners doing the course and as part of the program design itself."

Digital education projects often lead to the creation of learning assets that can be used in many contexts and classes. Digital case studies, immersive VR simulations, and TED talk-style presentations all engage learners in complex, real-life situations. They encourage understanding from a variety of perspectives. A digital case study on climate change, for example, can be used in courses and research in the sciences or on public policy or law. These high-impact digital learning assets are also modular. They can be inserted into a variety of classes. A course on environmental law, for example, can benefit from the insights of a leading scientist while also being used as a prompt for discussion in biology, economics, or public policy classes.

Digital case studies, or TED talk-style short video lectures, can be created with one course in mind but used for many others. High schools have been using evergreen course videos for years as teachers mix and match materials from Khan Academy, Crash Course, and other flipped class videos (Hua 2015; Koumi 2015; Nazir 2019). This flipping process has also begun to happen with content designed for graduate and postgraduate education. The idea of creating modular, sharable content has been somewhat of a Holy Grail for higher education. The digital case study offers one powerful format. Digital cases from Columbia's School of International and Public Affairs (SIPA) digital case collection have been downloaded and used by more than 300 professors and instructors from more than 200 universities, colleges, and nongovernmental organizations (figure 3.9).

Digital tools also connect scholars in "long-tail" specialties and create virtual communities of practice. The concept of the long tail refers to the ends of the bell curve where uncommon goods and ideas lie. Before online platforms, such as Google, Amazon, and Gutenberg, people had a hard time finding these rare assets. But the internet makes it easy to catalog all assets—and to connect people from all over the world with an interest in these obscure topics.

"I always say there are two reasons to be digital and online," explained Rovy Branon (2021), vice provost for Continuum College at the University of Washington. "One of those is big hits. With the OPMs, we focus mostly on the big hits—the MBAs, the data

Figure 3.9 Columbia's Public Policy Case Collection

sciences, and engineering." The other advantage of the internet is the long tail. "For fields of study that may only have a handful of scholars around the world, there's also a great benefit in connecting digitally," he said. "You may not have a critical mass in any physical geographic location, [but you] may have critical mass if you open that up to the globe."

With digital cases, flipped course videos, and other assets, scholars around the world can connect and learn from each other. The United Nations Development Programme (UNDP) has invested in digital learning and online courses for exactly these reasons. The UNDP trains and connects teams in different countries in the intricacies of "climate finance" and compliance with UN Sustainable Development Goals and climate accords. The program uses online courses and workshops that connect biologists and policy makers around the world. "We were able to connect with experts in the field from forty countries," explained Jamison Ervin (2021), manager of the Nature for Development program at the UNDP. Their course on Biodiversity Finance enrolled more than three thousand learners, 75 percent of whom were from developing countries. By investing in digital content created by "the people making the rulebook for biodiversity," the course created an international community of practice. Digital assets enabled a geographically diverse group of scholars and practitioners to connect. For Ervin, the stakes are nothing less than the fate of the world: "How do you use spatial data? How do you make trade-offs between food production, water, security, carbon, and biodiversity? We need to figure this out."

CONNECTING TO "REAL-WORLD" PROBLEMS AND OPPORTUNITIES

Modern university leaders feel a new urgency to connect on campus research and learning with off campus issues (Mebert et al. 2020). As Michael Crow of Arizona State University notes, the university's public purpose requires both training students in the skills and knowledge needed in today's world and undertaking cutting-edge, cross-disciplinary research needed to respond to the challenges of the global economy (Crow and Dabars 2020). This challenge has led to initiatives such as the Columbia Global Centers and Columbia World projects, which are designed to bring research close to the major issues confronting humanity.

This drive to connect universities to current problems and issues is fueled by two needs. One is the need for students to engage with the world and real-life issues to better prepare themselves for the workplace. The other is the need for research on and solutions for the key challenges that face humanity. Digital educational tools can help in both of these core missions. Digital tools can bring real-world issues, with all their messy complexity, into the classroom. These tools work for both online courses and traditional in-person classes. Digital tools can also help universities do their part in actively solving these problems by bringing the insights and knowledge of their researchers and faculty to those on the front lines of issues such as climate change and pandemic response.

Educators have long understood the importance of connecting students to real-world problems and challenges. In co-op courses, students combine classroom learning with internships and paid jobs at companies, public agencies, and nongovernmental organizations (NGOs). Northeastern University in Boston has made the co-op model central to their students' college experience. The imperative of real-world learning has become even more urgent with the rise of high-tech tools that automate and outsource jobs. Northeastern's president Joseph Aoun (2017) argues that education must focus on complex real-world issues that require skills and actions only humans can provide. Northeastern's curriculum mixes semesters of traditional classroom and lab study with semesters embedded in companies, public agencies, and NGOs.

These goals also drive Capstone and Portfolio projects at Columbia's School of International and Public Affairs. Student teams work as consultants to international companies and NGOs, often documenting this work in digital case studies for use in future classes. The Dean's Challenges at SIPA give students funds to start NGOs to address the problems they first investigated for their coursework.

At Arizona State University, digital tools bring real-world problems into the classroom using the Riipen platform. Through the platform, companies are matched to professors and classes, creating projects for university teams to study and work on (Jhaj 2021). This same logic is applied to the design and creation of new online certificate courses at the University of California Irvine, which works closely with a local industry advisory board to identify needs and gaps in training and create short online courses to teach those skills. It also draws heavily on local practitioners as subject matter experts in their courses (Matkin 2021). The University of Washington's Continuum College also focuses on creating certificate courses and programs that are closely aligned with the needs of the local economy. "We form an advisory board for those certificates," explained Rovy Branon (2021). "We run over eighty advisory boards . . . so we have a tremendous network amongst the local business community that we draw on."

At the University of Pennsylvania, digital assets created for on campus classes have been customized and delivered locally to train biologists and community members in the Galapagos. Other UPenn faculty teamed up with UNICEF to create MOOCs on social norms around the world. "The COVID pandemic revealed new opportunities to make an impact beyond Penn's borders," explained Nora Lewis (2021), vice dean for professional and liberal education in the School of Arts and Sciences at UPenn. "Increasingly I am seeing proposals coming through our faculty that are leveraging digital assets . . . to reach communities who may not be contiguous to the university," she said. "It goes to the heart of what faculty really care about. They care about social impact, and the global connectivity that creating these kinds of digital assets allows you."

Cornell University also uses its digital assets for international training and outreach. In embedded courses, Cornell offers its content to local colleges and universities. One international program in Africa, for example, uses Cornell's marketing and business management course materials to upskill young professionals. "It's an opportunity to take some high-quality education and get it to places that don't necessarily have it," explained Cornell's Paul Krause

(2021), "and provides access to areas of expertise that might not be locally available."

A Cornell program in Rwanda offers training in hotel management, an essential skill for the nation's nascent tourism industry. The program combines Cornell's digital assets with local content and on-the-ground instruction provided by Rwandan teachers (figure 3.10). "This is really the audience that was most impacted by the genocide that occurred in Rwanda," explained eCornell's Sally Berkowitz (2021). "They're really trying to upskill and train a population who weren't even residing in Rwanda at that time. . . . They may have grown up in a refugee camp somewhere else. They're bringing them back into the country and trying to create a positive, healthy future there."

Jason Healey (2021), director of Columbia's Cybersecurity Program at SIPA, explained that they work with partner universities and NGOs to develop content that can be used in multiple environments and campuses. These include projects with partners such as Brazil's National Public Management University, and work with ISTARI, a new university created in Singapore focused

Figure 3.10 eCornell Rwanda training program for hotel managers

on cybersecurity issues. Through these international partnerships, Columbia shares its digital assets, such as flipped class videos and digital cases, and creates new ones on local issues. Students and faculty benefit from these partnerships, and new digital content and digital cases from Brazil, India, Uganda, Vietnam, and elsewhere have been created. It also led to a new collection of cybersecurity case studies. "By creating and sharing small and accessible learning assets such as digital cases," Healey explained, "we are able to really make a big impact, both in academia and in the world of NGOs and think tanks who also use them. The process of creating these cases also really forces us to connect our scholarship with real-world issues."

Stanford has recently created an Office of Digital Education that reports to the provost with the specific mission of using new configurations of digital tools and teaching models to do outreach beyond the university. "What we are trying to do is reposition digital learning as part of the core of the university and to link it to the educational mission, the service mission, and also the research mission through collaborations with researchers," explained Matthew Rascoff (2021), Stanford's new vice provost for digital education. "Our mission is focused on extending the reach of Stanford and using our human and technological assets to spread educational opportunity more widely." Achieving this goal will require creativity and new partnership models. "Tech allows for wide distribution at great scale, but we need partners who share our goals and understand the needs of learners in ways we can't," Rascoff explained. "We are trying to connect the digital transformation conversation to the educational access and equity conversations. We hope to be the home where those two conversations can come together."

CONNECTING TO NONTRADITIONAL LEARNERS AND NEW REVENUE STREAMS

Digital tools are key to connecting universities to nontraditional learners. Doing so is both an ethical imperative and a key survival tactic for most universities and colleges. In the United States, the population of college-enrolled students peaked at 18.6 million students in 2008 (Davis and Bauman 2011). In 2020, before the COVID pandemic, that number fell by about 2 million students, to 16.6 million (Illing 2021; National Center for Education Statistics 2021). The pandemic has accelerated these trends in a dramatic way, with overall undergraduate enrollment from fall 2019 to fall 2022 down 8.2 percent, and community college enrollment down 15.1 percent.

To thrive, universities need to increase their pool of nontraditional and adult learners. At the same time, workers at all levels need to gain new skills and training throughout their careers. In a projected sixty years of employment, today's workers will face not only "evolving jobs with expanding skill sets" but "multiple careers" as technological change makes some occupations disappear and creates new ones (Dede and Richards 2020). "Higher education, and really good higher education, is becoming necessary for everyone to have a good life," explained the University of Washington's Rovy Branon (2021). "Even if you are not going to be in a position of leadership, if you are going to have economic survival, you need that level of education in the world today." As Gary Matkin (2021) of the University of California Irvine notes, workers need a "sixty-year curriculum"—a career-long process of learning and upskilling for the modern tech-oriented economy.

Ongoing professional development and executive education programs offer a crucial growth opportunity for MOOC providers edX and Coursera. After their initial boom in the early 2010s, MOOCs have focused on offering "stackable" certificates for working learners. For working professionals looking to move into a new position, Coursera offers short certificate courses that teach new or updated skills. When learners stack enough of these courses, they qualify for jobs in high-growth industries. "We recognized that stackability is really important for online learners," explained Betty Vandenbosch (2021), Coursera's chief content officer. "They can go to Coursera [and] take a certificate for a very low price, which has been created so that they have the skills they need for an entry-level position."

Google's certificate training is available for as little as $39 a month on Coursera. Coursera works with university partners to arrange college credit for some of its courses and to meet industry needs. More than one-third of the degree students at the University of London start with a Coursera Google IT certificate. "What's so great about that?" Vandenbosch (2021) asks. "It gives people confidence. It's inexpensive. It's worth something in the world, and it's worth something at the University of London."

Over a third (38 percent) of Coursera Google certificate students make $30,000 or less when they begin. Following the Coursera training, many earn $50,000 a year and gain college credit. "They get the job, then they have more resources. Then they can get a degree. That, to me, is stackability and certification at its best" (Vandenbosch 2021).

Programs for adult learning range from free or inexpensive entry-level certificate programs to more expensive competency-based education certificates offered by universities. University of California Irvine's 45,000 learners take seven- to ten-week certificate courses that cost between $600 and $900. The University of Washington's 55,000 students can get a blend of face-to-face and online certificate programs for $3,000 to $9,000 tuition. High-end executive education programs at Harvard, Stanford, UPenn, Columbia, and Cornell range from $3,000 to $30,000 for a twelve- to fourteen-week certificate program.

Tuition rates for these higher-end programs depend, in large part, on the level of faculty and support staff contact offered. Online project management providers such as Extension Engine and Emeritus provide support for universities creating a wide range of programs offered to students at very different price points, with different levels of ongoing involvement by senior faculty. One example of a less expensive program, which relies on less direct faculty involvement, is a 100 percent online ivy league business school program, created by the Boston-based Extension Engine OPM. The program offers completely online, asynchronous, four- to seventeen-week courses for tuition rates of $1,400 to $2,250 (more if college transferable credit is given).

A typical six-week online course in the program is "Disruptive Strategy," offered at $1,600. The course does not include "live sessions" or direct interaction with faculty; instead, it uses well-designed active and peer-to-peer learning tools to keep students engaged and participating in activities every three or four minutes during the time they are logged in. The program uses highly produced video case studies and active learning "teaching elements" such as interactive budgeting tools. It also includes advanced social learning elements in its platform. After students fill out extensive profiles, the course uses "cold calls" to initiate interactions between students.

"Community is a big part of it," says Extension Engine founder and CEO Furqan Nazeeri (2021). "In fact, the program looks more like Facebook than an online learning experience. You're introduced to your cohort, and you see people around the world, whether they are logged in or not. The profiles must be completed before you can actually engage with the material." With over 150,000 students completing classes in the overall program, the venture shows the potential for "high engagement at scale."

Another OPM focused on developing business school–based programs with elite universities is the Singapore-based Emeritus group, which serves 250,000 students a year (Damera 2021). Two-thirds of Emeritus's students come from the developing world. Courses in English, Spanish, Portuguese, and Mandarin provide a gateway to courses at MIT, Columbia, UPenn, Cambridge, and other elite universities. While the Extension Engine model uses well-designed cases and automated group activities to achieve its high engagement at scale, the Emeritus group prides itself on its layers of support and online staff and faculty. It offers certificate courses that range in price from $2,500 to $30,000, depending on length, degree of support, and exclusivity of faculty and peer groups.

One of Emeritus's high-end offerings is its CFO program, offered in partnership with the Columbia Business School (figure 3.11). It is designed to prepare chief financial officers to take over the financial management of major companies. It combines pre-recorded cases and exercises with "high-touch" events including interactions with

Figure 3.11 Columbia Business School CFO program website with virtual mentors

current CFOs and project-based group work. A key selling point of the $28,000 program is the chance to network with high-level peers and industry professionals and lean on the support of online "success coaches."

Ashwin Damera (2021), Emeritus founder and CEO, explained that Emeritus courses use digital tools to replicate the high-touch and live learning interactivity that the best MBA programs offer. These include role-playing, simulations, and real-world exercises. Creating digital courses, Damera explained, has now become a known science with "learning metrics that you can apply." For Damera, Emeritus's premium "digitally enhanced" online courses offer an experience equal or superior to the older, 100 percent analog, in-person executive education classes they replace. "We have found that these senior executive programs have been extremely well received in the market," explained Karen Mahon (2021), director of instructional design and learning experience at Emeritus. "They are arguably more rigorous than what the face-to-face workshops were previously. We are thrilled that participants want to . . . apply their skills and learn with their peers." Mahon feels that there is no going back now that participants have experienced what high-end, digitally enhanced, and supported learning can offer. She believes the digital transformation has "fundamentally changed the way these kinds of programs will exist going forward."

THE CONNECTED UNIVERSITY

Online or blended digital courses can provide sizable revenue streams for universities and, in many cases, their OPM partners. The process of creating these courses can also create digital assets and know-how that can be used in both on campus programs and as part of wider university outreach and engagement initiatives. But making these connections and realizing these synergies is not automatic. It requires bold leadership. Most universities have the components that a truly connected university requires, but they are located in separate schools, programs, and support units, without the management structures or faculty incentives in place to realize the potential of combining them.

The units set up to create and manage these online executive education certificate and master's programs are often run as separate entities, with at most loose integration with on campus teaching and learning. At times, they are run as entirely separate enterprises by OPMs or as "in-house OPMs" separate from on campus operations. At some schools, professors from the main campus also teach in the online programs and share digital assets with their on campus students and classes. At others, online programs feature separate adjunct faculty.

During the pandemic, the traditional barriers between on campus and off campus teaching and learning were taken down almost overnight. "It's pretty clear now that this line between residential and online education has completely broken down," explained Joshua Kim (2021) of Dartmouth. "There is no wall anymore. We are going to be doing it in person, we're going to be doing it online. It's going to change back and forth . . . so every course now, every program now is a blended program. And we must accept that."

Although the barriers between on campus and online programs seem to have fallen, students during the pandemic were organized into two very different categories of online courses. In a strange role reversal, executive education and adult learners often found themselves getting much better instruction than those enrolled in on campus degree programs. Students enrolled in traditional online courses—designed from the ground up to be delivered online, generally built around active learning concepts, and using high-quality digital assets—enjoyed the high-quality learning they had come to expect. Many students enrolled in traditional on campus programs received improvised Zoom University with all its shortcomings.

As universities move into the postpandemic world, students are demanding that the digital affordances offered during the pandemic be maintained (Kelly 2021; Top Hat 2021). Some students received high-quality digital education and want more. Citing a petition signed by thousands of University of Washington students demanding that all courses be delivered digitally as well as face-to-face, Rovy Branon (2021) wonders what this means going forward. "As someone who's advocated since the 1990s that our universities need to do more online, I never thought I'd see a day where traditional undergraduates across the board are standing up and saying 'We need more options in the way that you're delivering higher education to us!'"

The exciting potential that the new connected university offers is improved student outcomes through more active learning, improved peer-to-peer interaction, deeper connections across disciplines, and closer engagement with real-world issues and communities. It is possible, but it still must be built. Forging the new connected university requires moving external digital education units from the periphery to the center of university teaching and learning. It requires changes in budgeting and management structures. Digital education must be understood as a central and core piece of basic university infrastructure, which requires investment, planning, and time.

This movement is already underway. In many cases, the integration of digital learning into the center of teaching and learning began before the pandemic. In other cases, the pandemic has pushed forward these initiatives. Columbia, Cornell, Georgia Tech, Harvard, MIT, Stanford, the University of Washington, UPenn, and others have reorganized, moving previously external services into the central administration. These are the first steps in what will no doubt be a long and, we hope, successful process of digital transformation. In the next chapter, we explore some of the issues that leaders of digital transformation face, and describe some of the moving parts that must be managed to realize the potential of the connected university.

REFERENCES

Aoun, Joseph. 2017. *Robot-Proof: Higher Education in the Age of Artificial Intelligence*. Cambridge, MA: MIT Press.

Avida, Dan. 2021. Interview of CEO, Engageli, by Adam Stepan. November 9, 2021.

Avida, Dan, and Adam Spivak. 2021. Demo of Engageli platform to Adam Stepan, November 9, 2021.

Bain, Ken. 2021. *Super Courses: The Future of Teaching and Learning*. Princeton, NJ: Princeton University Press.

Becker, Jonathan. 2021. Interview of Executive Vice President and Vice President for Academic Affairs, Bard College, by Adam Stepan. October 22, 2021.

Berkowitz, Sally. (2021). Interview of Senior Director of Product Management, eCornell, by Adam Stepan. October 22, 2021.

Branon, Rovy. 2021. Interview of Vice Provost for Continuum College, University of Washington, by Adam Stepan. November 30, 2021.

Chou, Luyen. 2021. Interview of Chief Learning Officer, 2U, by Adam Stepan. October 27, 2021.

Cochran, Bill. 2021. Interview of Associate Director of Instructional Media, Wiley Education Services, by Adam Stepan. November 16, 2021.

Crow, Michael. 2021. Interview by Adam Stepan. November 23, 2021.

Crow, Michael M., and William B. Dabars. 2020. *The Fifth Wave: The Evolution of American Higher Education*. Baltimore, MD: JHU Press.

Damera, Ashwin. 2021. Interview of CEO, Emeritus, by Adam Stepan. November 8, 2021.

Davis, Jessica W., and Kurt Bauman. 2011. "School Enrollment in the United States: 2008." *United States Census Bureau*, June, 16.

Dede, Christopher J., and John Richards. 2020. *The 60-Year Curriculum: New Models for Lifelong Learning in the Digital Economy*. New York: Routledge.

Ervin, Jamison. 2021. Interview of Manager of the Nature for Development Global Program, UNDP, by Adam Stepan. November 4, 2021.

Hanson, Melanie. 2022. "College Enrollment & Student Demographic Statistics," July 26, 2022. https://educationdata.org/college-enrollment-statistics.

Healey, Jason. 2021. Interview of Senior Research Scholar in the Faculty of International and Public Affairs and Adjunct Professor of International Affairs, Columbia University, by Adam Stepan. December 1, 2021.

Heitzmann, Nicole, Ansgar Opitz, Matthias Stadler, Daniel Sommerhoff, Maximilian C. Fink, Andreas Obersteiner, Ralf Schmidmaier, et al. 2021. "Cross-Disciplinary Research on Learning and Instruction—Coming to Terms." *Frontiers in Psychology* 11 (May): 562658. https://doi.org/10.3389/fpsyg.2021.562658.

Hesford, Wendy, S. 2021. "Cross-Disciplinary Impact and Influence." *Global Arts and Humanities*, April 29, 2021. https://globalartsandhumanities.osu.edu/news/impact-and-influence.

Hua, Karen. 2015. "Education as Entertainment: YouTube Sensations Teaching the Future." *Forbes*, June 23, 2015. https://www.forbes.com/sites/karenhua/2015/06/23/education-as-entertainment-youtube-sensations-teaching-the-future/.

Illing, Sean. 2021. "Is It Time to Rethink the Value of College?" *Vox*, June 1, 2021. https://www.vox.com/policy-and-politics/21279216/higher-education-college-america-student-debt.

Jhaj, Sukhwant. 2021. Interview of Vice Provost for Academic Innovation and Student Achievement, Arizona State University, by Adam Stepan. November 1, 2021.

Kelly, Rhea. 2021. "Survey: What Students Want to Retain Post-Pandemic." *Campus Technology*, June 4, 2021. https://campustechnology.com/articles/2021/06/04/survey-what-students-want-to-retain-post-pandemic.aspx.

Kim, Joshua. 2021. Interview of Director of Online Programs and Strategy, Dartmouth College Senior Scholar at Georgetown University, by Adam Stepan. October 21 2021.

Koumi, Jack. 2015. "Importance of TikTok Type Videos for Learning." *Cogent Education* 2 (1). https://doi.org/10.1080/2331186X.2015.1045218.

Krause, Paul. 2021. Interview of Vice Provost of External Education and Cornell University Executive Director, eCornell, by Adam Stepan. October 22, 2021.

Lewis, Nora. 2021. Interview of Vice Dean for Professional and Liberal Education, School of Arts and Sciences, University of Pennsylvania, by Adam Stepan. October 26, 2021.

Linder, Kathryn E. 2017. *The Blended Course Design Workbook: A Practical Guide*. Sterling, VA: Stylus.

Mahon, Karen. 2021. Interview of Director for Long Form Programs on U.S. Design Team, Emeritus, by Adam Stepan. November 16, 2021.

Matkin, Gary. 2021. Interview of Dean of Continuing Education and Vice Provost for Career Pathways, University of California Irvine, by Adam Stepan. October 19, 2021.

Mebert, Laura, Roy Barnes, Jacqueline Dalley, Leszek Gawarecki, Farnaz Ghazi-Nezami, Gregory Shafer, Jill Slater, and Erin Yezbick. 2020. "Fostering Student Engagement Through a Real-World, Collaborative Project Across Disciplines and Institutions." *Higher Education Pedagogies* 5 (1): 30–51. https://doi.org/10.1080/23752696.2020.1750306.

National Center for Education Statistics. 2021. "The NCES Fast Facts Tool Provides Quick Answers to Many Education Questions." https://nces.ed.gov/fastfacts/display.asp?id=372.

Nazeeri, Furqan. 2021. Interview of CEO, Extension Engine, by Adam Stepan. November 9, 2021.

Nazir, Nazreen. 2019. "Dancing to the Tunes of Educational Content." *Entrepreneur*, June 29, 2019. https://www.entrepreneur.com/en-in/news-and-trends/the-sudden-rise-of-educational-content/336069

Nelson, Ben. 2021. Interview of CEO and Founder, Minerva Project, by Adam Stepan. October 14, 2021.

Rascoff, Matthew. 2021. Interview of Vice Provost for Digital Education, Stanford University, by Adam Stepan. October 29, 2021.

Reich, Justin. 2020. *Failure to Disrupt: Why Technology Alone Can't Transform Education.* Cambridge, MA: Harvard University Press.

Singh, Sharan. 2021. Interview of Senior Managing Director of Strategic Partnerships, Minerva Project, by Adam Stepan. November 2, 2021.

Top Hat. 2021. "3,052 College Students on the Good, the Bad and Learning Post-COVID." March 14, 2021. https://tophat.com/teaching-resources/interactive/3052-college-students-on-the-good-the-bad-and-learning-post-covid/.

Ubell, Robert. 2021. "Lacking Online Programs, Many Colleges Are Rushing to Partner with OPMs. Should They?" *EdSurge*, June 7, 2021. https://www.edsurge.com/news/2021-06-07-lacking-online-programs-many-colleges-are-rushing-to-partner-with-opms-should-they.

Vandenbosch, Betty. 2021. Interview of Chief Content Officer, Coursera, by Adam Stepan. October 22, 2021.

4

LEADING DIGITAL TRANSFORMATION

The American university model is unique. When Harvard University first combined the British model of the undergraduate residential college with the German model of the graduate research university, the modern American university was born (Christensen and Eyring 2011). By many measures, it has been successful. According to the 2021 Shanghai Ranking of world universities, forty of the one hundred top-ranked universities in the world are in the United States—the most of any country in the world (Shanghai Ranking 2021).

However, the modern American university is also a complex and unwieldy structure that is, by design, resistant to change. As Clay Christensen notes, the U.S. university combines the attributes of multiple "different and incompatible business models" within the same institution (Christensen et al. 2011).

University leaders committed to innovation must be skillful, powerful, and persistent. Despite almost two years of "pandemic teaching," a core resistance to the use of digital tools remains. The reasons for this resistance must be examined and understood by university leadership before any strategy to change these viewpoints can be developed.

Online tools and online education developed most rapidly in the early 2000s in the for-profit education world. The University of Phoenix, Corinthian Colleges, and the ITT Technical Institute enrolled hundreds of thousands of students online, often using predatory recruitment practices and accepting incredibly low completion rates (Shireman 2017). In 2015, the Obama administration stepped in with a major reform, leading to the closing of ITT, Corinthian, and similar organizations (Grasgreen 2015). This history has helped reinforce existing prejudices against online teaching, especially among elite universities and tenure track faculty. In a world driven by ranking and prestige, anything associated with such low-prestige, for-profit companies was to be avoided.

A second major challenge is that most universities provide few incentives for faculty to develop their teaching skills, learn digital competencies, or create online or digital classes. In the "publish or perish" world of higher education, teaching either in-person or online is generally not a priority. As Jonathan Zimmerman (2020) notes in *The Amateur Hour: A History of College Teaching in America*, few universities reward the quality of teaching in their tenure assessments or provide teaching training for new faculty. Nor do most universities mandate the level of class preparation that online education requires. "There is a perception," explained Nora Lewis (2021) of the University of Pennsylvania, "that if you have always taught your course, you can just walk in and teach it. . . . That's not the case online. . . . You really have to spend the time and effort to prepare and refine."

Rather than being seen as a plus on your résumé, time spent learning digital tools and prepping for online education classes can have a negative impact on one's professional opportunities. As Robert Ubell (2017, p. 50) notes, teaching an online course has often been seen as time "wasted" that could and should be used for original research and publication. "Teaching online can be a dangerous career move," Ubell stated, "departing from the comfortable respectability of conventional classrooms for the exotic, suspicious digital world."

The third obstacle to teaching innovation is that many older senior faculty members are unlikely to have had the experience themselves of taking or teaching an online course of any kind. In a comprehensive literature study of teaching online, it was shown that the negative views of digital teaching were especially strong among those who had never taught online (Lloyd, Byrne, and McCoy 2012).

But the actual impact of digital tools on the labor market is more nuanced than it first appears. A well-designed and delivered course requires new sorts of instructors, course designers, and facilitators. The best digital classes provide intimate learning experiences with the skilled guidance of instructors and assistants. Some forms of online courses, such as self-paced massive open online courses (MOOCs), can be scaled without hiring additional instructional staff. But the most successful courses maintain teacher-student ratios of one to twenty-five or less. Digital tools can expand access to learning by adding virtual seats and new career opportunities, providing thousands of new jobs for online instructors without new investments in buildings and physical infrastructure. Examples include Arizona State University, the University of California Irvine, and the University of Washington, which all created hundreds of new teaching positions with their shift to digital education (Whitford 2021).

There is also a need for a new conversation on how those whom Kim and Maloney (2022) have called "AltAcs," or alternative academics, can be recognized. As we explore in later chapters, digital course delivery is generally best done as a team effort. It often requires the work of trained academics who are not the "instructor of record" but who nevertheless are crucial to course design and delivery, and who combine content-area knowledge with expertise in course design, pedagogy, and digital tools.

If universities are going to improve on campus instruction, there is also a need for universities to recognize the contributions of "teaching professors"—professors who do not conduct original research but are content experts. "We need to be thinking about the career paths and lives of our nonfaculty educators, just as we think about our traditional faculty," argues Kim (2021) of Dartmouth. One solution may be to combine a move to new digital workflows with increased compensation. The investments needed for successful digital transformation are principally in the areas of human capital rather than in new IT infrastructure (Whitford 2021).

Focusing on the faculty's role in digital education could be a wise move, enabling university leaders to address these two important areas together. University leaders could provide financial incentives to adjunct instructors to undertake some new digital responsibilities. The key to implementing successful digital programs is support and training. It is possible that university leadership could solve several long-standing issues by embracing the creation of new digital instructor roles.

Another factor that might help leaders in their efforts to drive change is a rising generation of young researchers and instructors who have grown up as digital natives. Although they may not be in senior leadership roles, their presence can and will be felt. There is also the force of students themselves who increasingly demand more digital delivery options. "There is no faster path . . . to getting the door closed," explained Rovy Branon (20210) of the University of Washington, than saying "I'm here from the administration!" But when students say "this is an issue for me," faculty begin to pay attention. The pandemic has also opened the eyes of many faculty to the advantages of digital tools. "Faculty will begin to see the benefits of this as well," explained Branon, as they realize the "flexibility it brings to their own careers and their own teaching."

This trend should continue. The COVID moment will ensure that a whole generation of college students enter university with almost two years of online high school. As more and more of the current generation enter the workforce, issues that presently seem impossible and insurmountable may begin to fade away. If nothing else, the recent pandemic should remind us all that very different solutions are possible.

EXTERNAL OR INTERNAL DIGITAL ENHANCEMENT?

Another key issue that leaders of digital transformation programs must understand is the very different finances and structures of revenue-generating external programs compared to core investments in a university's own internal digital infrastructure. Digital initiatives and online education are often conflated. Some see online education as a cheap alternative to traditional learning, and others are wary of the steep up-front investments needed for the creation of good content and programs. Some see digital classes as a potential revenue stream that can bring in significant resources, whereas others see digital learning as a financial black hole without a viable business model. These common views all have some basis in reality, and untangling them is crucial for leaders trying to strategically plan their institution's digital transformation.

External digital programs have historically provided many universities' online education programs. Digital programs often are situated in executive education units at Ivy League universities, or in wholly autonomous digital "universities within a university" at major public universities, such as programs at the University of California Irvine, the Continuum College at the University of Washington, or Purdue Global. As explored in chapter 3, many of these programs have evolved as autonomous entities working in parallel with the traditional university and having separate management structures and staff. Many have become "mega universities" in their own right, with fifty thousand or more students enrolled who provide hundreds of millions of dollars in annual tuition revenues (Copley and Douthett 2020; Hanson 2019; Schroeder 2019).

What these units have in common is a business model that is very different from what would work in internal digital enhancement projects. External projects—be they an executive education project run by an in-house unit or a complete program run by an online program management (OPM) partner—generally have clear revenue streams. On campus digital enhancement projects generally do not. The tools used by units for these external student-facing programs— well-designed course websites on the learning management systems (LMS) model, recorded video lectures, well-planned and run Zoom sessions, digital case studies—are also needed for on campus delivery of digital course experiences. But new models for faculty compensation and budgeting must be developed if these tools and techniques are to be deployed at scale for on campus learning.

DIGITAL ENHANCEMENT AS UNIVERSITY INFRASTRUCTURE

An extensive review of successful digital transformations shows that they do not happen organically. Rather, they are led by leaders who embrace digital enhancement as a core goal and fund it from the central budget. Investing in digital tools can open new revenue streams and improve student outcomes, but it is not an overnight process and must be seen as a core and long-lasting investment in university infrastructure.

Michael Crow (2021), president of Arizona State University, was an early leader in this area, making decisions to invest in digital learning at the beginning of his tenure. "People born after 1990 have never known life without the internet," explained Crow. "Digital technology is an integral component of their daily lives . . . it was clear that technology would have to play a significant role in generating the kind of meaningful learning outcomes we wanted." Crow focused not only on making central investments but also on changing incentives for schools and programs to make it easier for them to embrace this digital transformation of teaching. "The design of our institution," Crow explained, "would need to anticipate these changes, allowing our organization to move quickly."

The good news for university leaders is that the funding needed for the digital enhancement of core classes is modest compared to university investments in new buildings and programs. Some investment in "hard infrastructure" is needed, mostly in terms of in-classroom lecture capture systems, but human capital is the most important investment. The digital revolution in teaching and learning requires hiring more teaching and learning support staff, as well as media creation experts. Even more important, it requires that faculty and their teaching assistants are incentivized to invest the time and effort needed to learn about digital teaching methods and pedagogies and to redesign courses.

Leaders must understand that such investments in human capital and course redesigns are often harder to "sell" to donors, boards, and funders than traditional investments in buildings and new research centers. They are relatively invisible and do not provide the immediately noticeable impact that new construction or a new center can provide. That said, they can and should provide positive outputs for students and leaders in a relatively short time frame. Making the payoff of these investments visible and demonstrating their positive impacts to key funders and stakeholders is critically important for leaders of digital transformation projects. "Where I think schools go wrong is when they look at digital and online education only as a cash cow," explained Josh Kim (2021) of Dartmouth's Center for the Advancement of Learning. "COVID made it very clear that the ability to create and deliver high-quality education across multiple mediums is a core competency . . . we need to have instructional design . . . we need to have media educators."

Well-run digital enhancement projects improve learning experiences for students on campus. Over time they enhance the university's prestige, increase new student applications, support fund-raising, and lead to other positive outcomes. Just as universities invest in core services—security, food services, fitness facilities, or even the hiring of famous new professors or department heads—universities must invest in improved digital course delivery systems to stay relevant. Making the benefits of these investments clear to key stakeholders—trustees, alumni, faculty, and students—is an integral part of the job for successful leaders of digital transformation.

GOVERNANCE

Another key issue leaders must address is the governance of digital transformation efforts. Should the university have a set of university-wide policies and mandates for digital education—as they generally do for many facets of university life, including research and gender and diversity guidelines—and should they leave these questions to the schools and individual professors? Should digital efforts be driven by a central unit, such as an "in-house OPM," or should it be outsourced? Should the university establish a set of core "digital competencies" that all classes and professors must follow? These are some of the crucial and difficult issues that leaders now face.

Faculty governance is at the core of many of these debates. So is the alignment of the incentives of professors and students. The U.S. university model is built on the core value of faculty independence. The tenure system itself, which many people assume is an ancient tradition, is a relatively recent invention, only institutionalized in the 1930s as a way of ensuring faculty independence during a time of global authoritarianism. Similarly, the model of the researcher-teacher is a nineteenth-century U.S. invention, built on the largely unproven assumption that good researchers are by definition also good teachers. "It goes back to the founding of the modern American research university at Johns Hopkins," explained Matthew Rascoff (2021) of Stanford, "where we bundle together research, teaching, and service in one institution" and hope that it works well.

In the university's digital transformation, administrators and faculty face difficult questions. Are the interests of faculty and students actually aligned? Does the faculty promotion system, which is based on the volume and prestige of research and publications, provide adequate incentives for faculty to invest in teaching and learning? Should the university adjust its incentive system to encourage better course delivery?

How should the university approach faculty governance and independence when it comes to curricular design and course delivery? Faculty need independence for their research, but as teachers they are part of organized programs of study. Many argue that in this area the needs of students must be paramount. Ben Nelson (2021) of the Minerva Project argues that the modern faculty's near-absolute control over what happens in the classroom is an "insane redefinition" of the professor's traditional and historic role. Should university leaders reassert greater influence over curriculum and course delivery? As leaders rethink their offerings in a digital age, these questions must be front and center in their minds.

Another set of governance issues revolves around the question of central versus distributed management and control of digital projects. Most large research universities are built on a federal model: individual schools and programs receive some orientation, guidance, and funding from the university's central administration but have considerable autonomy to design their programs. This includes, at times, creating their own units to fund and make external-facing revenue-generating programs.

Individual schools, be they engineering, law, or social work, have area-specific knowledge. They understand their subject areas and how to teach them, at least within the framework of traditional classroom lecture-based instruction. But rarely do individual schools have the bandwidth or the funding to take on the sort of investments that "going digital" requires. This decentralized federal approach has generally meant that certain schools with funding and activist administrators have been early adopters of digital tools, creating their own internal digital teams, and those who have not had the funding or mandate have not done so. Nina Huntemann (2021) of edX explained that many schools with federal systems have seen individual deans or programs "do something scrappily on their own" that would in turn then serve as a "catalyst" for others in the university. In general, most universities then eventually move toward a central system of support. "There can be real benefits to centralizing," Huntemann said. "You can keep costs down, you can prioritize. You can spread the love or really focus in one area."

Most universities that have had success with digital transformation have done so through the creation of a central unit that provides services and technical know-how across the university's schools. They also have generally created a mechanism to centrally fund some local school-level digital education staff who work closely with local faculty on projects. Many times, universities have begun their work in the digital space using a federal approach, allowing innovation to happen at the school level, and then deciding to organize these activities under a central unit.

INTELLECTUAL PROPERTY

Another key area leaders of digital transformation must address are questions of intellectual property (IP). Most universities have standing agreements in which all underlying course IP belongs to faculty. However, when funds are invested in the creation of digital learning assets, most universities have added riders to these agreements stating that the online and digital assets are owned by the university or their OPM partners, who have a perpetual right to use them in university courses and projects. These agreements have precedent; professors are used to signing similar agreements with university presses that publish their IP in books, but these agreements are complex to negotiate. Having a standard and accepted university-wide agreement on these issues is helpful.

The question of faculty compensation for their involvement in the planning, creation, and delivery of digital courses is fundamental. Building good digital programs requires additional work and time by faculty, and creating a system to incentivize and compensate this work is key. "Building a good online learning experience requires upfront effort from faculty," explained Paul Krause (2021) of eCornell. "Sometimes the incentive systems aren't really set up for this. How do you get focused time from a faculty member to do this work and do it well? It's certainly one of the fundamental challenges we have."

Most successful digital executive education and online programs to date have been built on the recognition that the work of creating digital classes is indeed additional "work," especially if this work must take place over the summer or other traditional university breaks. In programs run by external digital education units operating outside the normal university structure, the question of compensation has generally been resolved with additional compensation payments to the participating faculty that range from $3,000 to $25,000 or more, depending on the work involved and the time commitment required.

An instructor who creates an online degree program course with an OPM such as 2U understands that this is a time-consuming process that generally requires 150 hours over six to nine months (Hermalyn 2021). "We usually spend four to six weeks in the planning and really come up with the blueprint," explained Luyen Chou (2021) of 2U. "Then we spend three months on content development." Faculty who will record video course elements work intensively in 2U studios in Arlington, Virginia; Los Angeles; or Cape Town, South Africa. "We usually get the filming done in three to four days, really concentrated," Chou said. Faculty partners continue to contribute to the course-building process through to final course delivery.

For in-house course creation units at major public universities, it is also the norm to compensate faculty for their time in digital course design and filming. "The faculty member signs a memorandum of understanding (MOU)," explained Phil Regier (2021) of EdPlus at Arizona State University (ASU). The MOU says, "I'm going to build this course with the instructional design team at EdPlus. I understand that it's going to have to achieve a certain score on the quality matter rubric, and it'll be on this schedule." Course creation programs at eCornell, Georgia Tech, University of California Irvine, and the University of Washington all operate on similar principles: courses are chosen for "digital enhancement," and professors are contracted for the additional work this will involve. "We don't fly people to LA," explained Rovy Branon (2021) of the University of Washington, "but we do have two production studios actually in our building. . . . Not as fun as flying to LA, but we can reach them." The university's in-house OPM unit funds all project "year zero" costs, including faculty "buyouts" and compensation.

For most on campus digital enhancement projects, however, the mechanism to fund and compensate faculty for their involvement has not been in place. Work for on campus digital enhancement, along with workshops for using digital tools, has often been "voluntary." Professors can apply for in-kind support, and even for funds to help in digital course enhancement, but their own additional effort and time spent in class redesigns and the creation of digital assets has generally not been compensated.

There are exceptions. At the award-winning IMPACT program at Purdue, faculty are encouraged to participate in a semester-long training program to improve teaching. They generally receive course relief and an additional payment of $5,000. With funding from the provost's office, the program has helped to pay for the redesign of high-enrollment introductory mechanical engineering courses. The results have been impressive, with failure or withdrawal rates falling from 34 percent to 12 percent with the new digitally enhanced courses. "It was a lot of money that went to mechanical engineering," said Purdue Global's chancellor Frank Dooley (2021). "But you take a roughly 20 percent drop in the failure rate, and it has more than paid for itself."

At Michigan, a core unit was centrally funded with a focus on improving on campus teaching. Faculty who participate in digital course redesigns are compensated via course relief, and professors' "digital contributions" are directly considered in tenure review. For James DeVaney (2021), the director of Michigan's Center for Academic Innovation, such acknowledgment offers a real incentive. Professors seeking promotion, DeVaney said, can tell review committees: "Here are direct teaching contributions, and here are my indirect teaching contributions, because people have used my (digital) content in a variety of important ways."

Another area that must be explored by leaders planning new digital education initiatives is whether faculty and the schools where they work should receive some long-term financial compensation for the digital assets they create—and whether these royalties should be tied to the quality and success of their digital offerings. Such arrangements make sense in theory but are difficult to manage in practice: complex accounting is involved, as digital assets may be used in a variety of both revenue-generating and mission-driven courses. Arizona State University has developed such a system to compensate both faculty and schools for their investments in the creation of digital assets. As a university working to increase access and enrollment, ASU strives to have larger courses and has designed a compensation model in which schools that participate in digital course redesigns receive a residual payment for increased enrollments. Schools get a "flat rate per seat enrollment," explained ASU's Phil Regier (2021). "If it's a three-hour course, they get X. If it's a four-hour course, they get 1.3 times X. We want to incentivize them not to teach a course with ten students, but to teach a course with fifty or sixty students, and do it well."

But long-term royalty agreements are challenging to manage, especially as more and more courses use and share a variety of digital assets. Creating and delivering engaging digital education experiences is a team effort that often involves mixing and matching digital assets created by one professor with assets created by others in a course delivered by a team. That one course might use materials created by many others, adding extra levels of complexity. In many cases, the "authoring faculty member" is not available to also be the "instructor of record," explained Paul Krause (2021) of eCornell. "It changes the standard university teaching model. In the future, we will need a new model that balances the interests of the authoring faculty, the instructor of record, the university, and the students."

For all these reasons, most organizations have avoided making forward-looking financial commitments to faculty for digital assets created, at least until long-term markets and standards for exchanging and sharing digital assets are more developed. The key will be to find a fair and equitable system that is also relatively easy to manage.

PRICING AND REVENUE SHARING MODELS FOR HYBRID AND BLENDED PROGRAMS

Another key issue that must be thought through and negotiated between central administrative units and schools is the pricing for, and participation in, online and hybrid programs. There are many benefits to having one central unit handle all external revenue-generating programs. One is simply an issue of scale—running successful online programs requires a large staff both for content creation and for program management, marketing, and student support. Many in-house OPMs and external OPMs have a staff of more than two hundred professionals to handle these aspects of course delivery. Few schools or units within a university can fund and support such large teams on their own. But if marketing and management of a program are moved from the school to another unit—be it an external OPM, such as 2U or Wiley, or a central unit run by the university itself—the issues of how to price these programs and what part of revenue should flow back to the school where the program resides must be negotiated.

Traditionally, tuition for most online degree programs has been priced at a rate that is near or equal to the on campus in-person cost. There are several reasons for this. One is simply the worry that offering a for-credit online program will cannibalize the existing on campus program. Research has shown that this is generally not the case because students who gravitate toward fully online degrees generally cannot participate in full-time in-person programs due to other family and work commitments (King and Alperstein 2017).

However, the most important reason for maintaining online program costs at the same price as on campus programs is that offering small to medium size high-touch online degree programs with well-designed learning experiences and student services customized for online students' needs is costly. Some universities have set up university-wide units in charge of online programs. eCornell—a unit that has seen significant annual growth in revenues in the past five years—is organized as an enterprise unit whose operating results fund programs on campus. "We are expected not to be a unit that sucks funds from the university but rather returns [funds] to the university," explained Krause (2021). Online programs run by the OPM 2U are often priced at rates that are similar to traditional in-person program costs. Luyen Chou (2021) of 2U explained it this way: "When you order food delivery from a high-end restaurant, do you pay more or less for that? . . . You pay more to be able to eat when you want, where you want. That was very much the vision around 2U."

Not everyone agrees. Georgia Tech shocked the higher education world in 2014 when it offered a fully online master's degree in computer science for $7,000, about one-quarter of the rate of the on campus program. This move required complex financial modeling and discussions with university leadership and campus units. Some were worried about the impacts and the potential to lose residential students due to the cost. "It began with a market analysis, a market study," said Nelson Baker (2021), dean of professional education at Georgia Tech. "The research indicated that there should be different students and different types of interests at the different price points." The analysis showed that each course would initially cost close to $300,000 to build. But after a certain number of students enrolled, the program would pay for itself. "There's a decreasing cost as the course goes along, allowing you to scale," Nelson said. "So we modeled the variable and fixed costs to determine the sweet spot based on the amount of risk we wanted to take."

Eventually, in consultation with the University System of Georgia, the governing body for public universities in Georgia, the university determined that a degree for $7,000 was the right mix of risk to cover costs with projected enrollments. To respond to the concerns of the on campus program leadership, the venture, with philanthropic support from AT&T, signed an internal MOU saying that "if it did cannibalize the program, this program would offset the loss to the university." Fortunately for Georgia Tech and the program's funders, this never occurred, and Georgia Tech's on campus and online programs have both thrived in parallel.

Some observers agree with the approach to pricing taken by Georgia Tech even though it may mean lower-touch programs with limited access to full-time tenure track faculty. Other observers now feel that offering online or hybrid degrees and programs at the same price or a slight discount to on campus offerings makes sense. It increases enrollments without requiring new physical infrastructure, a win-win for both students and universities. Where these options are available, many students opt for a mix of online and blended learning programs, increasing student satisfaction. Georgia Tech's Nelson Baker (2021) credits the school's investment in digital tools for improving both online and on campus programs. "You can do things . . . that you can't do in the physical classroom . . . special effects . . . that will make higher education even better." The question for Baker is this: "How do we take this technology that's in front of us and make education more engaging for the student? . . . That is where we are headed."

CREATING A CENTRAL DIGITAL EDUCATION SUPPORT UNIT

Beyond questions of governance and program pricing, a significant question facing leaders of digital transformation is how to create an organization that can run and manage these activities. How should central units be created and organized, and what should their scope and mandate be? What should be done centrally, and what can be done at the school level? In most cases, central units have been created following one of two paths:

- **Bringing the outside in:** Choosing an independent executive education unit program—which traditionally operates outside standard university systems—and bringing it in-house. The program would expand its portfolio to support the "digitization" of on campus courses and instruction, with a new financial structure to pay for this effort. We call this the "in-house OPM" model.
- **Boosting the inside unit:** Expanding the resources and mandate of an in-house center for teaching and learning (CTL), and giving it increased funding and a mandate to acquire the digital content creation and digital delivery support skills most often found in external-facing units. We call this the "enhanced CTL" model.

The in-house OPM model requires important adjustments. Typically, external-facing executive education units tracked costs on a project-to-project basis; they did not provide services to the university or school on an as needed basis. They also controlled their projects, with a certain autonomy over program design, recruitment of instructors, compensation policies, and staffing. Pivoting these structures to support other on campus digital initiatives requires important cultural shifts and a new financial model.

The enhanced CTL model, in which existing CTL units are given new responsibilities for digital support and online course creation services, also requires adjustments. Most CTLs were set up to provide as needed professional development and assistance. They were not designed to coordinate digital content production or to support remote learners. Most lack project managers or professional media creation teams, and few CTLs have been designed to manage large-scale production of digital assets. If CTLs are to take on new responsibilities, they need new management structures, new staff, and digital production facilities.

Both organizational models have areas of strength and areas that require adjustments. Next we review some examples of organizations that have followed each of these paths.

THE IN-HOUSE OPM MODEL

Many universities want to take an existing executive education unit and turn it into a course production and management unit that can provide services across the university. One of the most interesting examples of this model is at Arizona State University, whose in-house OPM was designed from the ground up to provide services for both fully online and on campus digital classes (figure 4.1). Originally founded in 2009 and renamed EdPlus in 2016, the unit is unusual because it was not designed to create short-term executive education and certificate courses but to build credit-bearing courses. One of the distinguishing characteristics of ASU and EdPlus is that the same faculty and courses are offered in both in-person and online programs. "We don't think of them as separate," explained Sukhwant Jhaj (2021), ASU's vice provost for academic innovation and student achievement. "It's the same group of faculty who teach what we call 'campus immersion,' which is our way of saying 'in-person' and 'digital immersion,' which is what some might call 'online.'"

EdPlus leads course design and delivery, providing the media creation and course delivery services that schools cannot deliver

Figure 4.1 Arizona State University studio website

on their own. EdPlus has more than five hundred employees and its own board of directors. Its staff includes a course management team, "success coaches" who work with online students, and more than two hundred professionals in its central media production and course-creation units.

To cut through red tape, ASU established university-wide MOUs to cover digital education projects. If a degree program is approved by the academic senate, no new approval should be needed for online programs. "It comes from the central thesis that the learning outcomes are the same," said Phil Regier (2021), CEO of EdPlus, and the process is well defined. "The department chair has an MOU. The department chair knows what their responsibilities are and what EdPlus will do. The department chair works carefully with our schedulers to build a program on a schedule. . . . We have done it over two hundred times." A revenue-sharing agreement aligns with the interests of all parties. "When online student enrollment grows, money goes to the academic unit, which allows it to do a wide variety of things," Jhaj (2021) said. Regier (2021) adds that "some units are hiring tenure-track faculty on the proceeds that they have from online teaching and learning. So it's a big deal."

EdPlus runs three production studios, with online scheduling and training available to faculty and departments. The EdPlus website offers a menu of different approaches to course filming and production, including different options for filming lectures, conducting interviews, and staging simulations (figure 4.2). A central team of twenty instructional designers at EdPlus supports course design and production, as well as one hundred school-level instructional designers. They work with professors to build content using EdPlus's instructional design guidelines, with faculty coming to the EdPlus studios for video shoots and final course production (Harding 2021).

Another school with an in-house OPM model is the University of California Irvine (UCI), which also has a robust digital education content creation and delivery team, that serves approximately 45,000 online learners. Like ASU's EdPlus, it oversees all aspects

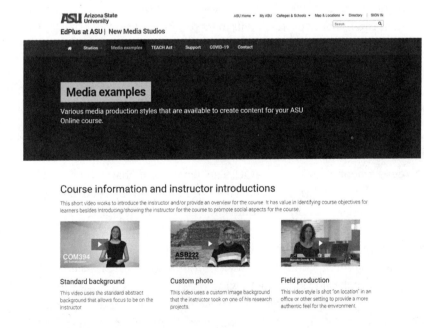

Figure 4.2 Arizona State University studio menu of filming formats

of content creation and delivery for online courses and sets formats for its video-driven online courses. Unlike ASU, UCI is an in-house OPM that focuses entirely on its remote learners, with less connection to on campus teaching or faculty.

Other schools have also developed large and sophisticated in-house OPMs that rival the outside OPMs in the size and sophistication of their digital content creation and delivery teams. eCornell, University of Washington, and Georgia Tech all have units of between one hundred and two hundred employees who manage the recruitment and support of their successful online student programs, as well as run sophisticated in-house content design and production facilities.

eCornell presents an excellent example of the potential benefits of a well-run in-house OPM model, and it is now beginning to digitally enhance some on campus courses as well. Set up as an external revenue-generating operation, eCornell is a separate legal entity that is 100-percent owned by Cornell. It was restructured recently to be more strategically integrated into Cornell's main academic operations, and its director, Paul Krause, was given the title of vice provost. The unit creates and manages both short-form certificate programs and fully online or hybrid degree programs.

Although eCornell's focus remains on its executive education courses, it is increasingly designing courses explicitly for multiple uses, explained Krause (2021). For example, video assets created for an online graduate course in data analytics are repurposed for undergraduate use on campus, sometimes requiring a reworking of certain planned activities. The repurposing is often simple. "In an active learning assignment for an executive education class, we design projects such that a participant typically works with a dataset from their organization," explained eCornell's Sally Berkowitz (2021). "For the undergraduate class, however, the dataset would be incorporated into a case study." Using instructional assets for multiple audiences requires some planning, but Krause (2021) explained that the concepts and principles in the videos largely still work in the new setting. Faculty with undergraduate students can choose to use eCornell's sophisticated animations and digital activities on issues ranging from economics to agriculture to biology to hotel management. Because these assets are modular, they are easy to insert into different courses. "Most of our videos are modular, well organized, and short—five minutes or less," said Krause.

Several other universities have also recently moved external-facing executive or continuing education units, making them part of their university's central administration. Now inside the central administration, they are often asked to provide in-house OPM services to the wider university. These include the University of Washington's Continuum College, whose director, Rovy Branon, was also given the title of vice provost. "We're sort of a not-for-profit internal OPM at the University of Washington," Branon (2021) explained. "We have about eighty degree programs. For degree programs, we provide the funding . . . we own all the risk as an OPM does. We do all the marketing . . . and we have a cost-recovery model that recovers investments in that degree program, makes us whole, and allows us to invest in the future." As with eCornell, the University of Washington unit's primary focus remains on executive education, but it is increasingly providing digital education support for on campus learning as well. Handling both sorts of projects—some funded through external revenues, some from central funding—raises management issues that the unit is still working through. "We provide both OPM-like services to our campus and have our own portfolio," explained Branon. "It's a bit of a challenge for us."

In most cases, the transition from an external-facing unit to an in-house OPM is still a work in progress. Many executive education and continuing education units have weak links with on campus professors and departments, and they must make a cultural pivot to begin offering support services to on campus classes. Despite these barriers, their developed workflows, media skills, and project management experience make many executive education units interesting candidates for universities that want to create central digital education units. Enrollments and staff numbers of the principal universities that have created in-house OPM's are shown in figure 4.3.

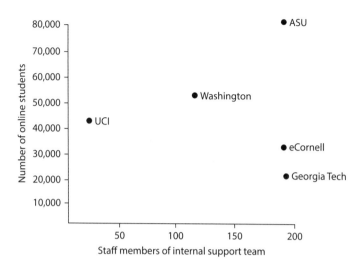

Figure 4.3 Universities that have created in-house OPMs

THE ENHANCED CTL MODEL

The second option that many universities have embraced for the creation of a central digital education unit is expanding the scope and mission of their own current centers for teaching and learning (CTLs). We call this the enhanced CTL model. With their focus on pedagogy and research, CTLs are close to the needs and desires of both students and faculty. CTLs were also the heroes of the pandemic, providing essential leadership and services to faculty struggling to take their courses online. "All of a sudden, our CTLs became the central player," said Joshua Kim (2021) of Dartmouth. "We had educational developers and instructional designers . . . we were comfortable in this world." Suddenly, the university community realized that the CTL's work on digital learning was "actually central and strategic for institutions."

Designed to provide voluntary solutions for professors, CTLs traditionally put a premium on being responsive to the immediate needs of instructors rather than organizing and directing coordinated programs. They have focused on offering a wide menu of options to professors who want to experiment and innovate instead of providing well-oiled and finely tuned models and workflows. They have often been optimized to support pilots and experiments rather than setting up production lines for the efficient creation of coordinated offerings.

Joshua Scott, the director of course strategy at 2U, previously worked at CTLs at Notre Dame and the University of Colorado, where he saw the constraints created by their limited funding and mandate. "I saw the disconnect," Scott (2021) said. "We were building out instructional guidance, but we weren't building the capacity to produce. We didn't have production studios and graphic design professionals and people with the hard skills to aid in production." Work was isolated and disconnected from the university's larger strategic vision. "Because there was no central mandate, we never knew how much support we were providing," Scott said. "Different schools would set up their own micro-units. . . . It was very siloed to a specific unit or specific purpose."

Despite the limitations of their current size and budgets, most CTLs are well-positioned administratively to make the transition to the role of central provider of digital services because they already provide central teaching and learning services. Many have begun to build successful in-house digital course creation teams. The University of Michigan offers perhaps one of the largest and most successful examples of the implementation of the enhanced CTL model, showing how successful it can be when backed by strong administrative support and central funding.

The project was launched in 2014, partly in response to the MOOC moment (figure 4.4). It was centrally funded from the start and given the mandate to improve teaching and learning on campus. "In 2012, Michigan became one of the first four partners with Coursera," explained James DeVaney (2021), director of Michigan's Center for Academic Innovation. The innovation center was championed by Provost Martha Pollack. The school made a strategic decision to focus on using digital tools to improve on campus learning. "Michigan is known for its breadth

Figure 4.4 University of Michigan biology MOOC also used in on campus classes

of excellence," explained DeVaney. "Having more than one hundred programs ranked in the top ten compelled us to think about how to create access to our breadth of excellence in the digital space and how to create and support interdisciplinary, intergenerational, and interprofessional learning communities. Importantly, missing from that charge was an overemphasis on revenue generation."

With an on campus enrollment of 44,000, Michigan has many of the same considerations as other mega universities. A top priority has been to provide new digital learning tools and support for a wide range of classes and to create assets that could improve both off campus and on campus learning (figure 4.5). "We have a really

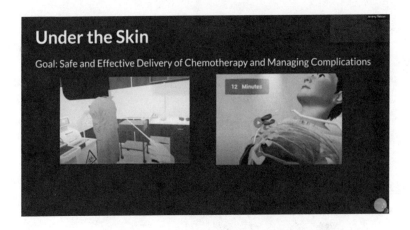

Figure 4.5 University of Michigan virtual reality class—under the skin

important focus on remixing and reusing content derived from MOOCs and other open offerings to complement, reinforce, and scaffold activities on campus," DeVaney (2021) explained. Senior university leadership encouraged leading professors to get involved in digital projects. "Having faculty engaged from the beginning was prudent and has paid dividends ever since. As the work began to grow both in volume, complexity, and impacts," DeVaney said, "the contributions of our president and provost have been critical. They put this work in the context of a public research institution and explained how we would explore new modalities of learning and leverage the power of novel educational technology and translational research in service of strengthening the quality of a Michigan education and enhancing our impact on society."

Columbia University has so far followed the enhanced CTL model as well. Its CTL was designated a central support unit for both pedagogy and technology-assisted learning in 2014. The CTL has created a sizable number of MOOCs across schools. Individual schools run their own executive education programs, sometimes in conjunction with OPM partners, and provide course support services. UPenn also followed an enhanced CTL model, with a central team running both MOOCs and school-based creation and production, as have other Ivy League schools, including Brown and Dartmouth. These and other schools are now considering how to expand the roles of centralized units for both online and traditional courses.

At Brown University the move toward digital education began with MOOCs in the early 2010s. One of the key questions, explained Catherine Zabriskie (2021), Brown's senior director of digital learning and design, was "how does Brown enter the MOOC space in a way that's authentic to Brown?" One motivation for creating MOOCs was sharing Brown's assets with a global audience, but another was to use the experience to "figure out how might Brown benefit its own community," said Zabriskie.

In 2020, during the COVID-19 pandemic, Brown decided to combine the team focused on digital education efforts (Digital Learning & Design) with the Sheridan Center for Teaching and Learning. Combining these teams into one unit helped "make a more cohesive experience for the faculty," explained Zabriskie (2021), and it also fulfilled the Brown provost's vision of "looking for opportunities to enhance any course with digital tools." The newly combined teams ensured academic continuity and a positive student course experience during the pandemic. Nina Huntemann (2021) of edX noted this trajectory of CTLs across the country. "The Centers for Teaching and Learning, which would support the occasional faculty member who wanted to do something interesting and experimental . . . became the heroes of 2020," Huntemann explained. Now the work they have long supported is moving to the center. University leaders are now asking how they can move forward so that "our whole approach to how we deliver education" can have the "things we learned from the center of teaching and learning at its core."

Some of the principal enhanced CTL model universities are shown in figure 4.6. They have generally not been the major "digital public universities" but rather are schools that have focused their digital education efforts on MOOCs, research, and digital enhancement efforts.

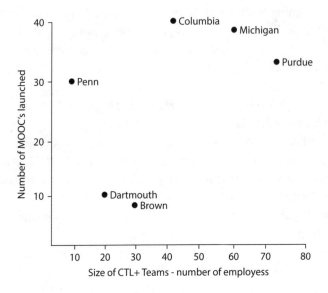

Figure 4.6 Enhanced CTL model schools—MOOCs

OPMs

In this new and fast-changing world, traditional OPMs continue to play an important role as program managers, thought leaders, and advisors as universities navigate these complex waters. On enhanced CTL campuses that have not yet developed their own in-house OPMs, traditional OPMs such as 2U, Noodle Partners, Wiley, Pearson, and Emeritus continue to play a large role in designing and managing programs. Although most OPMs have been focused on delivering online programs for external students, they have increasingly been asked to provide support and consulting services on the development of strategies for campus digitization efforts.

OPMs such as 2U, Wiley, and Extension Engine play a consulting role for universities similar to management consulting teams such as McKinsey does for corporate clients. With their wide networks of university partners and large production teams and facilities, they have positioned themselves as the experts in digital education and are recognized as thought leaders in program implementation. Without disclosing the secrets of other universities' programs, they can share industry intel and know-how with their clients that has been built through experience working across a wide variety of programs and projects. For a price, OPMs can help universities understand the various options and approaches that are available while handling the complex mechanics and finances of online programs.

Todd Zipper (2021), Wiley's executive vice president and general manager of university services and talent development, explained that Wiley works with universities through both revenue-sharing and fee-for-service models, depending on the partner's specific needs. For online education programs, Wiley uses universities' existing LMS and technology platforms. "We design courses and enroll students on D2L, Canvas, Blackboard, or Moodle for instance," Zipper said. Wiley is agnostic about platforms, preferring to work with whatever each university already has in place. "Universities are coming to Wiley more from a strategic and execution standpoint around online programs," Zipper added. Wiley has more than two centuries of experience in research and education services and draws on its team's expertise in career-connected online education. University Services employs close to 1,500 professionals among 7,500 Wiley employees worldwide. "We think about relationships in terms of long-term partnerships," said Zipper.

For universities building in-house units from scratch, working with OPMs such as Wiley enables them to get partners to run the operation until they build their own capacities. The OPM's financial resources are also a plus. Many OPMs fund the up-front costs of new online degree programs in exchange for a share of external revenue streams. To make the most of any partnership, universities must choose the partnership model that works best for them. "Twenty-eight percent of our partners use the fee-for-service model," Zipper (2021) explained, "so it's not always revenue share exclusively. Sometimes it's even a combination of the two."

In response to press reports of OPM contracts in which the OPM retained more than 60 percent of tuition revenues for periods of up to ten years, Zipper (2021) explained that most current Wiley revenue share agreements are close to 40 percent, with a commitment of less than seven years. "We always start with the partner's needs and work backward," he said. "If a partner requires a significant investment, accruing losses to get a program up and running, revenue share makes more sense for them in that scenario." More established programs may want to "outsource a number of services around the program," such as faculty development or retention support, which Wiley offers on a fee-for-service basis.

One OPM that has committed to a nearly 100-percent "build and transfer" model is the Boston-based Extension Engine, which designed and built the "high engagement at scale" Ivy League business school program discussed in chapter 3. "I believe that the capacity for delivering amazing virtual experiences for faculty and learners is something that should be owned by the institutions," explained Extension Engine founder and CEO Furqan Nazeeri (2021). "We don't take revenue share, and we don't do long-term contracts. . . . We work really hard with our clients to help them build up internal capacity and be successful without us. Success for us is that we bill the client for nothing in year two or three."

Unlike OPMs that focus on program management, Extension Engine focuses on creating unique and high-end websites, learning elements, and user experiences. Most projects are delivered using their own custom LMS and focus on using innovative design to drive engagement at scale. "The promise of great online learning is high engagement at scale, both together," said Nazeeri (2021), "and that's not just in learning, that's in all experiences that have been digitally transformed." The company seeks inspiration from transformative companies such as YouTube, Airbnb, and the Disney Institute. "Learning is everywhere," Nazeeri said. Inspired by the successes of some of these companies' practices, Extension Engine built its learning model for active learning, peer-to-peer learning, and high-end videos and digital cases. For Nazeeri, design is key.

The strategy is to "pick the best learning experience, thoughtfully design it from a pedagogical point of view, and then go pick the tech to deliver it," he said. "That's the big idea."

Another new player in the OPM and consulting space is the Minerva Project. Based in San Francisco, the 1,000-student Minerva University has no formal campus and focuses on a collection of high-end digital classes and support services. The venture-capital-backed enterprise has expanded its operations to add a consulting branch that helps universities create digital-first learning experiences. "We are not a technology company," explained Sharan Singh (2021), Minerva Project's senior managing director for strategic partnerships, "we are an education reform, transformation innovation company that has a technology tool." Minerva helps universities create brand new "institutions within institutions" based on a radical rethinking of how learning can be delivered. Using its proprietary Forum platform, Minerva takes the concepts of active learning and peer-to-peer engagement to their logical extremes in a package that involves overhauling curriculum and teaching and replacing most or all in-person classes with digital seminars and active learning projects. It has created small, entirely digital campuses within larger universities from Dubai to Miami.

Working with Minerva, Singh (2021) admitted, is not for everyone. Minerva's solutions are often the "most complicated" for universities to understand and implement. They require a "fundamental change" rather than just "putting things online and making money off it." After the pandemic's first year, Singh explained the "anxiety and uncertainty of leaders dissipated," and conversations with leaders began to be "more intentional about their long-term future." Institutional leaders told Singh at Minerva, "I figured out the pandemic technology thing. I'm even starting to work with an OPM for revenue generation. But I also want to work with Minerva to do Version 2 or 4 of myself."

OPMs will continue to provide a wide variety of engagement models for universities—some with the fee-for-service deals of Wiley and Extension Engine, others with the "total makeover" approach of Minerva. OPM leader 2U now also offers a variety of approaches, from fee-for-service to its traditional revenue share models. "Our partnerships with our universities are deep, they're strategic, they're long term," explained Andrew Hermalyn (2021), president of partnerships at 2U. "It's our job to really make or help make universities great digitally in the twenty-first century."

Hermalyn (2021) has seen universities move from a decentralized approach to one focused on creating "overarching digital strategy for the university." 2U offers "for fee" services but finds that most universities want the longer partnership model. "We do have a fee-for-service option, but almost no one is interested in it," explained Hermalyn. "They recognize the value of the sort of end-to-end student journey . . . where everything is within 2U. . . . It's really what generates great student outcomes, high retention rates, and ultimately quality."

In recent years, the lines between players in the OPM and MOOC spaces have blurred as companies seen as MOOC providers (i.e., offering their classes, certificates, and degrees) began to provide "OPM-like" services, such as offering platforms and "à la carte" course delivery partnerships. Some traditional OPMs that had previously focused on offering services began to directly offer classes and degrees. Distinctions were further complicated when 2U, one of the largest classic OPM operators, announced its purchase of edX in July 2021, a previously nonprofit MOOC platform. The fascinating chart in figure 4.7 was created by EdTech guru Phil Hill (2022), and it shows the complexity of the current OPM/MOOC/EdTech services landscape.

These lines will continue to mix and blur as for-profit (but often money-losing) OPM providers try to find common ground with nonprofit (but generally revenue positive) universities. In an attempt to define these murky waters, there has been a recent call for more transparency in these transactions, and a definition of what Georgetown's Ed Maloney and Dartmouth's Joshua Kim called a "Statement of Principles for Nonprofit/For-Profit Educational Partnerships" (Kim and Maloney 2022). As university leaders move ahead in their journey toward digital transformation, a great

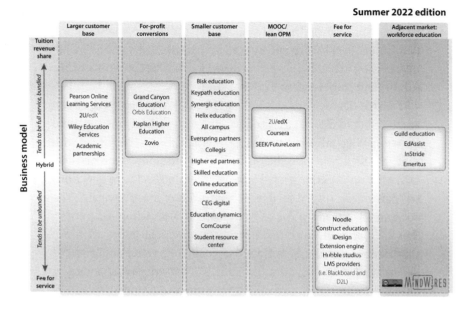

Figure 4.7 OPM market landscape

deal can be learned from the many OPM partners who now offer services. But many pitfalls must be avoided, especially those presented by long-term contracts that may inhibit the creation of the school's in-house expertise and control over digital learning. The OPM market is currently estimated at more than $5.7 billion a year in revenue, and it is estimated to grow to $13 billion by 2025 (HolonIQ 2021).

ACADEMIC SHARING AND MISSION-DRIVEN INITIATIVES

We cannot conclude a discussion about the strategic and planning issues related to digital education without discussing "mission-driven projects." These projects involve sharing digital assets for classes or group training beyond the university's walls, not as part of a revenue-generating tuition-driven program but as part of the university's broader public mission. Most universities recognize that sharing knowledge with the wider academic community is a core value. Faculty are encouraged to publish and share the findings of their research in peer-reviewed journals and open-to-public forums and conferences.

To what degree does this obligation extend to digital education assets? Should digital case studies, labs, and simulations—created for fee-paying online or on campus digital classes—be shared with others? Should they be shared as part of mission-driven projects or sold at online educational asset marketplaces? These questions are part of the digital landscape that leaders must navigate. The good news for educators is that there is a growing recognition that the value of educational programs is much more than the sum of the digital assets they use. The core value add of most educational programs is in program *delivery*—the value added by live discussions, mentoring, peer-to-peer work, and the degrees and certificates that their institutions can provide. In practical terms, this means that universities can "afford" to create and give away good online content for free or at low cost—for use by international partners or NGOs, for example—while still retaining the ability to use it and charge for its use in fee-paying classes that it runs directly.

Universities are increasingly adopting a hybrid model for their operations—using digital tools to develop online courses and programs but also providing traditional classes with varying degrees of digital enhancement. Well-managed, each kind of program can inform and support the other. Universities now create content to use in a number of formats: on campus digital credit-bearing classes (with all the support of an on campus class), fully online credit-bearing classes (for tuition), modules for executive education classes (for a fee), and free or low-cost programs offered in MOOCs or other mission-driven programs. As these models evolve, more universities are developing institutional digital strategies that allow them to generate revenue while fulfilling their wider mission of sharing knowledge and access to education.

DIGITAL CONVERGENCE

Although schools have followed different approaches to these issues, there is a clear trend toward bringing the digital education skills developed by external-facing units in-house, and also bringing the faculty and student-facing skills of the CTL to digital education efforts. The best approach might be some combination of these approaches whereby faculty support for on campus instruction (the traditional CTL area) and creation of assets for blended classes (traditionally a strength of external-facing units) is offered to academic units across the university, perhaps with the help of outside experts and advisors from the OPM industry.

The benefits are clear. On campus students demand more options in course delivery and want to experience the benefits and learning support provided by well-designed digital education experiences. During the pandemic, content created for MOOCs or fully online master's programs was increasingly used by on campus learners as part of blended course experiences. Students and teachers saw the benefits of these approaches and want more. Adding digital scaffolding to core entry-level courses is also an important equity play because it often makes them more accessible to a wide variety of students, including those with additional needs. "If we start focusing on the people with the least access and figure out how to best support them, we end up building systems that help absolutely everybody," explained Frederick T. Wehrle (2022), the associate dean for academic affairs at UC Berkeley's Extension Program.

Creating funding and management structures to support digital-first course experiences at scale is challenging. It will require a combination of approaches and profound changes in management and delivery teams as well as creation of new incentives for such work. Some argue that achieving this vision requires a radical rethinking of university structures themselves. Others argue that the benefits of digital tools and digital convergence can be brought to higher education with a more paced approach. Whether the movement happens in the radical overhaul vision of the sort proposed by the Minerva Project or at a steadier pace, the existence of synergies between on campus digital initiatives and off campus programs is here to stay. And this will drive the direction of university digital strategy in the years to come.

CREATING A STRATEGIC DIGITAL EDUCATION PLAN

The ancient Greek mathematician Euclid famously said that "there is no royal road to geometry." The same might be said about universities in the post-COVID age. There is no royal road to digitally enhanced education. That said, there are a few key questions that educational leaders will face as they plot their way forward:

Federal vs. Central? Most of our interview subjects agree that all schools and programs—and their instructors—need central funding and support, as well as support for in-school digital course design know-how. Ideally, schools develop programs to meet their unique needs, with funding from a central university "investor" and support from a central unit that establishes university-wide standards and a common framework for course planning and design.

Outsource vs. Insource Solutions? Most of our interviewees believe that digital tools should be seen as a core competency that must be built and managed in-house. That said, working with outside partners can be a great way to learn how this work is done, build new units, or seek expertise or support in areas that do not make financial sense to keep in-house.

Financial Models? Most experts agree that certain core services must be provided as part of central support. An internal accounting system must be developed to manage funding and support of core strategic projects, and a central university "digital education investment bank" must be established to invest in programs and cover up-front start-up costs. A system to recoup investments once new revenue-generating programs are operational would enable this bank to become self-sustaining. A certain percentage of all revenue can then be invested in operations that generate indirect, rather than direct, revenues, such as programs designed to improve on campus teaching or in mission-related projects.

Scale of Investment in Internal Digital Enhancement? Central support and investment are essential to improving core on campus classes. Large introductory classes offer a prime opportunity to bring digital tools to traditional college programs, and they can help improve the equity of learning outcomes for first-time college students and others in need of additional support. Creating high-quality digital assets for these courses will improve learning on campus and can also be used to raise revenues in online programs. The question is how much to invest and how quickly?

Rewarding Teaching and Prep Work? Good digital classes require planning and preparation. Universities need to offer faculty incentives to create great digital materials. Ideally, the partners will use a standard MOU for cooperation in this area.

Faculty IP Issues? Uniform, transparent policies and standard legal agreements on these issues reduce the transaction cost of new digital programs. We recommend a combination of a standard range of buyout payments, with a recognition of the professor's digital contributions in faculty promotions, and either additional compensation or "course relief" for those semesters when new materials are being created.

Pricing Policy of External Offerings? Most external programs are priced based on only a very slight discount from on campus rates. This protects against the cannibalization of traditional campus programs and ensures profits for schools and OPMs but limits the ability of lower income students to gain access to this learning. Is this policy to be maintained? Should public universities, especially, offer some classes at cost and expand access? Having a standardized policy in this area would be helpful.

Participation of Schools in Revenues from Hybrid and Online Offerings? If a central unit will be offering in-house OPM services that include online and hybrid degree program marketing and management, how will schools be incentivized? Having built-in financial incentives for schools to participate in such programs seems key to long-term success. As with faculty incentives, creating a standard university-wide revenue-sharing model in this area would greatly reduce administrative transaction costs for creating and offering new programs.

MOOC and Open Educational Resource Sharing Strategy Issues? Are MOOCs destined to be the digital textbooks of the future? If so, should faculty be encouraged to create and share some digital assets? What should the university's strategy be in this area? We explore these issues in more depth in chapters 9 and 10.

Service Mission and Public Good Strategy? Just as consulting and law firms take on pro-bono cases, shouldn't universities commit to creating and sharing some of their educational assets? Do universities have a wider obligation to share digital assets or classes as part of their mission to serve the larger community? How much should universities use digital tools to expand educational programs beyond campus-based and tuition-bearing online programs? How can this work be centrally funded and managed? Can local partners be found in other countries or geographic areas who can help localize and use content created? Ideally, all standard university-wide MOUs with schools and faculty should make clear that their assets will also be used in mission-driven projects that do not create new revenues and that these projects can be part of the university's wider public mission.

REFERENCES

Baker, Nelson. 2021. Interview of Professional Education and Professor of Civil and Environmental Engineering, Georgia Tech, by Adam Stepan. October 27, 2021.

Berkowitz, Sally. 2021. Interview of Senior Director of Product Management, eCornell, by Adam Stepan. October 22, 2021.

Branon, Rovy. 2021. Interview of Vice Provost for Continuum College, University of Washington, by Adam Stepan. November 30, 2021.

Chou, Luyen. 2021. Interview of Chief Learning Officer, 2U, by Adam Stepan. October 27, 2021.

Christensen, Clayton M., and Henry J. Eyring. 2011. *The Innovative University: Changing the DNA of Higher Education from the Inside Out*. Hoboken, NJ: Wiley.

Christensen, Clayton M., Michael B. Horn, Louis Soares, and Louis Caldera. 2011. "Disrupting College." *Center for American Progress* (blog). February 8, 2011. https://americanprogress.org/article/disrupting-college/.

Copley, Paul, and Carter Douthett. 2020. "The Enrollment Cliff, Mega-Universities, COVID-19, and the Changing Landscape of U.S. Colleges." *CPA Journal*, October 5, 2020. https://www.cpajournal.com/2020/10/05/the -enrollment-cliff-mega-universities-covid-19-and-the-changing-landscape -of-u-s-colleges/.

DeVaney, James. 2021. Interview of Associate Vice Provost for Academic Innovation and Founding Executive Director of the Center for Academic Innovation, University of Michigan, by Adam Stepan. October 29, 2021.

Dooley, Frank. 2021. Follow-Up Interview of Chancellor, Purdue Global, by Adam Stepan. October 27, 2021.

Grasgreen, Allie. 2015. "Obama Pushes For-Profit Colleges to the Brink." *Politico*, July 1, 2015. https://www.politico.com/story/2015/07/barack-obama -pushes-for-profit-colleges-to-the-brink-119613.

Hanson, Andrew. 2019. "Meeting of Mega-Universities and Online Educators Provides Clues About What Online Learning Might Look Like in the Future." *Strada Education Network*, April 29, 2019. https://stradaeducation.org /navigating-education/meeting-of-mega-universities-and-online-educators -provides-clues-about-what-online-learning-might-look-like-in-the-future/.

Harding, Justin. 2021. Interview of Senior Director for Instructional Design and New Media, EdPlus, Arizona State University, by Adam Stepan. November 30, 2021.

Hermalyn, Andrew. 2021. Interview of President of Partnerships, 2U, by Adam Stepan. October 18, 2021.

Hill, Phil. 2022. "OPM Market Landscape and Dynamics: Summer 2022 Updates." July 19, 2022. https://philonedtech.com/opm-market-landscape-and-dynamics -summer-2022-updates/.

HolonIQ. 2021. "Global OPM and OPX Market to Reach $13.3B by 2025." March 3, 2021. https://www.holoniq.com/notes/global-opm-and-opx-market -to-reach-13.3b-by-2025/.

Huntemann, Nina. 2021. Interview of Vice President of Learning, edX, by Adam Stepan. October 18, 2021.

Jhaj, Sukhwant. 2021. Interview of Vice Provost for Academic Innovation and Student Achievement, Arizona State University, by Adam Stepan. November 1, 2021.

Kim, Joshua. 2021. Interview of Director of Online Programs and Strategy at Dartmouth College Senior Scholar, Georgetown University, by Adam Stepan. October 21, 2021.

Kim, Joshua, and Edward J. Maloney. 2022. "Toward a Statement of Principles for Nonprofit/For-Profit Educational Partnerships." *Inside Higher Ed*, April 10, 2022. https://www.insidehighered.com/blogs/learning-innovation /toward-statement-principles-nonprofitfor-profit-educational-partnerships.

King, Elliot, and Neil Alperstein. 2017. *Best Practices in Planning Strategically for Online Educational Programs.* New York: Routledge.

Krause, Paul. 2021. Interview of Vice Provost of External Education and Cornell University Executive Director, eCornell, by Adam Stepan. October 22, 2021.

Lewis, Nora. 2021. Interview of Vice Dean for Professional and Liberal Education, School of Arts and Sciences, University of Pennsylvania, by Adam Stepan. October 26, 2021.

Lloyd, Steven A., Michelle M. Byrne, and Tami S. McCoy. 2012. "Faculty-Perceived Barriers of Online Education." *Merlot Journal of Online Learning and Teaching* 8 (1): 12.

Nazeeri, Furqan. 2021. Interview of CEO, Extension Engine, by Adam Stepan. November 9, 2021.

Nelson, Ben. 2021. Interview of CEO and Founder, Minerva Project, by Adam Stepan. October 14, 2021.

Rascoff, Matthew. 2021. Interview of Vice Provost for Digital Education, Stanford University, by Adam Stepan. October 29, 2021.

Regier, Phil. 2021. Interview of CEO of EdPlus, Arizona State University, by Adam Stepan. November 8, 2021.

Schroeder, Ray. 2019. "The Impact of At-Scale and Mega-U Degrees." *Inside Higher Ed*, September 25, 2019. https://www.insidehighered.com/digital-learning /blogs/online-trending-now/impact-scale-and-mega-u-degrees.

Scott, Josh. 2021. Interview of Director of Course Strategy, 2U, by Adam Stepan. November 30, 2021.

Shanghai Ranking. 2021. "2021 Academic Ranking of World Universities." August 15, 2021. https://www.shanghairanking.com/news/arwu/2021.

Shireman, Robert. 2017. "The For-Profit College Story: Scandal, Regulate, Forget, Repeat." *Century Foundation*, January 24, 2017. https://tcf.org/content /report/profit-college-story-scandal-regulate-forget-repeat/.

Singh, Sharan. 2021. Interview of Senior Managing Director of Strategic Partnerships, Minerva Project, by Adam Stepan. November 2, 2021.

Ubell, Robert. 2017. *Going Online: Perspectives on Digital Learning.* New York: Taylor & Francis.

U.S. News & World Report. 2021. "Best Undergraduate Computer Science Programs Rankings." September 13, 2021. https://www.usnews.com/best -colleges/rankings/computer-science-overall.

Wehrle, Frederick T. 2022. Interview of Associate Dean, Academic Affairs, UC Berkeley Extension, by Adam Stepan. June 20, 2022.

Whitford, Emma. 2021. "Online Learning Giants 2U and edX Will Merge." *Inside Higher Ed*, June 30, 2021. https://www.insidehighered.com/news/2021/06/30/online-learning-giants-2u-and-edx-will-merge.

Zabriskie, Catherine. 2021. Interview of Senior Director of Digital Learning and Design, Brown University, by Adam Stepan. November 9, 2021.

Zimmerman, Jonathan. 2020. *The Amateur Hour: A History of College Teaching in America*. Baltimore, MD: JHU Press.

Zipper, Todd. 2021. Interview of President, Wiley Education Services, by Adam Stepan. November 10, 2021.

5

DIGITAL COMPETENCIES

The COVID-19 pandemic brought into sharp focus the extreme range of digital competencies among universities. Prior to the pandemic, some universities had institution-wide strategies for the use of digital tools, advanced centers of teaching and learning, and clear standards and practices. However, many others did not have university-wide strategies, consensus on tools to be used, or plans in place to provide adequate professional development and support. At most universities, only a few professors had participated in online and hybrid programs, and only a select few had participated in the full process of designing and delivering blended content. But the pandemic forced nearly every professor into some form of digital teaching.

How can the university build on this basic knowledge, support current digital teaching, and entice holdouts to use digital tools in their classes? How can universities create ladders of skills, enabling faculty to climb from basic competencies at the lower rungs to expert-level mastery at the higher rungs? In this chapter, we provide our best answers to these questions.

DIGITAL COURSE ASSISTANTS

The fastest, most cost-effective path to improve digital literacy is to expand the traditional role of teaching and course assistants

(TAs and CAs). These assistants generally receive a stipend to teach small sections and grade papers and tests, but they could also play a key role in expanding the use of digital tools in classes. Today's student assistants are digital natives and are generally quick studies when it comes to learning and using a wide range of online tools.

This expanded digital role would require that TAs and CAs be hired earlier in the course cycle to help with course planning and preparation. Rather than starting work in September, for example, digital TAs and CAs should begin in early August or even earlier if more assets are to be created. Implementing this new schedule requires changes in business as usual, but hiring TAs a bit earlier in the calendar year and approving the relatively minor additional costs for increased prep time would provide an outsized return in terms of improved course websites and planning. With support from senior leadership, these should be relatively easy changes to make.

STANDARD TOOLS AND WORKFLOWS

Our core ideas stress the value of identifying the simplest and easiest digital tools to use, creating standard workflows for implementation of these tools, and supporting and encouraging faculty to follow these workflows in every possible way. Most online program management (OPM) models recognize the substantial benefits of standardizing workflows for professors. OPMs also seek to make things as easy as possible for professors, generally offering them a simple 1, 2, 3 system to get most things done. Centers for teaching and learning (CTLs) have traditionally taken a different approach. Their spirit of research and experimentation, with an emphasis on faculty independence, has led many CTLs to offer a wide variety of technological options. Although innovation and technical experimentation are supported, project execution is often not optimized because few faculty or support staff develop deep knowledge of the best practices for any specific tool or platform. Nina Huntemann

(2021) of edX stated that supporting myriad systems and workflows was untenable during the 2020 pandemic: "Having faculty across the university . . . using all these different digital tools is actually quite a mess because you don't know if those tools are being used properly."

Universities should support innovation and experimentation with new tools, but they must also recognize that many professors struggle with digital basics. Offering fewer and simpler options generally leads to more use and deeper engagement. As Einstein is reported to have said, "make everything as simple as possible, but not simpler." A variety of tools and approaches can confuse and overwhelm faculty and students, and it also makes it difficult to share learning assets across classes. As much as possible, programs and schools should work to standardize technology and its use.

ONLINE WORKSHOPS FOR FACULTY

Once standards, simple tools, and workflows are chosen, faculty and TAs need to have access to accessible and well-produced professional development opportunities. Self-paced video training and workshops can bring most faculty up to speed. The online training materials need to be clear, direct, dynamic, and relevant to the professor's immediate job as a teacher and a scholar. Some CTLs have produced overly complex theoretical guides, and most professors do not want to navigate hundreds of pages of instruction. Busy faculty generally want the basics described in step-by-step guides on using key tools.

Universities should create a central portal with an official, short, simple guide that details the approved and supported steps and tools for course design and delivery. Consider investing in the creation of a well-produced website, with professionally produced videos and attractive and simple delivery. Universities work hard and invest in producing professional-quality marketing materials to attract the best students, and they must also invest in the best possible training materials to convince professors of the benefits of using digital tools.

Examples include the Open Society University Network (OSUN), a group of more than forty institutions all moving toward the use of shared core digital tools. They have invested in creating a core set of professional development videos, which are presented by young OSUN students and are delivered in formats tailor-made for professors (on how to build classes) and students (on how to use these tools). Although videos about how to use most tools can be found on YouTube, they are often long and designed for a specific user interface that might be different from the one used at the university in question. Making custom guides is the answer. "People get lost easily," explained Philip Fedchin, chief technology strategist for OSUN. "You need to show the whole process." OSUN created these materials for both students and faculty who are using laptops (figure 5.1) and smartphones (figure 5.2). "We have a program for refugee learners . . . in camps in Kenya and Jordan, and now Bangladesh," explained Fedchin, and "50 to 80 percent of these learners are using Android phones . . . the whole idea is to support the community of learners." Specific videos for this

Figure 5.1 OSUN professor laptop training video

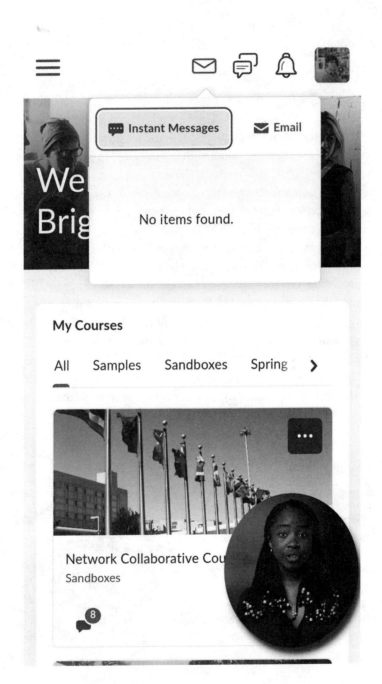

Figure 5.2 OSUN smartphone training video

subgroup of learners were made, showing how all key apps work on their mobile devices.

These video and PDF guides should be tagged and cross-referenced so they appear at the top of relevant Google searches with your university's name and the name of the tool. Additional information created by CTL teams should be clearly labeled as "Advanced Techniques" or "Guides to Learning Theory," so faculty looking for short and simple "how-to" guides do not inadvertently end up viewing long and complex theoretical readings. Outdated, competing, and overlapping guides and materials should be removed from official websites. Research and learning theory should be clearly separated from approved how-to guides.

Workshops should be offered several times a year during regular breaks between semesters. These workshops should offer both asynchronous and live elements, and faculty should be encouraged and incentivized to attend one such session at least every few years. During the pandemic, several universities and colleges made such training a university-wide program and had great results. Making training short, well-produced, fun, social, and engaging goes a long way toward making it palatable to most faculty members.

In the spirit of cooperation and support of teaching and learning across partner universities, Columbia and its partners offer a series of video training guides on the basics of digital course delivery in our massive open online courses (MOOCs): The Blended Learning Toolkit and Digital Case Method. These videos are discussed in chapters 7 and 8, are free to download, and can be used with any program.

ENCOURAGING DIGITAL TOOL USE

Some professors need a nudge to use available tools. Professional development is a key step, but so is the teacher evaluation process. Course evaluations should ask students to rate each course's digital education tool use on a scale of 1 to 10. Professors with average scores lower than 6 could be asked to improve their use of digital tools, and professors achieving a score of 9 or 10 could receive special recognition and perhaps a financial bonus or some sort of prize. Ideally faculty should be able to find help close at hand, with online materials, regularly scheduled workshops, and advice from digitally native TAs. But even with 24/7 help available, the best and easiest systems will not be implemented without adequate incentives.

LMS USE IS CRUCIAL

The learning management system (LMS) is the first and oldest piece of digital education infrastructure for most universities. LMSs began to appear in one form or another in the late 1990s, with many early-mover universities creating their own platforms using open source software such as Sakai or Moodle. In the 2000s, professionally built and supported systems began to take over, including systems from Pearson, Blackboard, and more recently D2L's Brightspace platform and Instructure's Canvas system.

An LMS is essentially an all-in-one platform focused on the delivery and management of courses, with a heavy focus on the "management" aspects and less focus on student and faculty user experience. It is unfortunate but true that nearly all LMSs have been optimized for administrative tasks such as enrolling students and grading, not for delivering engaging user experiences. When it comes to building course websites, most LMSs remain clunky and are not intuitive to use. Strange as it may seem, adding images and videos—key elements of 99 percent of websites in the wider online world—remains hard to do with most LMSs. The end result is that many course websites are at best functional but rarely thrilling and engaging. As EdTech commentator Phil Hill (2015) famously explained on Twitter, the "LMS is the minivan of education. . . . Everyone has them and needs them, but there is a certain shame in having one in the driveway."

LMSs tend to exhibit the same problems as other programs designed by committees. Rather than identifying a handful of key features needed to meet key learning goals and focusing first and foremost on the student user experience, most LMSs are the sum total of features requested by schools and departments, many of which are not needed. "People make a big list of all their requirements," said Furqan Nazeeri (2021) of Extension Engine. "The end product checks all the boxes but provides a very poor user experience because that's not front and center in the design process."

Chris Burns (2021) of Panopto notes the same problem with the purchase of video systems. "The technology buyer for most of our history has been a pretty technical team, usually running RFPs [requests for proposals] and checking boxes. That model incentivizes a bunch of complexity that will gradually check every feature box. But . . . the average instructor doesn't care so much. They care about reaching their students."

One LMS provider moving away from offering a wide variety of features and toward simplicity is Brightspace by D2L. "Making it easier for faculty to get things done online is critical," said D2L founder and CEO John Baker (2021), noting that this is also what students want. Just as WordPress has offered a number of simple tools for building websites, D2L offers prebuilt templates focusing on user experience. "We are the only learning platform that has templates built into the editor," Baker said. "Our whole philosophy is, 'How can we make it easier?'" Professors and support teams are "looking for the basics," and the goal is to make key actions possible with "only three clicks."

LMSs are showing signs of improving their products, but progress is slow. The fact that an LMS is a university-wide system makes changing from one platform to another a huge task, which most universities justifiably avoid doing unless huge advances in technology require it. For this reason, most schools stay with their LMS for multiple years, creating a sense of complacency for most LMS providers.

Despite these limitations, decent results are possible using most LMS platforms, but professors need to be guided in this process, trained, and held to some minimum standard of LMS use competency. Unfortunately, this generally does not happen. Most universities, working under the logic of faculty independence with regard to course delivery, provide LMS support and training on a strictly voluntary basis and do not require any minimum level of LMS use or proficiency from professors other than the ability to upload a PDF of their syllabus and post final grades.

The results are predictable: most professors only use the LMS provided for uploading PDFs and readings. Instructors frequently ignore tools for online discussions, creating and sharing video assets, and guiding students' online experiences. Most course websites resemble those of the early 1990s internet: lots of text and few images or interactive elements. It does not need to be this way. Universities' hands-off approach to monitoring and regulating how (and if) instructors use their LMS should change. The committees on instruction at most universities oversee, approve, and require changes to minutiae in most course syllabi. Why should this oversight and quality control not extend to actual course websites?

The current system means that the quality of classes that students experience in most universities varies widely, which has huge equity implications. "We need to up our games," explained Joshua Kim (2021) of Dartmouth, and deliver classes "of the highest quality and consistency." Students who enter top universities and come from privileged backgrounds are prepared to navigate a system in which some classes are much better in their delivery than others. "That system, with all that variation, mostly benefits those who are most privileged coming into our institutions," explained Kim. If you have a background in "prep schools and private tutors," you can compensate for uneven course delivery. "If you don't have those advantages, the quality of the learning experience has to be good across the board."

The fact that many instructors use the LMS in a limited way and inconsistently has a direct impact on student learning. "You have to look at the user experience of the students," explained Frank Dooley (2021), chancellor of Purdue Global. The evidence supports creating a standard template for LMS use and making sure professors take the time to use it well. "If we are there to support students in their learning, why would we want them spending a lot of time trying to navigate five different models or five different systems to learn where to keep your homework?" There is a "transactional aspect" of the course, said Dooley, that "I don't think has anything to do with academic freedom but can greatly enhance how students do." For Dooley, the key to modernizing university instruction lies in creating clear feedback mechanisms so professors can hear from their students about the importance of consistently well-organized course websites. In the case of Purdue, once this communication flowed in, the faculty understood how up-to-date course websites can improve their teaching, and they were eager to comply. "We brought in focus groups of students to let them hear it," Dooley said. Once professors heard from students, "it became much easier for them to buy into the idea that they're all going to use the same system and [that] having a standard template for the home page is fine."

Many executive education programs have overcome the limitations of LMS out of the box programs by creating customized course home page templates with HTML coding: For example, the Columbia Business School (figure 5.3), eCornell (figure 5.4), and the Dartmouth template created by instructional designer Sarah Cloud (figure 5.5). These visually appealing course websites stand in strong contrast to the home pages of most Canvas websites, which often consist of only a list a series of modules and folders. Columbia has also created the Canvas Coursebuilder—an open platform built by Bernhard Fasenfest, with user interface design by Siah Singh—that gives Columbia and partner universities a simple tool that allows nonprogrammers to design attractive course websites (see chapter 7).

Having an attractive and inviting LMS course website is an obvious plus for students, but even more important is having faculty understand and use the core LMS functionality. When faculty have

Figure 5.3 Columbia business school class template

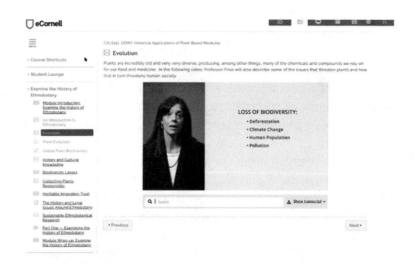

Figure 5.4 eCornell class structure template

Figure 5.5 Dartmouth class template

basic LMS literacy, students' learning experiences improve considerably. All professors should be able to complete the following tasks, with the support of campus online experts and a digital TA (if available):

- Create a welcome course home page with all core course information, contact information, and meeting times.
- Post readings and activities on an interactive calendar and syllabus.
- Post recorded lectures of course lessons; not just prerecorded lessons but also videos of in-person classes and Zoom meetings.
- Use course discussion tools actively.

The COVID-19 pandemic forced many professors to learn the basics of their LMS. With adequate support and incentives, universities should be able to help all faculty members achieve these basic competencies. Professors can then move beyond the basics through the use of custom course templates created by their teaching and learning teams or tools such as the Canvas Coursebuilder. These next steps will greatly improve the learning experience for students.

With leadership and incentives from university presidents, provosts, and deans, this improvement is possible.

LMS design and capabilities are constantly getting better. Simpler and more user-friendly interfaces are becoming available, especially in the corporate and for-fee online course market. Many of the simpler LMS formats offer cleaner and simpler interfaces and streamlined user experiences. In the final analysis, students simply need faculty to have basic competency in LMS use. Administrators need to ensure that instructors are trained and incentivized to provide this basic user experience and ideally more to their students.

IN-CLASS LECTURE CAPTURE

One of the most heated post-pandemic debates is whether in-class lecture capture—a new service that many universities expanded during the pandemic—should be continued, or whether making course recordings available undermines in-person classes. Capturing in-person lectures on video is relatively expensive to set up, requiring up-front investments in new cameras, audio, and IT systems. But the investment can pay huge dividends in student learning, especially if its use is integrated into a planned course of action. The investment is also generally popular with faculty because teaching in classrooms with this sort of room recording technology generally does not require much in the way of extra work for the instructor teaching the course. Once the system is set up and running, professors can teach their classes in the way they normally do.

Many schools, especially well-funded medical, law, and engineering programs, have offered video capture of lectures for some time. It requires installing high-quality cameras in classrooms, ideally with several angles such as a wide shot of the room, a close shot of the professor, and another recording of either the blackboard or the PowerPoint being shown. In the most sophisticated systems, all these angles are automatically captured online, stored, and linked to the course website on the university LMS, allowing students to view classes remotely live or as recordings after the fact. Once recorded, students can watch the lectures, stop them, and play them at various speeds, always staying in sync with course PowerPoint templates and blackboard examples. This approach enables both lecture review and asynchronous learning.

In the summer of 2020, universities across the United States expanded classroom video systems, enabling traditional lecture capture and adding new real-time two-way communication technology. The goal was to offer lectures both to students physically present in the classroom and to those who were remote learners. This has become known as the hybrid-flexible (HyFlex) mode of course delivery. Whereas traditional lecture capture simply records what is said in the physical classroom and broadcasts it to remote students (who often watch it as a recording after the fact), in the HyFlex classroom remote students also appear on in-class TV monitors and ask questions in real time. This new ability opens exciting possibilities (allowing people who travel for work to take some classes in person and some remotely), but it also adds complexity. For instructors, focusing on two sets of students—those physically in the classroom and those on Zoom—requires extra work and is best handled with the help of having digital TAs manage the various cameras and views needed.

In the HyFlex classroom, class presentations and discussions can get awkward with two separate groups present at the same time—one visible, the other mostly invisible (figure 5.6). Students in the classroom can ask questions and make comments by raising their hand and talking the old-fashioned way. Remote learners can ask questions and make comments in chat boxes, but a TA or other helper needs to convey the comments to the professor or "beam them in" by sharing their video and audio with the group. Doing this well requires practice and effort. In general, most agree that the flexibility it provides makes this effort worth it because these same tools also enable including remote speakers and presenters. One key point of agreement is the need for additional TA support in HyFlex

Figure 5.6 The HyFlex classroom

classrooms. Many also would also argue that faculty agreeing to teach in this useful but demanding format receive additional compensation for the extra work and prep time it requires.

Simple class lecture capture—without the real-time two-way communications of the HyFlex room—offers perhaps the greatest potential for improving learning outcomes with the least amount of additional effort for instructors. For Eric Burns (2021), the CEO of the video company Panopto, lecture capture also has very real equity implications: "We used to do this for accessibility reasons. . . . A student maybe had some reason why they needed to be able to watch an all-online version with help for the hearing impaired or the differently abled. . . . The real ambition should be educational equity for all students, that regardless of your background when you arrive at [university], you have the opportunity and the means to catch up or to overcome some equity disadvantage."

Studies conducted during the pandemic showed that lecture capture allowed students to turn live synchronous classes into asynchronous flipped lectures. A study conducted by a Stanford

Figure 5.7 UCLA protest against end of remote options (Wong 2022)

University student explored how students took advantage of a core math course offered at three different times (synchronously) as well as lecture recordings (asynchronously) during the fall 2021 semester: 50.2 percent of students moved to the asynchronous option over the semester (Gao 2021). Demand for this option is clear. A group of more than 10,000 students at the University of Washington signed a petition demanding that all classes be recorded. The petition, citing issues of equity, called this option a "moral requirement" (Bowyer 2020). Similar movements happened at other campuses, including UCLA, where 1,300 students signed a petition and held a strike against the mandatory return to in-person instruction (figure 5.7), demanding that remote learning options be kept available (Wong 2022).

Most universities offered class meetings on Zoom during the pandemic with recordings soon made available online, so it is hard for administrations to now argue that such recordings can no longer be made available. Using an in-class system for recording lectures, each course meeting produces content that can be edited and used again and again. "Asynchronous is a side effect of teaching synchronously," said Panopto's Burns (2021), "so there is no excuse for not at least opting into it." Putting cameras in most lecture halls would require an investment in the hundreds of thousands of dollars, but most schools that have installed this equipment say the benefits exceed the costs.

Recorded lectures create alternative delivery modes—including fully online courses. When Purdue began prerecording some lectures and recording other lectures in traditional classrooms, all sorts of new possibilities opened up. Some students chose to be in the classroom every day, and others preferred viewing recorded lectures online. After recording her lectures, one professor realized that she could easily create a fully online version of her course for remote students. "Once I have the lectures taped," she explained, "it's not that much more work" (Dooley 2021).

For schools with adequate class sizes and budgets, it makes sense to outfit classrooms with the technology to create lecture recordings. Capturing lectures might make the most sense in large introductory and required courses. These lectures should be uploaded to a course LMS to give students more options for learning. For in-class lecture capture, the core suggested digital competencies include the following:

- Cameras and other equipment for capturing and sharing recorded lectures for all core required lecture courses.
- Integration of recordings into the LMS.
- Searchable videos, in which both lecture and PowerPoint decks are available.
- Playback systems that make all videos available, searchable, with subtitles for accessibility, synced to PowerPoint decks and demonstrations, with playback possible at variable speeds.

Recording classroom lectures will no doubt be met with resistance from some quarters, including those who have privacy concerns. Keeping close control on recordings and ensuring that they can only be accessed from within the LMS by enrolled students should address most of these concerns. And private areas should be maintained—especially for one-on-one student-professor conferences in which recording does not take place. In the medium and large venues of most university courses, the benefits of sharing and making learning and debate available to students in a variety of ways would seem to justify the investment in hardware and in the privacy control systems needed to safely deliver these videos.

ZOOM+

Even before the 2020 pandemic, most universities created university-wide Zoom or other video conferencing accounts. They integrated these video meeting applications into their LMS and uploaded recordings onto video storage systems, so universities were able to quickly switch to remote learning in March of 2020. Traffic on Zoom and other meeting apps quadrupled (figure 5.8). From February to May alone, Zoom saw a 354 percent increase in the use of its tools ("Zoom Reports First Quarter Results for Fiscal Year 2021" 2020).

Forced to move online, professors mastered the basics of Zoom and found they could easily share their presentations, see gallery views of students, and replicate many aspects of their traditional lecture techniques. However, most professors used only the most rudimentary features of Zoom. For those who learned only the basics, Zoom was a workable but limited substitute for traditional lectures. For those who took the time to learn Zoom's advanced tools, a new world of rich online interactions was opened.

Zoom and its competitors were designed for business presentations, not classroom learning. But they offer intuitive systems for getting groups together for presentations and discussions. Making

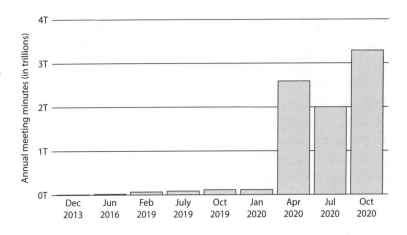

Figure 5.8 Zoom use during COVID-19 pandemic (Dean 2022)

sure that all professors understand the following Zoom features is key to a well-run connected university:

- Use of Chat feature to allow both private and public commentary during a video lecture. Chats offer a way for less outgoing students to share their questions and thoughts.
- Use of polling feature to get students involved, posing questions for all to answer at key moments—especially when everyone needs to understand a concept before the lesson continues.
- Use of breakout rooms to assign students to small groups for discussions, and then reconvene them with the main group to report their findings.

Digitally proficient professors, often with the help of TAs, use all of these tools and more. They make their online courses engaging, interactive events. Lectures and slides alternate with course discussions, Q&A periods, polling, breakout groups, guest speakers, and student presentations (figure 5.9). Professors and their TAs must develop a plan for this flow of activity so each action feeds smoothly into the next.

Figure 5.9 Zoom polling and breakout room

The most sophisticated Zoom alternatives—such as the Engageli platform and the Minerva Project's Forum platform—build "run of show" systems into their platforms, to use a term from live television programming. Professors can preprogram a series of actions and events, making actual course delivery much easier. Professors can monitor student activity, shift seamlessly from breakout room to breakout room, and share collaborative documents and projects in real-time. "Everything is in one place and prescripted," explained Sharan Singh (2021) of Minerva Project. "You can prebuild a class, an entire lesson plan with four polls, followed by a breakout, and debriefed by a particular group, [and] a summary by the professor." In the years ahead, these more advanced features—prebuilt lesson plans and run of show templates—will become a standard part of all video conferencing platforms used for teaching. In the meantime, professors must be incentivized and supported in using the Zoom+ tools that are available and receive training in developing a session plan for their Zoom-enabled classes.

Even with a return to in-person lectures, Zoom will continue to play a role in more and more courses. Zoom has shown the power of using guest speakers from all over the world to engage students, with chats and emojis that allow quick feedback. Some students will insist on connecting synchronously via Zoom, as well as asynchronously for lectures, projects, tests, and individual work. Zoom-inspired techniques now used in traditional classrooms include breakout rooms (which can happen both physically and digitally), chat (using either Zoom or WhatsApp groups), and real-time polling (using clickers or apps such as Poll Everywhere or Zoom).

Faculty and their TAs need tutorials that include the basics of lighting and audio in home "studios," sharing PowerPoint and other presentation slides, spotlighting guest speakers, and sharing video and audio from a desktop. The following Zoom+ competencies are essential:

- Knowledge of how to set up the computer camera, microphone, and a light of some kind so there is a clear view and good audio of the professor (use the "blur background" function to keep attention on the speaker).
- The ability to seamlessly share PowerPoint presentations in the "Slide Show" mode (showing just the slide, not the whole computer screen).
- The ability to share video and audio from the desktop.
- The capability to use remote speakers with Zoom or another meeting application.
- The ability to call on and "spotlight" student speakers and to set up and manage breakout rooms, live chats, and real-time polls.

A step-by-step breakdown of these and other skills is presented in chapter 7.

SOCIAL ANNOTATION TOOLS

One of the exciting growth areas in which universities are creating new ways for students to connect and collaborate is through the use of digital social annotation tools. These tools allow professors and students to comment on texts collaboratively or to create group documents, both in real time and asynchronously. Examples of these include Perusall, a text annotation tool, and Padlet, a group brainstorming platform.

Two pioneers in their use have been Bard College and OSUN, a network of universities and colleges dedicated to teaching liberal arts with writing as a central part of the learning process. Bard College privileges a "writing-rich pedagogy," explained David Shein, Bard's dean of students and the associate vice president for academic affairs. "Writing and thinking are connected." Bard began to work overseas with a network of colleges and needed tools that would allow group writing to happen online. Padlet and Perusall facilitated this. "A lot of what happened during the pandemic has not been good," explained Shein. People talk on the screen, but "there's no actual engagement happening." Padlet allows professors to post prompts, questions, images, and videos in a group collaborative space, and students can then respond in real time (figure 5.10). "Everyone's actually online, and we are writing together and sharing what we've written—everyone's engaged." The work happens in real time and is recorded and becomes an "artifact of the class,"

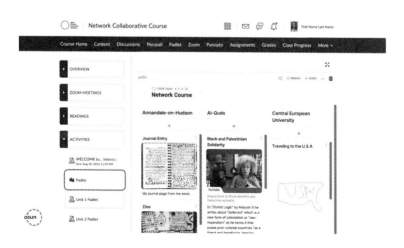

Figure 5.10 Padlet discussion

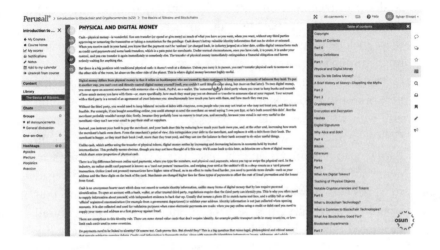

Figure 5.11 Perusall social annotation tool

explained Shein. "It's all about collaboration and engagement and talking to one another."

Perusall is another tool that allows for rich written exchanges. With Perusall, professors (or students) share a text and invite others to comment and notate certain portions (figure 5.11). "We used to do this when we were kids," explained Shein. "You're scribbling in the margins, except this is typed . . . everyone else in the text can read it and comment on people's comments." Like Padlet, Perusall allows for a set of exchanges that demand action and engagement and can happen both live or between classes. Perusall also allows for the purchase and sharing of digital books and other content (Hill 2015).

We recommend that universities add a few social annotation tools to their suite of platforms and technologies. As with all tools, there is an initial learning curve, so we recommend that universities choose a few standard tools and support them with guides, training, and tutorials. These tools should be integrated into the school's LMS, so it is easy for instructors and students to use them in classes. Our core recommendations in this area include the following:

- Choose a few standard social annotation tools.
- Make sure they are available and easy to connect to your LMS.
- Provide guides and tutorials on how to use them, and encourage professors to plan activities using them.
- Provide in-training concrete examples of course projects.

RECORDED VIDEO LECTURES

Prerecorded video lectures are a core tool for both asynchronous learning (in the style of many traditional online courses) and blended learning (the mix of asynchronous and live learning). Prerecorded video lectures allow classes to be flipped so that students can view lectures and do other activities online before coming to class, then participate in live interactive discussions and activities. But how should these videos be created?

For well-funded university programs, lectures for flipped classes might be created in a studio on campus with the help of a professional media team (often supplemented by student media interns). For smaller seminars, a less expensive do-it-yourself option could work well. Instructors simply need a basic system to record themselves and their PowerPoint presentations and upload them to the LMS.

The simplest system—recording a minilecture on Zoom and then posting the video to the course website—offers basic functions but little opportunity to control the visual quality of the presentation. It works well for most classes, especially if the video will not be widely available and shared with the general public. Other video lecture recording systems, such as Screencastify and Screencast-O-Matic, offer more professional options. Popular with K–12 teachers, use of these tools increased dramatically during the pandemic. These tools enable teachers to mix video and PowerPoint, and do basic video editing as needed. But university professors have traditionally been less likely to self-record video lectures with these

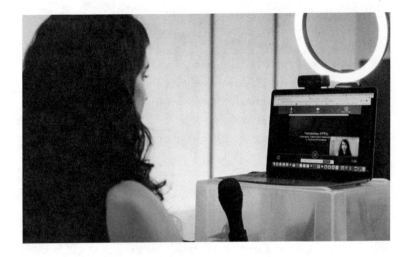

Figure 5.12 A professor self-recording a video

tools than their K-12 colleagues. Faculty often resist sharing videos that appear less than professional. They also say they have less time to learn the systems.

During the pandemic, leading OPM providers such as Wiley and 2U developed systems to allow record professors to record themselves in their homes. Professors received kits with basic lights and video equipment (figure 5.12). The vendors developed workflows to remotely create video recordings (Chou 2021; Zipper 2021). Similar systems were developed by Arizona State University, the University of California Irvine, Cornell, and Columbia (Funk 2021; Jhaj 2021; Krause 2021). To guide the recording of in-home studios, OPMs and university digital teams provided remote directors and online technical support. But for courses without these resources, other options are needed.

The browser recorder system developed by Panopto enables professors to upload a PowerPoint, choose a template with university branding, and record the lecture. After recording, the system allows instructors and TAs to add video transitions and graphics if needed. "It aims to be the self-driving car of digital education," said Eric Burns (2021), the CEO of Panopto. "We realized that the core creative element for the videos that most professors produce is the content, not the form. If we can automate and simplify the process of making quality videos, it will be a big step forward for many programs."

Built-in production and editing tools will grow even simpler to use in the coming years. Here are the key competencies your system should have now:

- Provide an easy self-recording tool that professors can use and integrate it into the learning management system.
- Make it simple to record with PowerPoint and other presentation software.
- Integrate high-quality cameras, lighting, and audio systems into the system.
- Provide intuitive editing tools that have a simple process for making decisions and automating actions.

Creating and sharing video lectures will continue to get simpler and tools will become more powerful. Faculty competencies can be expected to improve with the technology. Faculty in all fields should master the basics of making video lecture recordings, just as they have now mastered using computers, spreadsheets, and software programs.

OUR CHECKLIST FOR ACHIEVING
UNIVERSITY DIGITAL COMPETENCY

The following sections provide a quick recap of our suggested actions for achieving university digital competency.

Choose and Support Standardized Digital Tools and Workflows Consider including a standardized university-wide template for building class websites on the university LMS, and provide support for faculty and TAs to use it. Integrate that system into a universal learning management system. Encourage high standards for using Zoom and in-class lecture capture tools. To avoid confusion and overwhelming the faculty, do not offer additional options. Make sure faculty and others can easily find the university's core tools and systems on the teaching and learning website. Remove all competing, overlapping, and obsolete guides.

Provide Core Digital Skills for Faculty Teach core tools in short workshops during breaks between semesters and online. Set minimum standards for in-service training—perhaps workshops every several years. This model has worked in most other professions, including finance, law, medicine, accounting, and elementary and secondary education.

Include Review of Digital Class Plan in Curriculum Review Process Reviewing only a class's syllabus as a PDF will not lead to engaging and digitally enabled learning. Asking professors to actively participate in the creation of a decent course website and having a plan to use digital tools in course delivery are the first steps toward ensuring that students receive high-quality learning experiences that take advantage of modern learning science and techniques.

Include Digital Competency in Student Course Evaluation Nudge professors to up their game by including assessments of digital teaching in student evaluations. Give students a chance to evaluate use of the LMS, Zoom, and in-class lecture videos.

Invest in Creating Digital TA and CA Positions Give faculty the support they need by hiring digital teaching and course assistants while also investing in a new generation of scholars and teachers. By using the TAs and CAs who assist faculty in major lecture classes, the process of integrating technology into the curriculum becomes seamless.

Invest in In-Class Lecture Capture for Core Required Courses Invest in classroom camera and audio systems, hard-wired into the university's video management systems. These investments can be substantial for major university-wide programs. To phase-in this investment, start by wiring key lecture halls used for mandatory introductory classes.

Include Social Annotation Tools in Your Suite of Offerings
Look for and include in your package some social annotation tools such as Padlet and Perusall. Make sure these tools are available to all faculty and students, are integrated into your LMS, and are supported with training guides. Encourage professors to consider assigning projects using them.

Support Faculty Use of Self-Recorded Video Platforms Choose and support the simplest workflows possible while looking for new automated systems similar to Panopto. Whatever the system, make sure it is integrated into the university's LMS. Avoid needlessly complex systems. Support one basic solution and workflow for all classes.

REFERENCES

Baker, Nelson. 2021. Interview of Dean of Professional Education and Professor of Civil and Environmental Engineering, Georgia Tech, by Adam Stepan. October 27, 2021.

Bowyer, Rochelle. 2020. "UW Isn't 'Boundless' for Students with Disabilities." University of Washington. *The Daily*, April 13, 2020. https://www.dailyuw.com/opinion/article_2c8b2e90-7d1b-11ea-81ff-df2a491a4478.html.

Burns, Eric. 2021. Interview of Dean of Continuing Education and UCLA Extension, UCLA, by Adam Stepan. October 18, 2021.

Chou, Luyen. 2021. Interview of Chief Learning Officer, 2U, by Adam Stepan. October 27, 2021.

Dean, Brian. "Zoom User Stats: How Many People Use Zoom in 2022?" *Backlinko*, January 6, 2022. https://backlinko.com/zoom-users.

Dooley, Frank. 2021. Interview of Chancellor, Purdue Global, by Adam Stepan. October 25, 2021.

Funk, Camille. 2021. Interview of Director of Learning and Innovation and Instructional Design, University of California Irvine, by Adam Stepan. November 4, 2021.

Gao, Benjamen. 2021. "Zoom University: A Review of Fall Lecture Attendance." *Stanford Daily*, January 20, 2021. https://www.stanforddaily.com/2021/01/20/zoom-university-a-review-of-fall-lecture-attendance/.

Hill, Phil. 2015. "LMS Is the Minivan of Education (and Other Thoughts from #LILI15)." *ELiterate* (blog). May 7, 2015. https://eliterate.us/lms-is-the-minivan-of-education-and-other-thoughts-from-lili15/.

Huntemann, Nina. 2021. Interview of Vice President of Learning, edX, by Adam Stepan. October 18, 2021.

Jhaj, Sukhwant. 2021. Interview of Vice Provost for Academic Innovation and Student Achievement, Arizona State University, by Adam Stepan. November 1, 2021.

Kim, Joshua. 2021. Interview of Director of Online Programs and Strategy at Dartmouth College Senior Scholar, Georgetown University, by Adam Stepan. October 21, 2021.

Krause, Paul. 2021. Interview of Vice Provost of External Education, Cornell University Executive Director, eCornell, by Adam Stepan. October 22, 2021.

Nazeeri, Furqan. 2021. Interview of CEO, Extension Engine, by Adam Stepan. November 9, 2021.

Singh, Sharan. 2021. Interview of Senior Managing Director of Strategic Partnerships, Minerva Project, by Adam Stepan. November 2, 2021.

Wong, Jessica. 2022. "UCLA Student Organizations Lead Strike Against Return to In-Person Learning." *Daily Bruin*, February 1, 2022. https://dailybruin.com/2022/02/01/ucla-student-organizations-lead-strike-against-return-to-in-person-learning/.

Zipper, Todd. 2021. Interview of President, Wiley Education Services, by Adam Stepan. November 10, 2021.

"Zoom Reports First Quarter Results for Fiscal Year 2021." 2020. *Zoom*, June 2, 2020. https://investors.zoom.us/news-releases/news-release-details/zoom-reports-first-quarter-results-fiscal-year-2021/.

6

DESIGNING AND CREATING DIGITAL CLASSES AND PROGRAMS

In this chapter, we take a deep dive into the process of designing or redesigning both a program of study and a specific course within it to take advantage of digital tools and delivery methods. This process usually takes six to nine months per course, with faculty working with a digital education team to plan and create digital assets and activities, build a new course website, and plan delivery. These new digital assets can then be used as part of a 100-percent online program or as part of a digitally enhanced on campus class. In this chapter, we follow the steps of two workflows—one for overall program planning and one for specific course development.

IN-HOUSE TEAMS

The digital course design and creation teams employed by universities range in size from half a dozen to hundreds of people. The University of Pennsylvania employs six staff for one of its course design and media units. Rice University employs more than twenty. Major players eCornell and Georgia Tech have teams of two hundred professionals for full-blown "in-house" online program management units (In-House OPMs). These more ambitious programs handle both online and hybrid program creation and management for 20,000 or more learners every year. EdPlus, the in-house OPM at Arizona State University, has a team of more than five hundred, with 150 directly involved in digital course creation for more than 60,000 on campus students and 80,000 online learners. Other members of the team focus on program management and delivery (Krause 2021; Levander 2021; Lewis 2021; Regier 2021).

PHASE ONE: PROGRAM PLANNING

Planning for major digital programs is an iterative process. As team members discover new techniques and adjust their goals, they shift some of their approaches. Figure 6.1 tracks a sequence of steps universities often follow in a typical twelve-month planning cycle to design and plan a new digital education program.

Creating or Renting a Learning Framework

Success in digital program design requires a well-designed learning framework: an institution-wide agreement on mission and staffing that informs the planning and design of specific courses and assets.

Step #1	Step #2	Step #3	Step #4	Step #5
"Renting" or creating a learning framework	Program level planning	Defining delivery modes	Defining core courses	Faculty engagement
6 months	2 months	1 month	1 month	2 months
Define core approach	Define target students + overall program goals	Define modes of class delivery	Confirming specific courses	Confirming specific faculty involvement

Figure 6.1 Steps in a digital program planning cycle

This can be done by hiring an experienced external OPM team and "renting" their digital education learning framework or by using the expertise of an in-house team. Beware of entrusting this crucial task to in-house staff or outside consultants without a track record of managing successful projects. Education staff may have useful theoretical knowledge of digital education to faculty in seminars, consulting, and curricular guides and materials, but the key to success lies in the ability to coordinate large projects. This includes the ability to manage the logistical and financial aspects of creating media assets and delivering digital course experiences.

Whatever path is chosen, it is important that the plan of action is based on proven learning science and is geared toward results. In evaluating potential hires and partners, ask to review classes, websites, and educational videos they have overseen and produced. Compare them in design and build quality to the best online courses and programs described in this book and to the examples we share in chapter 7, The Blended Learning Toolkit.

2U's "Learning Experience Framework" (LXF), which is used in their work with partner institutions, is described in a forty-three-page downloadable brochure. The document identifies three core modalities of learning: feel, do, and think. To meet these key goals in its courses, 2U has developed a complex and detailed tracking system that maps actions with planned learning outcomes. "Our course building staff literally cannot build a course unless it adheres to the principles of LXF," 2U's chief learning officer Luyen Chou (2021) said. "We can actually tell that learners are learning at a higher rate than they are in a traditional learning setting," Chou stated. "Our partners are . . . relying on us to bring that science and art to the design of their courses."

Traditional educational publisher Wiley's Educational Services unit also uses a pedagogical framework—developed by D. Randy Garrison, Terry Archer, and Walter Archer—to guide its course design with its partner universities. It is based on three concepts: social presence, cognitive presence, and teaching presence (Cochran and Migliorese, 2021b). "The point of view that we attack learning with is through the community of inquiry," explained Bill Cochran.

For Wiley, successful course design is not "just a matter of taking your content and making it flashy and putting it online" but rather "designing a great learning experience."

The learning framework of the Boston-based OPM Extension Engine operates on the concept of "high engagement at scale." This concept has five key ingredients: learner-centered content, active learning, unbounded inclusivity, community connections, and real-world outcomes. Each online or hybrid program includes some combination of these "ingredients," explained founder and CEO Furqan Nazeeri (2021). Tactile interactions in simulations promote active learning. Collaborative learning offers "peer feedback [that] can promote engagement" and enables classes to be scaled. Connections to "real-world outcomes" equip students with actionable skills and tools.

These frameworks all embrace active learning, engagement through project-based and peer-to-peer learning, the use of digital cases or simulations, and connections to real-world outcomes and situations (Chou 2021; Cochran and Migliorese 2021b; Singh 2021). Most frameworks are designed to be flexible; the goal is not to create cookie-cutter courses but to provide a common set of goals and a shared language, with a menu of common options for course redesign and creation.

For 2U's Chou (2021), the ability to collect data on learning outcomes has been critical to refining techniques. "Today, we have thirty years of . . . research into how people learn," he said. In fact, 2U has collected data from more than 250,000 students. "What I'm super excited about is the opportunity for data science to inform in a deep way what works in learning and what drives student outcomes," explained Chou. "We have never as educators . . . had that kind of conversation."

Common elements used by most digital learning frameworks include the following factors:

- Active learning by design
- Social and peer-to-peer learning
- Connections to real-world outcomes

Thinking at the Program Level

Once your institution has decided on a general learning framework to drive course redesigns or agreed to work with an experienced OPM who can guide you in this process, the design process generally begins at the overall program level rather than on the level of an individual course (Chou 2021; Krause 2021; Nelson 2021; Regier 2021). If you want to design an online revenue-generating degree program, what core classes do you need to build out, and in what order? Which classes will be required for all students, and which ones will be used only by some? Are there program certification and accreditation issues that must be addressed?

If your focus is primarily on improving and "digitally enhancing" existing on campus classes, which classes are most strategic to focus on? Will this effort be funded by internal resources or by an OPM in exchange for a percentage of tuition revenue? Will the program generate revenue or enhance already existing on campus offerings?

Finally, consider the economies of scale. Digital assets can be used in more than one course or program. Can you digitally enhance a course for use in a fee-paying online master's program? Can the same online lectures, digital cases, or simulations then be used for other on campus classes? Can you create simulations or digital cases for use in on campus classes that can also be used in a revenue-generating executive education offering?

These strategic decisions fall under the purview of the leadership team: the school dean, the program department chair, and the leaders of the digital education unit. Wiley and other vendors assign a program strategy manager to coordinate the effort with the university team (Cochran and Migliorese 2021b).

Defining Delivery Formats

The online program team also generally decides on the delivery modes. Will students meet in person or online? Will the

	Meets in person ◄----------------► Meets on Zoom	
#1 Meets only in-person No pre-recorded content	#2 Meets both in-person + Zoom No pre-recorded content	#3 Meets only on Zoom No pre-recorded content
#4 Meets only in-person w/pre-recorded content	#5 Meets both in-person + Zoom w/pre-recorded content	#6 Meets only on Zoom w/pre-recorded content
#7 X	#8 X	#9 Never meets "Live" 100% asynchronous content

(Left axis: No asynchronous content ▲ ---------- ▼ 100% asynchronous content)

(Bottom axis: Meets in person ◄----------------► Meets on Zoom)

Figure 6.2 Digital class delivery modes

course meet at fixed meeting times, engage asynchronously online using discussion boards, or utilize some combination of the two? Frequently, content is designed for multiple delivery formats. Figure 6.2 is designed to help map out and make sense of the most popular course delivery formats so content can be designed for delivery and used in various ways over its life cycle. The list that follows describes the various modalities shown in figure 6.2.

1. **Traditional on campus lecture class:** The traditional approach to teaching and learning, with an on campus lecture, seminar, or lab class. All lectures and discussions take place at the same time and place. The asynchronous programs consist of assigned readings, research, papers, and reports.
2. **HyFlex class:** A combination of traditional class meetings and online meetings via Zoom or other meeting software that can be arranged flexibly depending on the needs of students and instructors.

3. **Teaching through Zoom:** All meetings and discussions take place in live sessions through online meeting platforms such as Zoom. This was the choice of most universities during the first year of the pandemic.

4. **Traditional flipped classroom:** Before class meetings, students view prerecorded lecture videos and other asynchronous content and then spend in-person class meetings engaged in active learning, with debates, problem-solving exercises, and presentations. This is the mode for on campus digital enhancement.

5. **Flipped classroom/hybrid version:** Similar to the flipped classroom, with one additional feature: Live sessions may meet in person, online, or with some combination of the two.

6. **Flipped classroom on Zoom:** The most common approach for online courses. A typical course might include assignments for asynchronous work before live sessions on Zoom when classes engage in active learning.

7. **Blank:** In-person 100-percent asynchronous modality does not exist.

8. **Blank:** Hybrid 100-percent asynchronous modality does not exist.

9. **Fully asynchronous class:** The classic self-paced online class, with all content produced ahead of the class and no regularly scheduled live meetings. In this category are two subcategories: (a) self-paced fully asynchronous classes generally 100-percent automated, or (b) cohort-based fully asynchronous classes, in which students do not meet in person but interact with each other and an instructor in online discussion boards and other activities.

Many programs and projects now plan and design content for use in several of these multiple delivery modes.

Core Courses

Once the issues of overall program design and delivery formats have been settled, the next question is what courses to "digitally enhance" or move online. To anchor an online program, it's often best to start by digitally enhancing required entry-level courses. This is an attractive option for several reasons.

One reason is that these courses are often very large, and the experience is already one of distance learning for most students. "We teach Chemistry in the fall to a ballpark of close to 5,000 freshmen," Purdue's Frank Dooley (2021) noted. In the traditional mass lecture class with hundreds of students, "you literally have to have binoculars" to follow lectures and demonstrations. To overcome the limits of the mass class, Purdue has created prerecorded lecture videos and detailed demonstrations of lab experiments.

Another reason to digitally enhance core entry-level courses is its impact on equity and accessibility. Very often, first-generation college students and others from underserved communities face challenges in these gateway introductory classes, which generally must be completed successfully to continue with a chosen course of study. This is especially true in STEM disciplines, where introductory math and science courses must be completed to pursue degrees in health or engineering fields. Investing in "digital scaffolding" for these courses in the form of recorded lectures, video cases, and other interactive assets can make these materials more accessible and improve learning outcomes, improving overall program equity and diversity.

Digitally enhancing core entry-level courses also pays other benefits. The material used in entry-level courses is often the same material needed for many executive education programs. Executive education and other programs can use the prerecorded lectures, case studies, and simulations created in this process. The "assets" for an introductory law class on property rights, Paul Krause (2021) of eCornell noted, can be used in an undergraduate summer course, a noncredit professional executive education certificate program, and as flipped class content at the university.

At the University of California Berkeley campus, Professor Armando Fox (2021) follows the same strategy in his computer science courses: investing in the creation of digital content that can be used in many ways. "Here's a piece of content that has some lectures, some exercises, some instructor-facing scaffolding," Fox said. "We're going to deploy that in a very low-cost MOOC, in a MOOC [supported by] student services, in a certificate program [with] coaching, [and] in a high-price exec-ed program," not to mention its value as flipped content for on campus classes.

The University of Michigan has added online materials in courses that require mastery of core course material, said James DeVaney (2021), the university's associate vice provost for academic innovation. In medicine and engineering, failure to pass an entry-level course can mean getting dropped from the program, which most often affects first-year students from underserved communities. For this reason, Michigan focused on creating digital materials for core STEM classes. Online lessons, videos, and tutorials offer remedial help for students with weak subject knowledge. "So, if someone is really interested but doesn't yet have the fundamental skills," DeVaney explained, "they can accelerate skill acquisition in order to succeed in that course."

The University of Washington also cites program equity and diversity as motivation for investing in digitally enhanced core classes. To increase diversity in its architecture program, the university created digital assets and is developing plans for summer programs and boot camps for high school students. "That's one of the least diverse STEM fields," said Washington's Rovy Branon (2021), "and we have a diverse group coming through this camp. We intentionally use our camp to diversify a pipeline of students into the field of architecture."

For the Minerva Project, thinking on the overall program level is so important that they refuse any consulting work that is focused only on digitally enhancing one or two classes. The key to the whole process, said founder Ben Nelson (2021), is to understand how one course flows into the other, with concepts from introductory-level classes providing a foundation for later study. Minerva Project sees itself as a curriculum reform company. "Reform doesn't happen . . . because of technology," Nelson said. "It is enabled by technology. But the real reformation has to happen in the curricular design."

Faculty Engagement

Ideally, key faculty members will be part of the degree program's overall planning and design team from the beginning. 2U's Luyen Chou (2021) explains that this part of the process at 2U generally involves "four to six weeks in analysis and really coming up with a blueprint" for the overall program. Then we would move on to specific options for professors and classes to work with: "Who do we need? What faculty members need to be involved with that?" At times, there are few options because only one professor teaches a key introductory-level course. At other times, various professors teach the same or similar material. In these cases, the question of which professors to choose to design a class and film content plays a key role in program success: Are they available? Open and interested? Do they have a skill set that works for digital delivery?

Good online or digital classes do not need professors to be slick TV personalities, but they do need to be people who understand performance and communication, who are passionate and enthusiastic about their subject area, and who are willing to work with media teams to learn how to best present their content online. Ideally, these factors are taken into consideration when choosing faculty to deliver digitally enhanced programs in which the university will be making considerable investments (Ubell 2021).

Another key question is what mix of junior and senior faculty to include. Junior faculty may have more flexible schedules, be more conversant with new technologies, and be more open to working with media teams. Senior faculty are more likely to be seen as authorities in their field. Junior and off-track faculty may be more open to delivering classes that feature video lectures from senior faculty experts (Krause 2021; Regier 2021). Digital classes are often delivered by teams. Ideally, the video lectures created will have a long shelf-life, serving as evergreen content that can be used for many years. For these reasons, having core fundamental material delivered by senior faculty may be a good choice. Either way, universities need standard policies and agreements that detail the intellectual property rights and prerogatives of both faculty and the institutions where they work, and allow for content to be created by one professor and delivered by another.

Universities' digital teams need a streamlined design and production system that makes the best use of everyone's time and expertise. "Number one, we recognize that the professor is not doing this and only this," 2U's Andrew Hermalyn (2021) said. "They have their teaching on campus, they have their research—we recognize that first and foremost."

Faculty engagement also requires frank discussions about what is possible online. Many faculty historically begin with skepticism, believing that online learning can't be as good as in-person teaching. "There's a wide variety of quality and effectiveness to online teaching," eCornell's Paul Krause (2021) explained. "There are some courses that are not particularly effective and engaging, but also some courses that are transformative for a student." At the beginning of any process, the instructional design team needs to show professors what well-designed online learning looks like and contrast this with the often subpar "emergency remote learning" common during the pandemic.

Getting senior faculty involved early in the process pays dividends down the road, explained Michigan's James DeVaney (2021). Faculty involved in digital class creation at Michigan receive a package of benefits, including course relief from some of their normal teaching load in semesters when new digital assets are being designed and created. Michigan also includes participation in digital efforts in promotions and evaluations. "It's being acknowledged in their tenure review, it's being positioned as accomplishments when they are pursuing external grants," DeVaney explained. With this effort, digital learning becomes central to faculty. "It [has] become integrated [as] top research and teaching priorities, as opposed to a space where they might focus in their spare time."

Arizona State University (ASU) offers a two-week boot camp to introduce first-time online teachers to the core concepts of digital course design. Faculty that participate in boot camps incorporate their new skills into traditional classes, said Phil Regier (2021), of

ASU's EdPlus team, and "90 percent of the people that go through the process say 'It has made my on campus teaching and learning better.'"

Another interesting model for faculty engagement is that followed by the Open Society University Network (OSUN) in the creation of their network collaborative courses, which are created by a team of professors and are delivered on multiple campuses across the network. Some of the learning happens locally during in-person seminars, and other parts occur online. When doing a class redesign, key faculty are brought together for a multiday, in-person Faculty Meetup. During OSUN's intense three-day workshops, faculty review course goals and new technologies and discuss collaborative assignments. They also bond as a team and lay the basis for their ongoing online collaborations. "It's not about just creating a model that's handed off to other campuses," explained Bard's David Shein, who often facilitates these workshops. "It's about developing partnerships and building on them." A key part of the process is questioning the ways each course has traditionally been delivered. "Why do we do it that way? What does that mean?" are typical questions raised by new team members. Seasoned professors who have offered previous versions of the course must confront these questions. "That's super important," explained Shein.

PHASE TWO: INDIVIDUAL COURSE DESIGN OR REDESIGN

After developing a mission and strategy for digital learning and engaging with a key group of faculties to confirm how specific courses work within a general program of study and their delivery modes, it's time to work on the design or redesign of individual courses. We often think of this process as a course redesign because the job usually involves taking a traditional lecture-based course and reimagining how it can be delivered as an online or digitally enhanced course. But the process also works for an entirely new course being designed from the ground up. The process follows the steps shown in figure 6.3 and generally is spread over a six- to nine-month period.

Step #1	Step #2	Step #3	Step #4	Step #5	Step #6	Step #7
Mapping learning outcomes/ backwards design	Confirming delivery formats	Planning class activities	Designing and creating content	Filming w/professors + others	Building class website video editing	Class delivery
2–4 weeks	1–2 weeks	2 weeks	4–6 weeks	1 week	6 weeks	Variable

Figure 6.3 Steps in individual course design or redesign process

Mapping Learning Outcomes

For most digital education teams, this part of the process takes place over a period of four weeks, during which the lead professor or professor team educates the instructional design team on current course content and learning objectives. The instructional design team then offers options for delivering content, creating exercises, and planning digital delivery. Most programs use some version of what is known as "backward design"—first mapping the final learning outcomes that the course is designed to deliver and then working backward to design activities that achieve these outcomes. For Joshua Scott (2021), director of course strategy at the OPM for 2U, course design is paramount. "We firmly believe that you can design the flashiest content, but if it's not quality learning design, then it's going to be a garbage course."

Scott (2021) explained that the process begins with the learning design team understanding as much as it can about the current course, its instructor, and its students. "Can we look at the syllabus? Can we look at any kind of draft materials they have? Is there any kind of student feedback we can learn about?" These are all questions the team asks at the beginning of the process. Ideally, the learning design team is managed by someone who has experience with the content area and has worked on similar courses with other partners. "It's not that everyone is a former professor in any particular topic," explained Scott—himself a former professor at Notre Dame and the University of Colorado—but ideally the lead instructional designers are people who have "built up a base of knowledge about a particular set of disciplines." The course designers identify the core ideas and skills that students must master and how these objectives fit into the overall program of study: "What does this course connect to and build on, and what does it lead to?" This work requires an understanding of how the course will be delivered: How much will students work apart from course meetings? How will students join together to learn? How often? Over what period?

At the center of the course is the curriculum: the knowledge and skills students will explore, as well as how they will be evaluated. "We then map the outcomes," explained Scott (2021). "We talk in really great detail." Students need to understand their learning goals and how they will be assessed. As planning moves into weekly assignments and activities, 2U gets granular. "What learning objectives are we meeting in week one?" Scott asks. "We have a taxonomy of learning category, event, and action before we get to the actual modality that it's being delivered on."

For each course, 2U creates a map detailing each week's learning goals and activities, which are assessed against the rubrics of its Learning Experience Framework (figure 6.4) The core idea of backward design—"do the outcomes, then you map it to the assessments, and then you map it to the course, and then you create the content"—is developed iteratively. Each new addition or change in the course affects what happens before and after. This up-front work is fundamental to ensuring a solid foundation for building the course before entering the production stage. Scott (2021) points out, "We want to make sure that before we do that investment, it's going to be a quality course with quality design."

Wiley also uses a backward design process. The instructional design team's role is to "really understand the faculty's goal for the course, their understanding of the challenges of the curriculum and the students," said Bill Cochran, Wiley's associate director of instructional media. "We have a reverse design concept," he said.

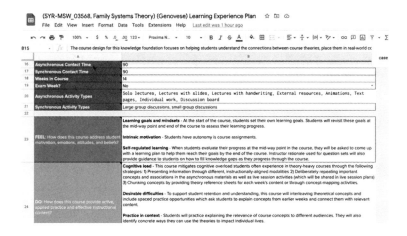

Figure 6.4 Course map using 2U's Learning Experience Framework

"What is the outcome we want to see? What is the vision for the program?" (Cochran and Migliorese 2021b). As with 2U, the process begins with mapping learning outcomes, moves to assessments, and from there to designing potential activities.

EdPlus at ASU uses metrics called Quality Matters to plot the course plan (figure 6.5). These metrics allow EdPlus to confirm that the course content follows the principles of good course design. "Are the activities identified?" Justin Harding (2021), the senior director for instructional design and new media at EdPlus, explained. "Are there activities and content that support the objective? Are there formative learning opportunities, so that students can self-access their learning along the way?"

Mapping Class Activities

Following backward design and course mapping of learning outcomes, course design teams move on to designing specific course activities. What part of the course is best delivered as prerecorded content, and what makes more sense as an active learning project?

ASU Online Course Design Standards

The ASU Online course development checklist was adapted from the QM Quality Matters research-based rubric and the Peralta Online Equity Rubric for equity and inclusion. Click the number next to each standard for annotations on how a standard is met vs. exemplary met in online courses. Your ASU Online Instructional Designer can provide consultation and support to meet these standards (video).

ASU Online Course Design Standards Checklist	*- Adapted from Quality Matters & Peralta Rubrics*
ASU Online	1. Course uses ASU Online Canvas course template and design theme and includes required syllabus criteria 2. Course is organized and optimized for student success to be delivered in the scheduled time frame (typically 7.5 wk format) 3. Course setup information is included for future instructors (course structure, to-dos, instructor guide notes) 4. Course includes videos (mini-lectures, demonstrations, interviews) to engage students
Course Overview & Introduction	5. Students are introduced to the purpose, navigation, structure of the course, and how to begin (QM1.1,1.2) 6. Course welcome & introduction encourages personal connections and demonstrates that each unique student's participation & success in the course is valued. Video highly encouraged (QM1.8,PE8) 7. When possible, human biases are acknowledged and information is provided on how to address (PE6)
Learning Objectives	8. Course and module learning objectives describe outcomes that are measurable and course level appropriate (QM2.1,2.2,2.5) 9. The relationship between learning objectives and learning activities is clearly stated (QM2.4)
Assessment & Measurement	10. Assessments measure stated learning objectives (QM3.1) 11. Course grading policy is stated clearly at the beginning of the course (QM3.2) 12. Clear instructions and specific and descriptive criteria (rubrics) exist for evaluation of student work (QM3.3) 13. Assessments are sequenced and varied, providing multiple ways to demonstrate progress and mastery (QM3.4) 14. Course provides learners with multiple opportunities to track their progress with formative assessments (QM3.5)
Instructional Materials	15. Instructional materials clearly communicate to students how they align with course and unit objectives (QM4.1,4.2) 16. Instructional materials (readings, images, activities, etc.) reflect and demonstrate the value of diversity and encourage students to analyze course content from multiple perspectives (PE4) 17. Instructional materials/activities invite students to connect course content to their own lives and/or reflect on course content as relevant to their future (PE7) 18. Instructional materials are appropriately cited and adhere to copyright (QM4.3)
Learner Activities & Interaction	19. Learning activities promote the achievement of stated learning objectives (QM5.1) 20. Learning activities provide opportunities for interaction that support active learning (QM5.2)
Course Technology	21. Tools used in the course support learning objectives (QM6.1) 22. Course tools promote learner engagement and active learning (QM6.2) 23. Resources to support the use of course tools are provided (PE1)
Learner Support	24. Technical support information and how to access it is provided and easily located (QM7.1) 25. Accessibility policies and support services are provided and easily located (QM7.2) 26. Academic support services and resources that can help learners succeed in the course are provided (QM7.3)
Accessibility	27. Course navigation and design facilitates ease of use readability (QM8.1,8.2) 28. Digital textbooks and course materials are prioritized (QM8.2) 29. Course provides accessible text and images that value and represent the diversity of online learners (QM8.3,PE4)

Figure 6.5 Arizona State University's Quality Matters metrics

What content is best delivered in live synchronous sessions? What group projects can help students engage with the material and each other? How long will these activities take? What elements of the course are best delivered by a classic video lecture with a professor and a PowerPoint or whiteboard? What would a student learn best by reading? How can live sessions drive debate and discussion? If no live sessions are planned, how can students explore and debate topics on asynchronous discussion boards?

During the planning process, professors need to be deeply involved, exploring options for delivery methods and viewing and testing examples from other classes or mockups. ASU has developed a menu of delivery options for filmed classes, with instructor intros, professor and PowerPoint options, group interviews, simulations, and labs. "It's like when you go to a restaurant," ASU's Justin Harding (2021) said. "The restaurant says 'These are the ingredients we have to make this.'"

ASU has invested heavily in process-based videos, moment-by-moment depictions of lab experiments and detailed hands-on demos for engineering classes (figure 6.6). "You're looking, you're identifying, you're going through something," said ASU's Harding (2021). These videos are scalable, reusable learning assets. Even better, the

Figure 6.6 Arizona State University lab demo video

videos can be more useful than live demonstrations. "If you are five or six people deep around the demonstration table in a classroom, you're not going to be able to see the intricacies of what's going on," points out Harding. But a multicamera video shoot offers a "close up, first-hand viewing experience."

For ASU and others, the key to deciding how much to invest in the video production of a given course depends on the size of the student audience. One of the key questions the team asks when evaluating filming plans is impact. "Is this for a twenty-person per year course that we are looking at spending hundreds of hours developing content for?" asks Harding (2021), or is this a "10,000 student per year class?"

The University of California Irvine (UCI) follows a similar approach for its largely self-paced classes. "We start with the course map and really outline all the modules," explained Kris Velasquez (2021) of UCI's DesignPlus shop. "For each module, we isolate the topic that would benefit from media." From there the team explores options: "What's the best strategy? What's the best format? Would it be an animation? Would it be live action?" As with ASU, both budgetary and course considerations inform the options. "We have two main processes, a limited and a premium," explained Camille Funk (2021), UCI's director of learning innovation and instructional design. The limited option follows a shorter development cycle, with content created by professors with templates and guides. The premium option deploys UCI-DCE's live action and animation team.

The process requires imagining the final course delivery before mapping the video assets needed to achieve that delivery. For an online course on finance at Georgetown University, Wiley chose the classic blended approach with recorded video lectures. "We have a Master's in Finance program there which is centered on a lot of video lectures, and then live weekly case-based teaching sessions," said David Migliorese, Wiley's vice president of academic services. Students view video lectures before class meetings, which sets the basis for lively debates when the class gathers. "They do a sort of 'Paper Chase'–style Zoom session every week, where [faculty] are

Figure 6.7 eCornell law lectures used in multiple delivery formats

cold-calling students to analyze cases," explained Migliorese. "That really is the main event" (Cochran and Migliorese 2021a).

Assets created for blended classes generally also work for asynchronous classes that offer online support and activities. For example, eCornell often uses the same video assets for two versions of the same law course—one with weekly live sessions and the other self-paced (figure 6.7). In the self-paced version, discussions are moved to an online discussion board where a course facilitator guides discussions (Berkowitz and Krause 2021). Most of Cornell's professional master's programs designed for nontraditional students use a low-residency format. Students attend short in-person sessions "where students do an intensive week or long weekend or series of coursework on campus," explained Sally Berkowitz of eCornell. These in-person intensives complement the majority of the coursework that occurs online.

ASU uses a similar system. The university created a series of videos and demos for a neuroscience course in ASU's online and asynchronous digital immersion program. With these assets, some professors flip their on campus classrooms, with students viewing videos online before class. "We don't want to use lecture time to distribute that information," says ASU's Harding (2021). "When you come to class, we are going to do active learning-based activities." The course mapping design phase is also a great time to see what asynchronous assets can be used that are available for free. Many classes mix and match videos from open educational resource collections that include TED Talks, films from PBS via PBS Learning Media, or digital case studies such as those produced by Columbia and our partners at OSUN.

The consultant's task, says Bill Cochran of Wiley, is to help partners find these resources. "We are content agnostic," he said. "Even though we are owned by a giant publishing company, the academic freedom of our partners is paramount," citing examples such as a course for George Mason University that uses elements such as TED Talks (figure 6.8). Assets include interactive "learning objects," online text, PDFs, and interactive quizzes (Cochran and Migliorese 2021b). A business law class at eCornell includes a tool that allows students to calculate risk. "Here's an example of a rather complex tool . . . on risk calculation in the compliance world," explained eCornell's Berkowitz (Berkowitz and Krause, 2021). "We've created

Figure 6.8 George Mason University course with TED Talk content

this flow chart that students can use that really tracks them through the whole decision matrix and decision tree." For Berkowitz, the asset supports the video presentation of the concepts: "By providing both a verbal and visual description of the process, we are able to reach several different learning styles."

An eCornell medicinal plants class uses an interactive animation that allows students to add names of plants in a "drag and drop" activity (figure 6.9). Another eCornell course uses an online tool to develop and track a group project over the course of a student's studies. Many eCornell courses use these assets—prerecorded videos, animations, online tools, and exercises—in different versions of the course. Planning for multiformat delivery is key to the course design process. A semester-long class for credit can be broken into smaller modules for two-week classes (Berkowitz and Krause 2021). Likewise, a series of two-week modules can be combined into a larger course. With these shorter courses, working professionals can earn certificates in manageable blocks of time. "It's what we call structured flexibility," explained eCornell's Paul Krause (2021). This planning process creates a detailed roadmap that includes the

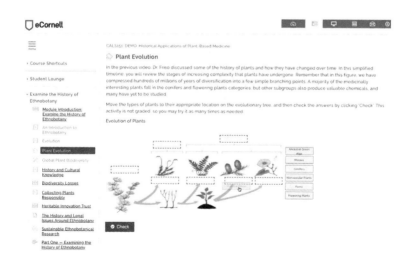

Figure 6.9 eCornell medicinal plants class with a drag and drop activity

number and size of the various sorts of learning assets to be created, licensed, or found, mapped to the learning outcomes identified in the first phase of the design process.

Luyen Chou (2021) of 2U described a typical mapping process. "We work with the professors and say, 'Okay, great. One of the key courses in this degree program is going to be a course in financial accounting. . . . Here are the topics that we think need to be covered. Here's the percentage of [time] that should be a live lecture over Zoom. Here's the percentage that we think should be asynchronous. . . . Here's what we think should be a lecture video. Here's what we think should be an interview. . . . It's traditional backward planning." After this detailed activity mapping, 2U presents the final plan to the professor for approval. "We get a sign-off and then we have this historical record of what has been decided upon," Scott (2021) explained. The project is then handed off to a production team. "It then takes on a more Henry Ford-esque approach to producing the course," said Scott.

In OSUN's collaborative courses, a similar intensive course mapping process happens, often with a focus less on designing prerecorded video elements and more on planning and preparing real-time interactions and activities to be done in class using tools such as Padlet and Perusall. A course might choose a specific text or video case study for group work, and then produce a series of activities that are developed around this content over a period of weeks. Making this work well requires detailed planning.

For UPenn's Nora Lewis (2021), this up-front work and investment in course planning pays huge dividends for the various versions of the course to be delivered. "If you want to do it right, it's a lot of work," explained Lewis, noting that such up-front preparation and planning is what has always defined quality teaching. "Great teachers do that, whether they're teaching in front of a huge lecture or small seminar online." The good news for teachers and students is that, if done correctly, this up-front preparation work can result in digital learning assets that can be used for years to come, improving the class experience for professors and students alike.

Nina Huntemann (2021), of edX, agrees that the process is time-consuming but that most professors who go through the digital course mapping and design process with a good instructional design team come out feeling that they learned a great deal and grew as instructors. "No matter how you cut it, it takes more time to develop that kind of learning experience," explained Huntemann. "People say 'Well gosh, first I need to record all my lectures. Then I have to come up with discussion prompts. And then I have to anticipate what students are going to say!'" Huntemann's response is, generally, "That sounds like a really good in-person course!" For Huntemann, the extra planning that the digital course design requires "actually sounds like really good practice all the time," noting that this level of thought, preparation, and planning "definitely takes more time and effort regardless of the modality."

Creating Asynchronous Content

Once the course map and activity plan have been approved, course building moves to the production phase, be it video lectures, digital cases, or planned group activities and projects that require scaffolding and prebuilt support. For some digital education teams, this means a formal handoff from one team to another. For other teams, the same head designer simply changes focus. Production is the nitty-gritty of course asset creation: scripts, shoots, graphics creation, editing, and delivery.

It is at this stage that the digital education process becomes very much like the television production process. It moves from areas that most universities have experience with and that are comfortable—course design, teaching, and learning—to media production and delivery. Learning how to recruit and retain gifted media professionals is a key part of the process. The skills needed to design and create quality educational videos require more than the jobs traditionally assigned to school AV teams, who are generally only asked to set up a camera and record a talk or a lecture.

At Columbia, we have brought in a number of TV producers with track records of producing content for PBS, Discovery Channel, and other conventional television outlets to help with course and case study creation. They generally have been happy to have a chance to apply their skills to content they often find more interesting and meaningful than that of traditional TV shows. We also involve film and media students who are almost always thrilled to have a chance to use their creative energies on media projects that will benefit other students. This process requires a strong project management system to handle studio scheduling and video editing as well as strict deadlines for script development and approvals.

The team at the University of California Irvine uses project management and tracking systems that would be familiar to anyone with experience at a busy TV production company. The team tracks the number of days for each project's scripting, filming, and editing as well as the allocation of resources such as studio space, animation, and graphic design (figure 6.10). The fact that it is located in southern California helps the UCI team recruit media talent. "That's one benefit of being in California," explained Camille Funk (2021). "We just added an editor from Netflix who also produced a Peabody Award–winning show!"

The UCI team is also very willing to look out of the box in how it conceives and designs its video course content. One area it looks

Figure 6.10 University of California Irvine media production tracker

to is the world of open educational videos available to young people for free on YouTube. "When you look at popular social media and YouTube educational resources that are often free for students," explained UCI's Velasquez (2021), "these components have now become their own genre of free educational materials that are engaging, that are memorable, that are effective, and often short." This has driven the UCI team to invest in simulations with actors and other formats. "We've got live-action, where a scenario is acted out," Velasquez explained, along with "animated explainers," such as those created by Khan Academy and others.

Although these options are intriguing, most universities that produce videos for online courses focus their efforts on creating content that closely follows traditional lectures. Most professors are comfortable with this approach, and it is generally most efficient to produce at scale. The key step in the process is to think about how to compress the content of a thirty- or forty-minute lecture from an in-person course into five- to seven-minute blocks of key information. At Columbia, we frequently cite the TED Talk format to explain the power of the short but dynamic lecture. TED Talks succeed because they are meticulously planned around simple ideas with dynamic visuals. The length of TED Talks—from seven to eighteen minutes—holds the attention of audiences while presenting compelling ideas in stunning detail. Often, these videos complement other course content and are inserted into preplanned active learning projects. These might involve students completing a simulated counseling session using 2U's prerecorded social work sessions or watching a student-created video case study and using a social annotation tool to reflect on how it applies to issues under study.

It is important to keep the length of class video lecture modules at five to eight minutes. A study of more than 280,000 students found a significant drop-off in the engagement at the six- to nine-minute mark of educational videos—a length of time much shorter than the typical college lecture. "This is literally when every one of those 280,000 students hit 'stop' on every one of the videos," said Luyen Chou (2021). Compressing a lecture takes work, as the French philosopher and mathematician Blaise Pascal famously noted: "I would have written a shorter letter, but I did not have the time" (Lamy, Armauld, and Nicole 1676).

A big part of the planning that goes into creating compelling lecture videos involves working with professors on compressing lectures to their core essentials, remembering that in most cases students will also be reading book chapters and papers and perhaps watching digital case studies or other video content on the same issues. Compelling videos require compelling visuals, and this is often delivered using especially prepared-for-filming PowerPoint decks. Carmine Gallo's 2014 bestseller *Talk Like TED* can provide inspiration, and other online guides explain how to produce effective visual presentations. The key is to keep presentations clean and simple, with illustrative images and few words or numbers. Too many PowerPoint slides are overloaded with information, making them difficult to read. Even worse, they distract from what is being said. Student interns have a lifetime of experience online and can assist in creating clean and simple PowerPoint presentations for filming based on professors' outlines.

To create video lectures, presenters often stand in front of a green screen so a variety of backgrounds can be shown (figure 6.11).

Figure 6.11 Behind the scenes of green screen filming at Columbia University

Figure 6.12 Edited green screen video, Columbia University

PowerPoint and other graphics can be added to the image of the professor speaking (figure 6.12). Professors can also "screencast": narrating as they share their computer screens. They can also draw, perform calculations, and mark slides in real time on digital whiteboards designed for use in filming.

Digital education units offer different formats for these short lectures. The recorded lectures at Arizona State University offer PowerPoint, whiteboard, and animated images to accompany lectures (figure 6.13). The University of Pennsylvania's course creation team films on location, in the studio, and directly from classrooms or labs. "We have multiple ways we produce content for courses," said Zachary Humenik (2021), of UPenn's Online Learning Studio. "For some courses, where it is more PowerPoint-driven or more screencast-driven, we might do it that way. For courses that teach abstract issues, there is more room for us to be creative." Teams at eCornell, Georgia Tech, and the University of Washington follow similar models and workflows. Budgets often dictate the level of editing for recorded lectures. The simplest model is for professors to interact with PowerPoint graphics in the shoot.

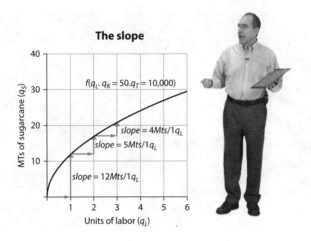

Figure 6.13 Arizona State University green screen lecture with graphs

Animation, which can be added after shoots, brings the discussion of complex concepts to life (Berkowitz and Krause 2021). For example, an eCornell business course uses an animated graphic to show the market entries of new products by different companies (figure 6.14). The University of Washington makes lecture videos

LSM525 DEMO: Introducing New Products: Successes and Failures

▶ The Diffusion Process

How can your customers help your new product gain market share? As you will see. research shows there is a very consistent process in which a new product enters the marketplace.

Figure 6.14 eCornell market entry animation

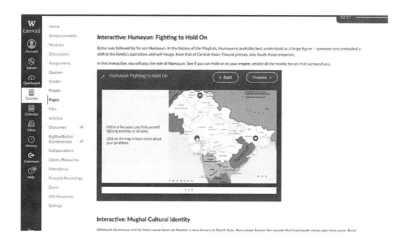

Figure 6.15 University of Washington course with interactive maps

more dynamic with images, polls, and questions. A lecture on Islamic history is supplemented with maps and interactive questions (figure 6.15). These extra features encourage students to pause and interact with the content (Branon 2021).

Increasingly, schools are looking for ways to film with professors that move away from the standard PowerPoint lecture. These include interviews, group discussions, or even simulated Q&As with students (Harding 2021). 2U has developed a category called "creative videos" that includes a variety of labs, simulations, and digital case studies. These videos may take the place of field trips or on-location research projects; they bring real-world situations to students digitally.

The digital case study format works for in-person and online courses equally well. In a course on development issues at Columbia's School of International and Public Affairs, students watch a video case on development issues in Rwanda and the Congo, along with the companion written case document. In course meetings, students debate strategies for foreign aid and investment. "It's an exciting active learning opportunity," Columbia professor Glenn Denning says (2021). "It comes at a point in the semester where

Figure 6.16 2U social work virtual field placement

we have researched these issues in depth. This video case allows students to apply the concepts they have learned to a real-world situation, presented in detail with all its messy complexity."

Videos also can be simulations using actors. Videos produced by 2U used simulations of clinical situations for social work classes during the COVID lockdown (figure 6.16). The videos included visits to a virtual social work agency where students could observe simulated interactions between patients and clinicians. Students then participated in virtual roundtables and discussions, with a follow-up set of live online activities. The simulations were expensive to produce, but they have proven effective and have more than paid for themselves because they are used in multiple classes. Many students rate the program as more effective than actual clinical placements, which are often poorly supervised and not connected to the planned learning outcomes of the course (Scott 2021).

These assets are used in clinical psychology courses offered by several 2U partner institutions. Investing in well-produced content can pay huge educational dividends, especially if it's something that can be used in various courses and settings. "What we developed . . . is a virtual field experience in their first year, [which] would essentially replace the first two hundred hours" of clinical placement, said 2U's Scott (2021). This same logic drives lab demonstrations at Arizona State University on topics ranging from frog dissection

Figure 6.17 Purdue engineering course video site visit

to electrical transistors. Increasingly, virtual reality and 360-degree videos allow students to enter and interact with environments that embed learning objects for student interaction. Wiley and Purdue University have collaborated for the Master's program in engineering technology to teach students about the gears used in boilers. The professor said: "I don't want someone to go to a job site and be thrown by a piece of unfamiliar equipment" (Cochran and Migliorese 2021a). Working with Indiana-based engineering firms, Purdue was able to create useful lessons and strengthen its partnerships with engineering and manufacturing partners (figure 6.17). The videos are used in both online and in-person classes.

Filming with Professors

Although a wide variety of creative videos is possible, the core of most digital course content remains some form of the video lecture. The reasons for this are both practical and pedagogical. The lecture, which presents one professor's take on the issues at hand, serves to guide students in their study and analysis of other readings and other video content. The filmed lecture is also generally the easiest and cheapest form of content for busy professors to plan and produce because the core content is already available in one form or another in their traditional in-person classes. That said, there are other interesting options to use with professors.

One common format is the Introduction Video. This is a two- to three-minute scripted introduction to the course filmed either in the studio or on location. This video will be seen by many students, including those "shopping" for a course, so media production teams often include stock images of things covered in the course, making the video into a short promo for the course as a whole. For courses that are 100-percent online and sold on MOOC platforms, these videos are essential.

Another common format is the Weekly Update video. These informal self-recorded videos are created by the professor from home or in the office that comment on or set up the coming week's class (figure 6.18). The key issue here, explained ASU's Justin Harding (2021), is timeliness, especially for asynchronous online courses that do not have weekly Zoom sessions or in-person meetings. "If you are a political science professor, you may want to just fire up your webcam," Harding explained, and say "this just came in on the news, this is really relevant to what we are talking about in this course, let's talk about this" as a way to

Figure 6.18 Arizona State University informal Weekly Update video

drive asynchronous discussion on the course website. These videos also help create a sense of community in a mostly online class. "I'm at my office, you can see my family pictures here, I'm a real person, I'm not a robot" is all part of the messaging of this sort of informal video communication.

Harding contrasts these informal quick update videos with the formal, filmed in the studio, higher investment, higher quality videos that make up the main content in the course. These videos are planned and filmed with care, generally including the best graphics and editing the course can afford. "Ideally, it lasts for years, if it's structured right," explained ASU's Harding (2021). Having shorter modular lectures helps ensure a longer shelf-life. By focusing on core concepts accompanied by some nicely produced graphics, your program can create evergreen videos that can be updated each year by adding new text intros and new readings to the course website. This has been the approach followed by eCornell, which produces short modular videos with content that can be used in various ways.

In all filming with professors, some basic media training is important. Professors need to be given the same basic media advice that any guest on a television news program or talk show would receive. Some of the key suggestions include making conservative wardrobe selections (wear solid, dark-colored shirts or suits—no white shirts or bright colors), avoiding patterns or anything that is overly informal (unless that is very much that professor's style), and using basic makeup powder (the $10 makeup kit bought at any pharmacy). At Columbia we advise professors to dress as if they were giving a keynote address at a major academic conference. We also insist that basic makeup powder be used. If not, they inevitably have the classic shiny face that we have all seen in poorly produced films.

Beyond this, most professors benefit from some degree of coaching and direction. This can be somewhat awkward at times, especially if a senior professor or college administrator is being filmed by a relatively young or less senior video technician. Most professors are used to public speaking and believe they know how to do it. However, speaking for a live class is very different from performing in a studio for a camera. Having an experienced and more senior video producer in the room can really make the difference between a deadly boring presentation and one that engages and pulls in the viewer. Professors being filmed soon learn what most people who perform on camera or on stage have long known—energy and focus are everything. When communicating on camera, professors must deliver content with more passion and conviction than may initially feel "normal." Using hands to gesture, and generally having and sharing a range of emotions, can be key in bringing an on-camera presentation to life.

It is often helpful for the video director to read parts of the script to show the professor the level of energy and focus that translates well when filmed. It is also helpful to watch examples of good presentations by other professors before filming—most of the MasterClass videos available online are very good and helpful here, as are the better TED Talks. If the professor refuses to take any of this advice, record a bit and then have the professor watch some playback video of the recording. Camille Funk (2021), of UCI, explained that many professors just assume that their success in the classroom means they will automatically succeed on the small screen. But when they see the results of filming—if it was done without effort and rehearsals—"most change their mind." Throughout this process the media team must let professors know that they are the star and that the media team's job is to make them look and sound fantastic.

To Script or Not to Script . . .

One of the essential questions and debates about filming with professors is whether to create a complete script or to use PowerPoints as a reference and let the professor deliver the content more naturally, as in the classroom. There are various schools of thought on this issue.

Most lecture video filming studios use a green screen background together with a teleprompter, which is a device that scrolls text (and PowerPoint slides) so the professor can read it while filming.

For many videos—including short, scripted, two- to three-minute Course Introduction videos—having a full script is essential. It keeps professors focused and on point and is easier to edit.

For the longer videos, scripting can become a huge burden and can lead to very stilted results. This is partly because the scripting must be done by the professor, and most professors do not have experience writing for video (or the time to do it!). The result is often the sort of terrible presentation we have all seen when someone reads a poorly scripted speech or a word-for-word talk at a conference. As most experienced public speakers know, it is better to have a clear outline and then speak naturally with emotion and empathy.

One alternative to creating a complete word-for-word script is to film with professors using the teleprompter that shows them PowerPoint slides rather than a full script (figure 6.19). This has the added advantage that a complex, multipage script does not need to be written. This is generally a huge time saver, but its success depends very much on the professor's comfort level with reading bullet points from a slide deck and improvising, as well as the professor's ability and availability to write complete scripts for each

Figure 6.19 Filming green screen with a PowerPoint rather than script

lecture. The choice of method depends on "the comfort of the instructor," explained UPenn's Zachary Humenik (2021). "Some instructors really prefer to go strictly off script, so they take a Word document, and we pop it into our teleprompter. Some folks like to have their PowerPoint file or PDF and advance [it] using a clicker."

eCornell generally avoids asking faculty to read scripts when creating videos. "When the professor is not scripted, they are speaking naturally," explained Sally Berkowitz of eCornell, reviewing a law professor video (Berkowitz and Krause, 2021). "We try to guide our faculty to deliver more in talking points than in a heavily scripted manner to enhance their authenticity and create an engaging environment more similar to a classroom." The University of Washington takes the opposite approach to combat professors' difficulty in keeping their talks short and focused. "We have had folks try to come in and riff, and typically it does not work very well," said University of Washington's Bryan Blakeley (Blakeley and Branon 2021). With scripting, the production team can help the faculty adjust a presentation to fit the desired five- to eight-minute format. "If we have a history professor come in and ad lib off a PowerPoint, we are easily looking at a forty-five-minute lecture."

For Wiley, the choice comes down to the instructors and their ability to block out the content into clear seven- to eight-minute modules. "Our guiding principle is what makes the instructor most comfortable," said Wiley's Bill Cochran (Cochran and Migliorese 2021b). "Some like to script everything out. . . . Other times, we'll just use bullets." Either way, the goal is to come to the set organized and rehearsed. "We go through a pretty rigorous preproduction process so that when we show up to the shoot we're organized and we know what we are going to get."

The effort and stress involved with creating PowerPoints and scripts lead some programs to use simpler ways of introducing professors and their content. The University of California Irvine treats the professor less as an instructor and more as a subject matter expert. They interview the professor for thirty or forty-five minutes on the issues, then edit the responses into seven- to nine-minute videos (Funk 2021).

At Columbia our experience with this technique is that it works well for a general overview of a subject but less well when carefully covering a set of planned lessons or ideas. It also effectively transfers the work of compressing and focusing the material from the professor—who should know what is most important—to the video editor or producer. However, it is an excellent way to bring in guest speakers and experts, and it works very well in certain situations.

Another way of filming with professors that we use at Columbia involves multiple-camera, live, in-class capture combined with documentary-style interviews. If the in-class lecture uses the same sort of graphics that the final video will use, these images can be edited easily and put together in a compelling video lesson. The final result is similar to a filmed music performance documentary in which live concert footage (the classroom) is intercut with an interview with the artist (in this case the professor). We have found it to yield very appealing filmed class videos.

On the other end of the technology spectrum, we have also developed a do-it-yourself, film-at-home workflow with our partners at Panopto, creating professional videos without using a full green screen studio. In chapter 7, we discuss both of these techniques and workflows in more detail.

Building Course Websites

With the course designed, student projects and activities planned, videos filmed, animations completed, and readings selected, the final phase of course development is reached: creating a website with the learning management system (LMS). In most cases, the choice of the LMS is not up to the individual school or program. Some federated universities still allow different schools to use different systems, but it is generally not considered a best practice because it makes sharing assets across classes complex and makes central support and planning of digital education projects difficult.

One exception to this general rule are courses built and run by outside OPMs, which often build and run on their own LMS. This is important for OPMs because they are responsible for course delivery and need to have the power to adjust and fix any issues with course delivery without needing to first get permission from the host university's IT department. Also, most OPMs recognize that most LMS out-of-the-box layouts are not great, and they want to add their own formatting. And finally, OPMs want full control over student enrollments because their revenue-sharing deals are directly tied to each fee-paying student enrolled.

2U generally builds classes using its own proprietary LMS, but in recent years it has begun building classes using Canvas, Blackboard, and Brightspace, the three most popular LMSs used by universities. "For example, [if] the university was heavily invested in Canvas," explained Josh Scott (2021) of 2U, "we may be able to use that as the LMS that we are building in, but it will be the 2U instance of that platform." Building their courses on the same core LMS that the university uses is a big plus for the university partner, making it much easier for the university to eventually "take over" and run the courses on their own once an OPM's five- to seven-year contract is over.

Increasingly, 2U is moving toward organizing its assets using a "content management system" rather than being tied to one LMS. This makes it easier to "mix and match" assets across platforms and partners. "We are trying to move toward a platform-agnostic . . . digital learning ecosystem approach," explained Scott (2021), noting that this would be "centralized in a content management system rather than dependent on any single LMS."

One of the key issues independent of the LMS system used is the degree of formatting for course websites. LMSs are notoriously clunky, and most do not offer good out-of-the-box options for creating attractive course home pages or layouts (chapter 5). Most LMSs continue to deliver a product that creates pages of folders and modules that look like they were created in the 1990s, not in an era of social media and video-heavy websites. For new students not familiar with the system, where they should go, how to navigate pages, and how to find content can be unclear.

How programs deal with this issue varies. Executive education offerings for adult learners—who may be taking only a course or two and do not have time to learn how to navigate a clunky interface—often hire HTML programmers to create attractive page layouts built on top of the core LMS. This creates clearer and cleaner systems to guide students through their learning experience, such as the examples shown in chapter 5. These customized pages "drive the student to focus exclusively on the learning material we are delivering to them," explained eCornell's Berkowitz (Berkowitz and Krause 2021). Columbia, Dartmouth, and UPenn also create customized templates to sit atop Canvas. OPMs for Wiley, Extension Engine, and Emeritus follow this path as well. The problem is that these customized pages, which require a skilled HTML programmer to create, are tricky to update. For this reason, most university-wide programs stick with the templates offered by the LMS despite their flaws and limitations.

To address this issue, Columbia University and a group of partner institutions have developed the Canvas Coursebuilder, an open resource that simplifies Canvas page customization. We also hope that LMS providers themselves will step up and realize they need to offer students better experiences and schools easier workflows, especially in the post-COVID context.

Using Canvas, UPenn created a template that welcomes students and provides guides to using the course's navigation system, accessing readings and videos, and participating in class discussions. "We have a little bit of templating that we are doing in Canvas in terms of a dynamic home page," said Angelina Conti (2021), director of digital learning at UPenn's School of Arts and Sciences. UPenn's customized Canvas template simplifies finding information on accessibility, tech support, and academic integrity. These courses include an introductory module that welcomes students to the course and provides information on course navigation and conduct. The standard course template shares basic information for all students: "Here's what it means to study online. Here are resources that are key for online learning."

Each art and sciences course at UPenn includes a guide for future instructors, available to them only. These instructors' eyes-only modules offer a quick guide to teaching the class and handling a wide variety of student issues. Topics include student activity and support, student conduct, thinking about digital literacy among diverse student populations, using key tools, Zoom, and discussion boards. 2U also offers "instructor only" modules, with guides on how to deliver the content for those courses with multiple professor teams (Scott 2021). As more courses are centrally designed and built, creating such a system for sharing knowledge and tips on course delivery is crucial. These guides also offer tips on using live class time to best effect. The goal is not to dictate all details of course delivery but to guide instructors on the intended purpose of the design of the course, and provide the best possible learning experience for students. These tools improve the quality of course delivery, student experiences, and equity. "For years . . . you would have two sections of a course, and you would just assume that one section would be better or worse than the other section," said Scott. "People just assumed that was okay. In the online space, that's not okay."

Student-facing websites should also encourage student engagement, social interactions, and peer-to-peer learning. Most interactions take place on discussion boards; students respond to prompts and participate in peer-to-peer interactions and projects. To help students know each other, this tool may prompt students to tell each other about themselves. Extension Engine created Facebook-style student profiles for one of its client's programs. eCornell uses a "Student Lounge" for this purpose. "We're trying to get students to meet each other and introduce themselves," said eCornell's Berkowitz (Berkowitz and Krause 2021). "It's really, 'Come, meet the classmates, share a bit about yourself.'" With photos and LinkedIn-style biographies, students can network and collaborate.

Course website design might also include quizzes, scenario-based games, and group projects. "We're trying to drive engagement between students, students and the content, and students and the instructor," said Bryan Blakeley of the University of Washington

(Blakeley and Branon 2021). Like eCornell, 2U, and others, Washington's custom templates add interactive quizzes and other activities to make the learning experience come alive. "We are really trying to drive this engagement in new and interesting ways that go beyond your typical 'Read this. Watch this video. Post on a discussion board' kind of approach," explained Blakeley.

Digital Class Delivery

The same care and attention that goes into course design and building must be devoted to course delivery. This is true both for traditional in-person classes that have digital elements and fully online courses. For classes that scale up to large numbers of students, online support is generally provided by a team of TAs and other support staff, whose work must be carefully coordinated.

An added factor that must be taken into account is that many courses will be delivered by a team that may or may not include the "authoring professors" who created the original digital course content. Large introductory courses are offered in many sections, with various professors all pulling from a collection of prerecorded lectures, video labs and case studies, and common activities, and this material must be customized and adapted to each instructor's class delivery style. This is a new concept for many universities, and it needs to be handled with care by leaders.

One argument for filming video lectures for key introductory classes with each department's most senior professor is that junior professors are likely to be more willing to teach using their department's most senior faculty's digital content. As more and more professors record their own content, the idea of using and sharing digital content will become more common and understood to be like sharing peer-reviewed academic papers. On campuses where a critical mass of professors has joined the digital revolution, this sharing is generally more accepted. "We want to be agile and support all sorts of remixing and reusing of content," explained James DeVaney (2021) of Michigan, especially when complex and expensive digital artifacts are created. "I think one of the breakthrough moments is just pointing out the obvious to faculty," he said. "If there is a resistance point about using someone else's content, you can point them to all the syllabi they have ever created where they have pulled articles and publications from a wide range of experts."

DeVaney, the University and Michigan, and other "digital first" schools view sharing digital content and learning objects as much a part of the academic process as giving papers at conferences or publishing peer-reviewed academic articles. Professors will learn to see this as part of their overall academic output. Creating short modular content—filmed with a similar style and format—makes it much easier to mix and match digital elements in a way that feels natural. The role of the professor or instructor then becomes that of a curator of this content, using class live sessions and online discussion boards to interact with students on projects, and explore complex issues.

Beyond using and sharing content, another key issue is hiring and training support staff. Delivering online courses, especially to large numbers of students, requires that digital TAs and other support staff help with grading and the management of online discussion boards. These are not trivial roles, and they need to be handled with care. So, too, is training all professors and their digital TAs in the proper use of the course website and how to teach using Zoom, Padlet, Panopto, and the other digital tools reviewed in chapter 5.

Having a well-staffed and trained team of online support providers is crucial. Many of the hundreds of people working at leading OPMs or in-house OPMs are trained digital instructors and support staff whose role is to support and enhance the online presence of the lead instructor of record. It is also important to recognize that teaching online requires more faculty and staff support, not less.

Arizona State University has invested heavily in this idea, with a student-to-support faculty ratio of 18:1 in its online classes, compared with a ratio of 25:1 in traditional in-person classes. It is also crucial to plan to offer online student support, including career counseling, mental health support, and other student services.

Often OPMs such as Wiley and 2U can provide this kind of support until the university can hire and train its own online support staff. "We don't teach the courses. They're always taught by faculty," explained Wiley's Migliorese, "but we would be the ones that build the course in the LMS, maintain it, and support as they teach" (Cochran and Migliorese 2021a). Georgia Tech has invested heavily in training and maintaining a large staff of digital TAs. Its online master's program now reaches more than 7,000 students, with a TA-to-student ratio of 1:50.

Training and guiding instructors is critical to creating and delivering successful online programs. The key is to make the process enjoyable. Discussion boards can produce surprisingly deep engagement. "Professors say that they have some of their deepest interactions with students when they are teaching asynchronously, because those students have time to think," said the University of Washington's Blakeley (Blakeley and Branon 2021). "They have time to digest the material, collect their thoughts, and put it down."

PROGRAM SUSTAINABILITY

Creating a culture of digital teaching and learning on your campus is not done overnight. The good news is that as more and more professors build digital classes and deliver them more and more others will learn about this process. Then others, seeing their success, will want to be part of it. Program leaders can help make this a sustainable activity by celebrating victories. Holding campus-wide symposiums and events to share and celebrate successful digital projects can go a long way toward creating a culture of digital innovation.

Leaders should also provide funds and incentives for training and hiring paid student interns to work in the digital course creation process, both as digital TAs and as part of course design and creation teams. Student media team members are almost always very creative, dedicated, and fun to work with! They also can share the student's perspective on what really matters and works in class delivery. Their contributions in the project design room, on the filming set, and in the final course delivery phase can be crucial and make the difference between a course that just gets the job done and one that truly inspires a new generation of learners.

KEY TAKEAWAYS

Creating good digital classes is a huge subject in itself, and the ideas and suggestions shared here only scratch the surface. As technology and delivery models evolve, so too will these workflows. Here are a few key takeaways.

Team Size and Roles This will depend on the size of the program and the services delivered. Digital course creation and delivery units can easily eventually grow to two hundred people at larger universities.

Learning Frameworks Create and share a detailed and clear guide to the learning framework. This guide should be based on research and evidence-based best practices, including active learning, peer-to-peer engagement, and connecting learning to real-world outcomes.

Program-Level Planning Begin with program-level planning to choose which courses to develop and how much to invest in their production. Invest most in the courses with high enrollments and with content that can be used in multiple formats. These are often entry-level and required courses.

Faculty Engagement Recruit faculty who are open to working with the instructional design and media teams and who are eager to learn how to effectively deliver content on digital platforms. Design workflows to make the best use of their limited time. The average faculty time commitment to create a completely new online or digital course is 100 to 150 hours over six to nine months.

Course Design Follow "backward design" principles. Map content to meet learning outcomes. In the mapping process, match the learning assets with the different needs of live and asynchronous activities. Brainstorm the right mix of student projects, recorded lectures, digital cases or simulations, and "live sessions."

Content Creation To produce high-quality videos, provide a "menu" of options for filming and activities. Begin content creation and production only after completing the course design and getting the signoff from key partners. Explore a mix of video content formats, including filmed lectures, interviews, role-playing, and demonstrations. Include student interns in your teams, and allow them to innovate and create.

Filming with Faculty Faculty need basic guidance on wardrobe and makeup before filming. Rehearsals can also help the filming go smoothly. Faculty need honest feedback and support to deliver in this medium. Consider whether scripting is needed or if a more improvised approach using PowerPoints or other forms of outlines can work.

Course Delivery A strategy is needed for course website creation and handoff to the delivery team. The support staff is needed for ongoing updates and live sessions. Design courses to be easily copied and updated and delivered in new versions. Creating course websites with module numbers—rather than specific yearly calendar dates—saves time when the content is used again the following year.

Prototyping, Testing, and Assessments Before rolling out websites for large courses, test new classes with small cohorts.

Program Sustainability As more professors go through the process, you will create a strong foundation. Celebrate victories, share insights, and hire paid student interns to help build and update classes.

REFERENCES

Berkowitz, Sally, and Paul Krause. 2021. "Demo of eCornell Courses, presented to Adam Stepan. November 11, 2021.

Blakeley, Bryan, and Rovy Branon. 2021. "Demo of University of Washington Continuum College Courses, presented to Adam Stepan. November 30, 2021.

Branon, Rovy. 2021. Interview of Vice Provost for Continuum College, University of Washington, by Adam Stepan. November 30, 2021.

Chou, Luyen. 2021. Interview of Chief Learning Officer, 2U, by Adam Stepan. October 27, 2021.

Cochran, Bill, and David Migliorese. 2021a. "Demo of Wiley Services, presented to Adam Stepan. November 16, 2021.

——. 2021b. Interview of Associate Director of Instructional Media and of Vice President of Academic Services, Wiley Education Services, by Adam Stepan. November 16, 2021.

Conti, Angelina. 2021. Interview of Director of Digital Learning, University of Pennsylvania, by Adam Stepan. November 16, 2021.

Denning, Glenn. 2021. Interview of Professor of Professional Practice in International and Public Affairs and Director of the Master of Public Administration in Development Practice, Columbia University, by Adam Stepan. December 1, 2021.

DeVaney, James. 2021. Interview of Associate Vice Provost for Academic Innovation and Founding Executive Director of the Center for Academic Innovation, University of Michigan, by Adam Stepan. October 29, 2021.

Dooley, Frank. 2021. Follow-up interview of Chancellor, Purdue Global, by Adam Stepan. October 27, 2021.

Fox, Armando. 2021. Interview of Associate Dean for Online Education, University of California Berkeley, by Adam Stepan. October 19, 2021.

Funk, Camille. 2021. Interview of Director of Learning and Innovation and Instructional Design, University of California Irvine, by Adam Stepan. November 4, 2021.

Harding, Justin. 2021. Interview of Senior Director for Instructional Design and New Media, EdPlus, Arizona State University, by Adam Stepan. November 30, 2021.

Hermalyn, Andrew. 2021. Interview of President of Partnerships, 2U, by Adam Stepan. October 18, 2021.

Humenik, Zachary. 2021. Interview of Associate Director for the Online Learning Studio, University of Pennsylvania, by Adam Stepan. November 16, 2021.

Huntemann, Nina. 2021. Interview of Vice President of Learning, edX, by Adam Stepan. October 18, 2021.

Krause, Paul. 2021. Interview of Vice Provost of External Education, Cornell University Executive Director, eCornell, by Adam Stepan. October 22, 2021.

Lamy, Bernard, Antoine Armauld, and Pierre Nicole. 1676. *The Art of Speaking*. London: W. Godbid.

Levander, Caroline. 2021. Interview of Vice President of Global and Digital Strategy, Rice University, by Adam Stepan. November 10, 2021.

Lewis, Nora. 2021. Interview of Vice Dean for Professional and Liberal Education, School of Arts and Sciences, University of Pennsylvania, by Adam Stepan. October 26, 2021.

Nazeeri, Furqan. 2021. Interview of CEO, Extension Engine, by Adam Stepan. November 9, 2021.

Nelson, Ben. 2021. Interview of CEO and Founder, Minerva Project, by Adam Stepan. October 14, 2021.

Regier, Phil. 2021. Interview of CEO EdPlus, Arizona State University, by Adam Stepan. November 8, 2021.

Scott, Josh. 2021. Interview of Director of Course Strategy, 2U, by Adam Stepan. November 30, 2021.

Singh, Sharan. 2021. Interview of Senior Managing Director of Strategic Partnerships, Minerva Project, by Adam Stepan. November 2, 2021.

Ubell, Robert. 2021. "Lacking Online Programs, Many Colleges Are Rushing to Partner with OPMs. Should They?" *EdSurge*, June 7, 2021. https://www.edsurge.com/news/2021-06-07-lacking-online-programs-many-colleges-are-rushing-to-partner-with-opms-should-they.

Velasquez, Kris. 2021. Interview of Assistant Director of Media, University of California Irvine, by Adam Stepan. November 4, 2021.

7

THE BLENDED LEARNING TOOLKIT

In this chapter, we provide an overview of tools and workflows for designing, creating, and delivering digital classes that we use at Columbia University and with our partner universities around the world, including those in the Open Society University Network. These videos are made available free of cost in the edX, Coursera, and Canvas Common's MOOC: "The Blended Learning Toolkit." Used together they provide a complete set of training videos and open educational resources for you to use in your program. All tools are licensed under Creative Commons and can be used at no cost, either in the MOOC itself or as downloaded content to be uploaded and used in your university's own LMS.

All modules include prerecorded video lectures and downloadable PDF handouts that include the core lessons. This overview describes the workflows for specific technology platforms (Canvas, Panopto, and Zoom), but it can be applied to a variety of software. All modules are presented by colleagues from Columbia's Center for Teaching and Learning, along with professors, media professionals, students, and other partners. The following sections provide a guide to using this content, which can be used as a self-guided class or downloaded with the Creative Commons license and used as part of a blended delivery class or workshop.

MODULE 1: INTRODUCTION TO DIGITAL COURSE DESIGN AND DELIVERY

This module provides videos on the core concepts of blended learning: what is blended learning, what is active learning, peer-to-peer engagement, best practices for building and designing course websites, and options for the creation of various forms of professor videos, digital case studies, and lab filming. The videos present examples from the programs discussed throughout this book, including Columbia University, Michigan, Dartmouth, University of Pennsylvania, Georgia Tech, University of California Irvine, Purdue, and OPM providers 2U, Wiley, Extension Engine, and Emeritus. The videos cover the following topics:

Introduction to Digital Education Tools (7 minutes): An overview of the digital course design and delivery, with examples from across academia and leading OPMs.

Course Website Design (7 minutes): Provides examples of course websites built on Canvas, Brightspace, Blackboard, and other platforms, including options for layout, navigation, and activities.

Prerecorded Video Lectures and Other Professor Videos (5 minutes): Presents formats for prerecorded video lectures and other video formats for filming with professors (figure 7.1).

Special Videos—Digital Case Studies, Labs, and Simulations (5 minutes): A brief introduction to digital case studies, video labs, and simulations.

Teaching on Zoom and in the HyFlex Classroom—Demo (4 minutes): Demonstrates how to connect in-person and remote students on Zoom and the HyFlex classroom.

MODULE 2: BLENDED AND ACTIVE LEARNING

While some courses are offered as 100-percent self-paced or "asynchronous" courses, most classes are far richer and more

Figure 7.1 Module—Self-recorded video lectures

meaningful to students when they include live or synchronous interactions. Rather than using class time for passive lecture presentations only, the goal is to use these live sessions, in-person or on Zoom, for active learning, discussions, and activities. Creating blended classes with active learning requires teamwork. Ideally, professors work with their TA and a university digital education group to redesign the whole course experience.

The module presents an overview of blended and active learning, with suggestions for faculty, TAs, and digital education support staff on how to best work together to redesign classes and create digital assets. The videos illustrate how students can use content before course meetings to improve live class sessions, in person or online. The videos and materials can be used for self-paced training or as part of a workshop.

Active Learning and Blended Design (5 minutes)
Amanda Irvin, the senior director of faculty programs and services at Columbia's Center for Teaching and Learning, introduces the concepts that drive blended course planning and design. She explores

the concepts of backward design, blended learning, peer-to-peer engagement, and active learning.

The Instructor/TA Partnership (7 minutes)
Mark Phillipson, the director of graduate student programs and services at Columbia University's Center for Teaching and Learning shows how instructors and TAs can collaborate in the creation of asynchronous course content. This includes planning class activities and group projects, finding educational resources such as TED Talks or readings, and creating video lectures.

MODULE 3: CREATING AND FILMING DO IT YOURSELF (DIY) PRERECORDED LECTURES

Self-produced and recorded lectures by professors are the most prevalent core of many online and blended classes. These self-recordings are an efficient way to share the professor's perspective on the material being covered and can serve to guide students through readings, video cases, and other assets.

For courses with sufficient funding and support, the easiest way to create these videos is to partner with the university's digital education unit and film in a green screen studio with a professional video crew. For courses with limited budgets or when filming professors who are physically remote, creating videos in a DIY home studio is a good option.

This module describes how to create five- to eight-minute videos combining the professor's lecture, slides that illustrate key ideas, and video clips. The presentation can be recorded with an online meeting platform such as Zoom. For a more sophisticated recording setup, a slide deck that includes a script for filming with simple PowerPoint animations and transitions can create compelling video presentations. After recording the presentation in the right sequence, edit the mistakes and upload the final video. Using a good webcam, proper lighting, and a good microphone can dramatically enhance video quality. These techniques follow the workflow for Panopto but can easily be adapted for other popular screencast software.

Creating PowerPoints for Home Recorded Lectures (4 minutes)
Sean Steinberg of Columbia's Picker Center Digital Education Group
(PCDEG) and Eduarda Zoghbi of Columbia's School of International
and Public Affairs (SIPA) present a workflow for creating slide
presentations in self-recorded video lectures. The video describes
how to design a slide deck specifically to use in filming. Some
slides are designed to appear alongside the professor, other slides
fill up the full screen without the professor, and others show only
the professor (figure 7.2).

Setting Up Your DIY Office Studio (4 minutes)
Cinematographer Brian Miller of PCDEG and Eduarda Zoghbi review
the setup and use of a remote camera package of webcam, microphone,
lights, and accessories. A light, external webcam and microphone
enhance the quality of Zoom calls and video recordings. Another
useful accessory is the hands-free "clicker" to advance slides.

Self-Recording and Editing with Panopto (8 minutes)
Brian Miller and Eduarda Zoghbi walk through the process of self-
recording, editing, and posting a video lecture to a course website.
The whole process comes together using a slide deck along with a
script and screen-capture software.

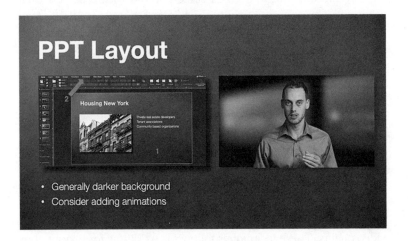

Figure 7.2 Module—Designing PowerPoints for filming

MODULE 4: FILMING IN THE GREEN SCREEN STUDIO

For videos that will be viewed by larger audiences, it makes sense to film in a studio with a professional crew if possible. A studio with a green screen—the kind of backdrop used for weather reports on local TV news—can be used for a variety of approaches. The most expensive and sophisticated workflows add video animations after filming, but you can create captivating videos with the core PowerPoint templates outlined in Module 3.

In this module, we detail the process of filming in a green screen studio with a professional crew, including lighting, audio, graphics, and the use of a teleprompter for the presentation's script. These videos are intended for production teams new to these techniques and for producers and instructional designers working with studio crews for the first time.

Green Screen Studio Filming (10 minutes)
Brian Miller explains how to set up for advanced green screen filming using existing PowerPoint slides. The video provides suggestions on where to set up cameras, lights, and microphones; tips on working with and directing professors as on-camera talent; and options for using a teleprompter during the shoot. The teleprompter can accommodate a written script or a PowerPoint with the professor while filming, just as newscasters or politicians do on television. The video also includes access behind the scenes of a typical green screen filming set and suggestions on eyeliners, framing, hair, and makeup (figure 7.3).

Green Screen Shoot Editing with Adobe Premiere (15 minutes)
In this advanced video, editor Elijah Zulu of PCDEG explains the workflow for taking the PowerPoints used in filming and syncing them with the professor's video using the Adobe Premiere video editing software. Elijah presents a step-by-step workflow from importing the footage to syncing video and graphics, editing out bad takes, and adding smooth transitions. He then shows how to upload the professional final product.

Figure 7.3 Module—How to film with a green screen

MODULE 5: THE COURSE WEBSITE FOR A BLENDED CLASS

The course website plays a central role in a blended class. It is a virtual classroom where students engage with content and each other. In this module, we describe best practices for course website design, including communications with students, content delivery, managing online discussions, and grading. These lessons use Canvas, but the methodology can also be used on any other online learning platform.

The Course Website in a Blended Class (7 minutes)

Amanda Irvin introduces course website design using the Canvas platform. She shows how to use online tools to connect with students, set course objectives and learning goals, share content online, and manage evaluations and grading. She also covers how to design and lead online discussion forums. After establishing ground rules for online conversations, she explores how to build a welcoming and inclusive online community of inquiry.

Figure 7.4 Module—Planning for asynchronous content

The Instructor/TA Team: Course Building + Management (7 minutes)

Mark Phillipson of Columbia's Center for Teaching and Learning reviews how instructors and their teaching assistants can work together as a team to create and manage online courses. The video explains how TAs can help build course websites, find asynchronous content, and assist in managing and directing online discussion forums (figure 7.4). The video also explores the important role TAs can play as "super-learners," sharing the perspective of students with the professor and helping guide and manage course content delivery.

MODULE 6: USING THE CANVAS COURSEBUILDER

Coursebuilder enables professors and instructional designers to easily build sophisticated class HTML web pages on the Canvas platform with no prior HTML training. Users can customize their websites with their school's colors and branding. To get the latest version, visit canvascoursebuilder.org.

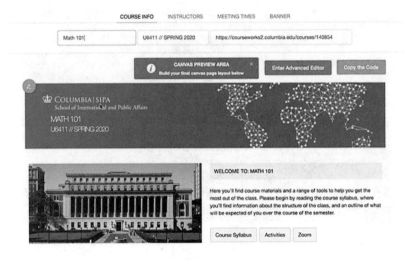

Figure 7.5 Module—Introduction to Coursebuilder

Introduction to the Coursebuilder Class Template (3 minutes)

Eduarda Zoghbi introduces the layout and features of a course created with Coursebuilder, including the home page and weekly activity pages (figure 7.5).

Using Coursebuilder (12 minutes)

In this step-by-step video guide, Columbia University/SIPA's Sean Steinberg introduces the features of the Coursebuilder tool. With a syllabus in hand and access to images, a new course website can generally be built in about one hour using this tool.

Year-to-Year Course Updating (4 minutes)

Sean Steinberg takes the viewer through the step-by-step process of updating courses built on Canvas Coursebuilder.

Advanced Coursebuilder for Instructional Designers (5 minutes)

This video describes the advanced features of Canvas Coursebuilder, including tools to create new templates, home pages, layouts, and other features.

MODULE 7: LIVE SESSIONS, ACTIVE LEARNING IN FACE-TO-FACE, ZOOM, AND HYFLEX CLASSROOMS

Active learning and blended classrooms go together. By moving some content online, classroom time can be used for active learning activities. This module explores how live sessions can maximize student engagement in face-to-face, Zoom, and HyFlex classrooms.

Live Session Overview (13 minutes)
Amanda Irvin explains how to set up and run active learning sessions in face-to-face, Zoom, and HyFlex classrooms. She illustrates how success depends on a strategic plan of activities with clear expectations for student participation. Activities include debates, role-playing, individual and group presentations, breakout groups, and polling.

The Instructor/TA Team: Face-to-Face, Zoom, and HyFlex (10 minutes)
Mark Phillipson of Columbia's Center for Teaching and Learning shows how to enhance the instructor's presence on Zoom through community-building activities, often with breakout rooms and presentations. TAs play a key role in live sessions, especially those delivered on Zoom or in HyFlex classrooms. Phillipson emphasizes the importance of teamwork and planning. Practicing and testing are especially important for HyFlex classrooms with complex cameras and audio setups. Phillipson also explores options for creating and managing chat and polling tools.

Active Learning on Zoom (4 minutes)
Columbia's Sean Steinberg explains best practices for running a live session over Zoom, including camera and audio setup and lighting, options for Zoom backgrounds, sharing slides and videos, using the chat tool, pinning and spotlighting speakers, and managing breakout rooms and online polls.

Active Learning in the HyFlex Classroom (7 minutes)
Eduarda Zoghbi joins Brian Miller and Sean Steinberg to explain the elements of the HyFlex classroom (figure 7.6). In a HyFlex

Figure 7.6 The HyFlex classroom

classroom, some students attend a live class meeting and others join the meeting via Zoom. This approach expands the number of students who can join a class but also presents new challenges for everyone. The video also explores how HyFlex classes at Columbia connect in-person and online students through discussions, chats, breakouts, and polls. Sitting in on a live class session, the viewer can see how active learning takes place across multiple formats.

8

DIGITAL CASE STUDIES

The value of small modular content has been clearly demonstrated in the K–12 learning space. Groups such as Khan Academy, Class Central, and others have produced thousands of high-quality short videos that students use for independent study and that teachers readily drop onto their course websites. When well done, these assets can be shared and reused in a variety of classes, providing support for digitally enhanced in-person classes as part of blended or partially online executive training or used in fully online courses. But the creation and sharing of smaller modular content across the higher education space is far less developed.

Open educational resources (OERs) have been around for more than twenty years, but few websites offer quality digital content. In higher education, most online content is created as fully packaged classes, often on MOOC platforms, with little room for mixing and matching. This is about to change. An explosion in sharing smaller modular content in the higher education space is coming, and many believe that the digital case study will have a major role in this movement. The case study connects learning with real-world experience, and students can play a major role in co-creating these assets as part of their own experiential learning projects.

In this chapter, we explore the history of the OER movement and of digital case studies. This chapter also has a free companion massive open online course (MOOC) that can be used to create and share digital case studies at your institution. This MOOC, "Digital Case Method," is available on edX, Coursera, and the Canvas Commons platforms. It contains videos and guides that can be downloaded and used free of charge under the Creative Commons license.

THE OPEN EDUCATIONAL RESOURCES MOVEMENT

The idea of modular, sharable educational assets can be traced back to the invention of the printing press. For the first time, books could be mass-produced and shared with audiences near and far. These asynchronous assets could be used at any time, and they became the heart of formal learning. In fact, all academic books and peer-reviewed articles are themselves open educational resources: they are designed to be mixed and matched, read, and shared (Butcher, Kanwar, and Uvalic-Trumbic 2011). With the rise of the internet, suddenly millions of books, videos, simulations, slides, games, lesson plans, testing systems, DIY kits for learning hands-on skills, and course management systems could be accessed with the click of a mouse.

Traditional distribution required a massive infrastructure of publishing, with armies of editors and marketers and printers, warehouses, brick-and-mortar libraries, and vast distribution systems. Digital technology enabled sharing these educational resources without this infrastructure. The relatively low cost of electronic reproduction and storage shrinks every year. The educational challenge today is identifying and curating the right pieces and assembling them into a compelling learning session.

MIT's OpenCourseWare was an early mover in this area. Launched in 2001, OpenCourseWare encouraged professors to make their teaching and learning materials available to a wider audience. MIT professors published and shared their syllabi, teaching guides, and lesson plans and also made select lectures available online for free. MIT OpenCourseWare would directly influence and inform the creation of MITx, the precursor organization to what would become one of the first and largest MOOC platforms, edX (MIT News 2012)

Anant Agarwal's MIT Circuits course, captured in a free online lab called MIT WebSim, was the basis of one of the first MOOCs. Agarwal (2021), who became the founder and CEO of edX, recalls that "MIT had launched MIT OpenCourseWare in 2000. Even in 2004, 2005, well before the MOOC movement, on an average day two hundred to three hundred people from around the world would come and take my free Circuits course online through WebSim," Agarwal said.

MIT OpenCourseWare shared syllabi and lesson plans online, but the joint Harvard/MIT entity that would become the MOOC provider edX shared complete online courses. Revolutionary though edX was, it was still stuck in the old-fashioned idea of the traditional twelve- to fourteen-week course as its principal unit of delivery. Students had to sign up and attend the entire semester-long MOOC class to access the content. MOOC providers edX and Coursera did not break the classes in their systems into modular educational assets that instructors of other courses could search and use in their own courses as needed.

Meanwhile, in elementary and secondary education, teachers were developing, finding, and sharing all manner of modular educational assets online. With millions of K–12 students all needing to learn the same basic subjects—algebra, biology, chemistry, and history—their teachers represent a huge market for digital assets. In response, groups such as PBS Learning Media, National Geographic's Educational Resources website, Khan Academy, and Crash Course created and posted short videos and other assets on YouTube that could be integrated into classes as teachers saw fit.

Khan Academy led the way. Sal Khan, a Wall Street financial analyst, spent weekends creating math videos to help his cousin with her schoolwork. He used minimalist videos to show the process of working out problems. When he began uploading his videos on YouTube, he discovered a mass market for these short introductory films. By 2022, he claimed 130 million users in 190 countries (Hua 2015).

When Khan formalized his lessons as an online academy, he registered it as a 501(c)3 nonprofit organization and attracted multi-million-dollar grants from Google, AT&T, and the Bill and Melinda Gates Foundation. YouTube pays content providers a percentage of ad revenue, so successful online teachers like Khan can earn significant revenues with their lessons (figure 8.1). By 2019, Khan Academy reported $28 million in revenue, mostly from YouTube AdSense ("Khan Academy Annual Report 2020" n.d.).

Khan's success on YouTube soon inspired others to create and upload short explainer-type videos. The number of platforms for online content expanded to Facebook, Instagram, TikTok, and other social media sites (Marketing Charts 2019; Nazir 2019). Typical K–12 video content providers were Hank and John Green of Crash Course, whose videos on math, science, social studies, and other subjects gained more than three million subscribers. These videos use innovative and entertaining animations and fast-talking millennial presenters. Students often use these videos on their own to understand assignments outside of school. Teachers eventually caught on and began to drop them onto their course websites (Genota 2018; Hua 2015; Koumi 2015).

Traditional educational video content providers such as PBS and National Geographic soon saw the potential of bite-sized video lessons. PBS Learning Media, formed in 2009, offers four- to seven-minute excerpts of PBS programs including *Nature, Nova, Wide Angle,*

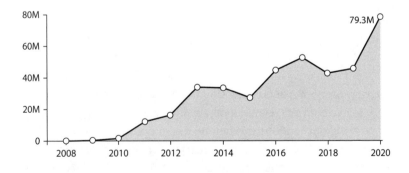

Figure 8.1 Growth of Khan Academy Revenues, 2008 to 2020 (Shah 2022)

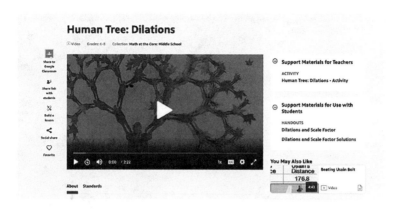

Figure 8.2 PBS Learning Media

and *American Experience* (figure 8.2). Video topics range from volcanic eruptions to the Nicaraguan revolution. The platform also offered lesson guides and handouts. These offerings are available as Google Classroom packages that can be downloaded and inserted into any K–12 course website at no cost and include teaching notes and guides. National Geographic also created its own education platform in 2018, using the freemium model: offering some content free of charge and adding other content that school districts can purchase along with online teacher training.

Perhaps the most popular and recognizable player in this genre of short and modular educational videos is the TED Talk, which began as a series of upscale conferences on Technology, Entertainment, and Design (TED) in, Long Beach, California in 2006. At these gatherings, experts presented tightly produced eighteen-minute lectures on topics that ranged from skateboarding to brain surgery (figure 8.3). TED Talks attracted millions of viewers online, making celebrities of once-obscure figures Ken Robinson and Brene Brown. In 2009, TED franchised its concept as TEDx, and local organizers at universities, museums, and theaters staged TEDx events following TED Talk guidelines for talk formats, staging, filming, and marketing. Final event videos were all shared online using the TEDx platform (Fidelman 2012).

Figure 8.3 TED Talk

TEDx produced an explosion of user-generated educational content. The number of TED and TEDx talks posted online increased from six in 2006 to over 3,900 in 2022. TED Talks reached their billionth view in 2013 (figure 8.4). Similar to peer-reviewed academic articles, TEDx talks succeed by following an established curation process. Educators could include them in classes, knowing

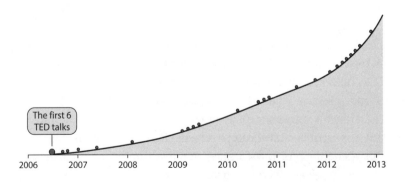

Figure 8.4 Growth of TED Talk views from 2006 to 2012 (TED 2012)

that the content had been reviewed and vetted. When presenters make claims that have not been vetted by academic researchers, TED puts a disclaimer on the video. Viewers of TED videos can depend on a standard format that students can follow and content that can be applied to people's lives and learning.

But beyond PBS Learning Media and TED Talks, few OER platforms offer free high-quality digital assets for higher education. Higher education OER websites mostly share syllabi and readings but not flipped course videos or digital case studies. Such assets are often embedded in MOOC classes, and few are available à la carte to be added to other courses.

THE WRITTEN CASE STUDY

Sharing digital assets lags, but sharing written or analog assets is firmly established. One ubiquitous modular short form learning asset is the written case study. After the academic book and the peer-reviewed academic article, the traditional written case study is the oldest and most successful format for sharing academic research and information. Professional schools have long used written case studies to engage their students in lively discussions that connect academic issues with real-world problems. Case studies as a format were first developed at the Harvard Law School in the 1920s; faculty discovered that students learned complex concepts better when they were applied to real-life situations. Soon case studies were developed for programs in business, public policy, medicine, public health, and even the liberal arts (Jack 2018; Lang 2011).

A Harvard written case study typically runs from five to fifteen pages. The text offers the narrative and background information students need to understand a key event or problem. Cases combine elements of journalism with academic concepts and controversies. Unconstrained by the requirements of a typical peer-reviewed paper, most cases avoid extensive citations. Instead, they focus on a rich description of a dilemma, with commentary by the actual participants in the issue. The best cases offer a gripping read, with

rich accounts that engage students emotionally as well as intellec-
tually—almost like a chapter in a novel (Fried et al. 2006; Herreid
and Schiller 2013; Lundberg 2015).

Often working in small groups, students analyze how the case
should be resolved and present their findings to the class. Law
students debate actual court cases in the classic *Paper Chase* style
rather than passively listening to a lecture. In a public policy course,
students engage in debates on issues such as the privatization of
prisons, local economic development, policing strategies, and the
use of big data in government. The interview subjects of the case
study, if still alive and available, are often invited to join the class
discussions via Zoom (Fried et al. 2006).

Case studies take many basic formats. In decision-forcing cases,
the basic facts of a complex problem are presented without
sharing with students how the specific issue or problem was in
fact resolved (Lundberg 2015). Students then debate the best
resolution of the controversy. Comparative cases offer accounts
of how people in two or more similar situations responded to
common issues or challenges, such as the best way to use big data
in policing or how to best outsource certain city services. Students
then debate which approach works best for certain goals and circumstances (Lundberg 2017).

The research and writing of case studies follow a workflow that
most journalists would find familiar. Once a case study subject
is identified, key actors in the story are contacted and invited to
participate. If they are willing to share their stories, and if the
organizations where they work do not raise objections, researchers conduct interviews and obtain relevant documents. The cases
use interviews to create a powerful narrative. Before publication,
case writers often share the case with those profiled as part of
their fact-checking process. In some cases, the subjects' identities
are masked to protect the participants and prevent students from
researching the right answers before class debates (Lundberg 2015).
Despite variations, the basic format of the written case study has
remained the same for more than seventy years (Jiang, Ganoe, and
Carroll 2010).

CREATING A FORMAT FOR DIGITAL CASE STUDIES

While the traditional written case study format has remained relatively unchanged since the 1920s, in recent years universities and other entities have experimented with new approaches to case creation that take advantage of digital tools. The most compelling of these formats is what we now call the digital case study—a collection of videos, written summaries, documents, and other materials about an issue or controversy—delivered as a "package" of content on an LMS.

In The Telling, a Colorado-based documentary film and online education company, was an early mover in this area and developed a multimedia platform that combined video with text. In The Telling used its proprietary Narrasys platform to offer links to these video interviews and other online material (figure 8.5). Beginning in 2008, Columbia University's Case Consortium experimented with a similar format, with interview videos posted on an interactive course website. For example, a case study on a newspaper story would be presented as a series of web pages, with links to additional interviews that can be watched.

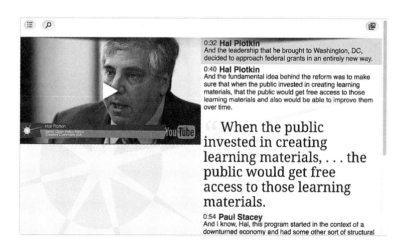

Figure 8.5 In The Telling video case study format

Figure 8.6 Extension Engine case website

Elsewhere, the Boston-based OPM Extension Engine uses a high-end version of this model, with detailed web pages and graphics, interviews, and other interactive elements for its web-based cases (figure 8.6). For cases on real estate development for MIT, Extension Engine built interactive websites with text, site photos, and videos. Similar approaches were developed by Wiley and 2U that integrate these case pages into the course website itself (Cochran and Migliorese 2021; Scott 2021). As more online courses use video labs and other versions of the digital case study—some even using virtual reality, the immersive experience—the "case as website" model will continue to evolve.

THE COLUMBIA DIGITAL CASE STUDY MODEL

Our team at Columbia University began an internal review of case studies and options for digital case delivery as part of a major digital education initiative in 2014 and 2015, developed in partnership with Jorge Paulo Lemann and Denis Mizne of the Lemann Foundation of Brazil. The review evaluated the lessons learned from the

Figure 8.7 Columbia Global Centers

MOOC experience of 2012 to 2014, and included a study of digital tools that could be used for classes to train the public sector in Brazil, and across the growing Columbia Global Centers network, which by 2013 included centers in Amman, Beijing, Istanbul, Mumbai, Nairobi, Paris, Rio de Janeiro, Santiago, and Tunis (figure 8.7). As part of a digital education program designed for use across the network, we wanted to create a format for smaller and shareable educational resources.

The "case as a website" model offers certain benefits, but our team wanted to modernize the traditional case study without embedding it in a specific website or platform. We wanted a model that our partner universities could use in their own ways and share on several learning systems rather than one tied to a specific LMS or web-based platform. We aimed for a system that could use videos and have a simple interface that could be used on a variety of platforms. We also wanted to create a simple template for producing digital cases, as well as a means for curating this content, so we could create new digital cases at scale and share them in the same way the TEDx movement shares TED Talks.

Our team finally decided on a format that contains a five- to fifteen-minute documentary video (which our students now often create) with a five- to twelve-page case study. With this new format, we combined two established popular formats: the PBS-style documentary and the traditional written case study. This format is platform agnostic and can be dropped into any LMS or website and used in a variety of ways. Figure 8.8 illustrates the elements of Columbia's digital case format in Columbia's Canvas LMS, including documentary style videos, edited interview excerpts, and the written case study.

Our team produced its first digital cases in 2014 and 2015. With grant funding, we hired a team of experienced PBS documentary film producers and experienced writers of traditional written cases. The writers conducted initial research and outreach and worked with the producers to schedule video interviews. With funding from Columbia's Office of the Provost and an award from the President's Global Innovation Fund, professors from different schools worked with our team to create cases on best practices in public health, public safety, and elementary and secondary public education around the world.

These initial video case studies were filmed on location in the United States, Brazil, and India and were featured in our online programs and in a 2015 international conference on Technology and Innovation in the Public Service (Columbia SIPA 2019). The cases proved popular with professors and students alike, and they were especially effective when teaching groups of learners from diverse backgrounds, providing them with a shared experience they could reference and discuss. "When you have students from a variety of diverse backgrounds, actually seeing the video of a specific location and place can really ground the discussion," explained Yumi Shimabukuro (2021), a professor of international affairs at Columbia's School of International and Public Affairs. Faculty generally assign the cases to be viewed and read before class meetings. The case materials form the basis for simulations, memo assignments, and debates. "The video cases often provoke the most intense debates in the classroom," stated Shimabukuro. "Especially when you have a class with adult learners, using cases helps us to connect theoretical concepts to real-life examples, which enables them to bring

Public Private Partnerships for New York City Parks ⚡

Due Mar 19, 2016 by 11:59pm   **Points** 100   **Submitting** a file upload
Available Mar 5, 2016 at 12am - Mar 23, 2016 at 11:59pm

This assignment was locked Mar 23, 2016 at 11:59pm.

Instructions: Please watch the video case on Public Private Partnerships in New York City, read the written case and accompanying documents, and follow the case assignment directions ↓; then submit your memo by clicking on the "submit" button to the right of the page.

CASE STUDY: Public Private Partnerships for Green Space in NYC

Beginning with the Central Park Conservancy in 1980, public private partnerships (PPPs) have played a crucial role in strengthening parks and green spaces throughout New York City. This video explores both the benefits and drawbacks drawbacks to the PPP model.

Written Case	Original Documents	Interviewee Bio & Transcripts

📄 Download the case ↓   📄 Annex A: Original Documents ↓   📄 Parks Case - Annex B - Interviewee Bios and Transcripts ↓

Case Assignment Directions ↓

DISCUSSIONS

For a more in-depth look at the issues touched on in the Public Private Partnerships in Urban Green Spaces documentary, watch the extended interviews below.

Davis, Rogers, Blonsky, Cohen, Gerafola *Creation of Central Park Conservancy*

Switkin, Holtz, Cohen *The High Line*

Rogers, Cohen, Davis, Blonsky, Gerafola *Equity in Parks*

MEMO ASSIGNMENT

Please view the attached PDF for memo assignments. Remember to answer the questions, be specific, and support your assertions with evidence from the case.

To submit your assignment, follow the below steps:

1. Click on **Submit Assignment** in the right navigation pane.
2. In the **File Upload** box at the bottom of the page, click on **Browse** and locate the Word document that has your memo.
3. Feel free to leave a note in the **Comments** field. When you are finished, click **Submit Assignment**.

Figure 8.8 Columbia digital case: "Public Private Partnerships for NYC Parks"

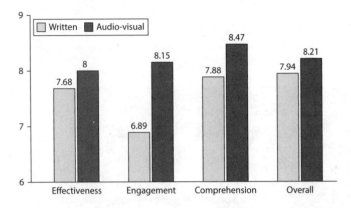

Figure 8.9 Learning outcomes for students in face-to-face classes

this knowledge to the classroom." The case videos help students overcome differences in background and perspectives. "As the whole class has watched the same video, and read the same case, they suddenly have a shared experience that they can all relate to," explained Shimabukuro.

In a series of tests conducted in 2015 and 2016, we compared learning outcomes for in-person and blended cohorts of the same course with one class using only the written case method (figure 8.9) and the other using fully digital cases with both videos and written materials (figure 8.10). We found that fully digital cases improved

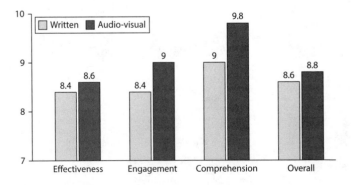

Figure 8.10 Learning outcomes for students in blended classes

student engagement and comprehension across all courses, with the largest improvements shown in students whose classes met online (Stepan and Eimicke 2016). These data support the qualitative evidence that we have gathered over eight years. Video cases are especially helpful in creating a community in courses that meet online, where making connections between a group of learners is especially important.

DIGITAL CASES AND STAKEHOLDER ENGAGEMENT

As our case study program developed from 2014 to 2017, we found it also brought benefits to Columbia as an institution over and above the value the cases brought to our in-person and online classrooms. Through the case creation process, we expanded ties to and connections with key partners and stakeholder organizations in our city, our region, and around the world. Our cases are generally about government, social organizations, and private companies, often working in cross-sector partnerships on complex and important challenges and issues. We have generally found that the organizations featured in our cases are thrilled to see their work documented and shared.

In creating the cases we are careful to follow traditional journalistic rules, and we seek to be neutral in our review of organizations and projects. Our digital case studies explore key problems and document both the advantages of a certain innovation or program and its limitations. We also share our semifinal cases with the key stakeholders featured for fact-checking. We do not allow outside groups to have editorial oversight, but we give all groups filmed a chance to review and comment and correct any factual errors. Our cases have also proved useful to the groups and organizations we profile, providing them with insight into what others in their field of practice are doing. Examples include Columbia's collections of digital cases on issues such as Social Impact Investing and Cybersecurity, which are used widely by companies, consultants, and think tanks and have helped advance debate and learning in these important areas (Columbia SIPA 2019).

We also share video footage with the groups we film to use along with our cases in their own outreach. By profiling NGOs, government groups, and companies involved in interesting and important work, we have deepened institutional connections with government agencies in the United States, Brazil, and India; NGOs working in development; and innovative investors working in the social impact investing space. All of these groups appreciate the opportunity to share their work with our students and those at our partner universities. Many of these groups have subsequently worked with us on research projects, guest-lectured in Columbia courses, or hosted student capstone projects.

In 2018, we opened our collection to the public as the Public Policy Case Collection on a free-membership model (figure 8.11). We also presented and shared our case collection at leading international teaching and learning conferences in the United States and Europe, including Learning with MOOCs in Madrid, the edX Global Forum in Boston, and the Sciences Po Teaching and Learning Conference in Paris. Today, Columbia's digital cases are used by more

Figure 8.11 Columbia's Public Policy Case Collection, "Digital India" case

than two hundred universities and NGOs around the world and are included in both online and face-to-face courses in all leading LMS solutions, including Canvas, Moodle, Brightspace, and Blackboard. Many cases will also available on the edX MOOC "The Public Sector Innovation Lab," scheduled for launch in 2024.

We continue to expand our case program on this model and receive funding from leading philanthropic organizations interested in seeing cases produced on issues that range from public health to conservation agriculture to the use of big data in city management and cybersecurity issues. Our team of case writers and producers travel to Latin America, Africa, and Asia interviewing senior officials in government, the private sector, and the development community to provide information that forms the basis of these in-depth case studies.

SCALING ACTIVE LEARNING:
STUDENT-CREATED DIGITAL CASES

As our case program grew, we began to think of ways to expand its impact—not only sharing our final cases but also sharing the details of the process we use to create digital cases so others could create and share their own. From the many professors who downloaded our courses, we saw a growing demand for short-format, high-quality academic content. We began to think of ways to expand the program while reducing the costs involved.

The key to expanding the digital case format, we realized, was to involve student filmmakers and researchers. The logic was simple. Creating cases generally involves a deep study of a particular issue or problem, finding data, and interviewing key actors. It also involves a great deal of passion and effort. In their fieldwork and research for papers and capstone projects, students were already doing this work. Columbia students often spend spring break or summer sessions doing on-location research projects, working in groups to create written research papers. Many students document their work with photographs and videos.

We found that many students were also eager to learn the skills of journalism and filmmaking. They were on the lookout for good stories and issues to explore. If we could connect these groups, train them, and provide equipment, support, and expenses, we could produce high-quality digital case studies at a fraction of the cost of hiring professional crews. The process would also provide an invaluable learning experience for budding researchers and filmmakers.

Our first experiments began in 2018. We offered an intensive "boot camp" on the basics of documentary film technique and partnered with graduate students doing capstone projects at Columbia's School of International and Public Affairs and the Technology, Media, and Communications program at SIPA (TMaC) created and run by Professor Anya Schiffrin.

Begun in the early 2000s, the Capstone program at SIPA oversees about seventy-five capstone research teams annually. Every spring break second-year students travel to overseas sites to study development issues. Students work with client organizations including the United Nations, ministries of health or the environment of developing countries, and major international NGOs. "These are real-world projects that are solving real issues for our client," explained Suzanne Hollman (2019), director of the Capstone program at SIPA. "I always highlight to our students that the client is asking the question because they don't know the answer." Hollman and her team identify client organizations and define the scope of the work for the student teams. Work begins in the spring semester, with two months of research and planning, which often includes early video interviews with key stakeholders. Student teams organize their work, allocating different tasks to each team member and plotting plans for their fieldwork. "There is no predetermined destination we want you to get to," Hollman tells the capstone teams. "It's your job to work together as a team, to develop the methodology and the approach, and as you hit stumbling blocks, like incomplete data sets to inaccessible information, [find out] how you pivot and find ways around that."

In January and February 2018, we ran hands-on media workshops for capstone teams going to Peru and Costa Rica. We offered training in using video equipment that eventually became the basis of the MOOC "Digital Case Method," which we now also run as a class with the Open Society University Network. The student teams created engaging digital cases about their field research projects, which professional producers edited into digital case studies that are used in classes around the world to this day such as "Internet-in-a-Box" (figure 8.12) and "Private Rainforest Reserves of Costa Rica." In the fall of 2018, we offered the same training in a for-credit course at SIPA. Student teams worked together to create a new case on the U.S. midterm elections and student activists in New York, Pennsylvania, and Florida (Columbia SIPA 2019).

The following spring and summer we repeated the cycle. As more students were trained, new capstone teams traveled to Haiti, Nepal, and Uganda to create digital cases. In the spring of 2019, we held an awards event at SIPA honoring six student video cases created the previous year. The event featured student filmmakers and key stakeholders, with guest speakers from the United Nations, PBS, and key research institutes at Columbia who had partnered in case-creation projects.

Figure 8.12 Student-created case "Internet-in-a-Box" filmed in Peru

UNDP STUDENT-CREATED CASES

An early sign of the success of this program occurred in the summer of 2019 when a group of six SIPA students were contracted by the United Nations Development Programme (UNDP) to help create video cases and documentaries. They would be working with a group of twenty Indigenous leaders around the world, creating video cases about their groups for the "Equator Prize," part of United Nations' annual Climate Week activities in New York. The films would be made in Tanzania, Indonesia, Bali, Bolivia, and Guinea Bissau, and other global locations, and would document the work of Indigenous groups combating climate change.

Most of the student producers hired were graduates of our Visual Storytelling course and were able to bring their experiences from previous projects to the endeavor. The projects involved working with local Indigenous leaders and filmmakers to co-create stories about nature-based ways to mitigate the impacts of climate change. The project grew out of an idea pitched to the UNDP by Columbia graduate student Louise Contino, who would go on to be the senior producer of the twenty-two films created for that year's event.

Jamison Ervin (2021), the manager of the Nature for Development Programme at the UNDP, saw the program as a great way to capture and share the stories of various groups being honored in the ceremony. In previous years, the groups honored had been presented in videos using archival footage, but without images or interviews from their actual communities. With the cases produced by students and local groups, "suddenly the communities were able to tell their own story in a way that's never been told before," explained Ervin. "Suddenly they could access, they could influence, they could show, and it had life."

The twenty-two student and local group co-created films were shown at a gala event before more than 1,500 people in New York City's historic Town Hall Theater in September 2019 as part of the UN's Climate Week, and the films were shared by UNDP on

Figure 8.13 UNDP Equator Prize YouTube channel

their websites and educational channels (figure 8.13). "Humans learn by storytelling, we're storytellers," explained Ervin (2021). "We used the video exercise to help communities tell their story . . . these videos have been incredibly powerful." The videos have been used as part of the UNDP's online education program and by local groups. "We reached 100 million people with the hashtag Equator Prize," explained Ervin, "and forty thousand people watched it live" (figure 8.14). The videos have also been used in national ceremonies in many countries. "They were so powerful," explained Ervin, "because suddenly it's the community saying 'this is our story.'"

Figure 8.14 UNDP Equator Prize awards ceremony in New York

OSUN STUDENT CASE PROGRAM

The movement toward student-created case studies took another huge step forward in 2020 with creation of the Open Society University Network (OSUN). OSUN, with forty universities and NGOs across the world, prepares students for "current and future global challenges" (Burton 2020). OSUN has long been dedicated to the idea of active learning, with students documenting how issues from water access to agriculture to local development shape their different geographies and communities.

As the new network expanded after 2020, OSUN reached out to our team at Columbia to explore how we could collaborate on student-produced case studies. To train students at OSUN campuses across the world, we realized we needed to provide online training in video case production. The result was a self-paced course on visual storytelling for civic engagement—now the core content of our MOOC, "Digital Case Method" (figure 8.15). With a series of how-to videos, the course provides a comprehensive overview of filmmaking with smartphones and digital single-lens reflex (DSLR) cameras. The course includes examples of

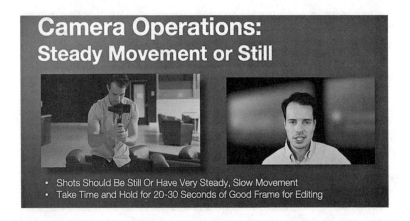

Figure 8.15 Video from Digital Case Method MOOC

Figure 8.16 OSUN's Visual Storytelling for Civic Engagement website

student-produced cases from Columbia and the UNDP projects as well as interviews with award-winning documentary filmmakers and students. It is now available on edX, Coursera, and Canvas Commons platforms.

We offer the course in different formats—as a stand-alone self-paced course or as part of a larger training process (figure 8.16). At local partner universities in the United States, Germany, Bangladesh, Lithuania, Belarus, and Kyrgyzstan, local documentary filmmakers each teach for-credit courses for local filmmakers using the same shared curriculum. Using the forty videos from the Digital Case Method MOOC as flipped course lectures, the whole group of almost one hundred young global filmmakers meets several times during the semester to share works in progress. OSUN provides students with gear, training, and modest financial support for on-location filming costs. The course concludes with an online film festival.

In the first two and a half years of the partnership between OSUN and Columbia, teams produced seventy-six student-created case studies and films on issues that include the policy challenges of Afghani refugees, squatters in Berlin, and Indigenous rights in

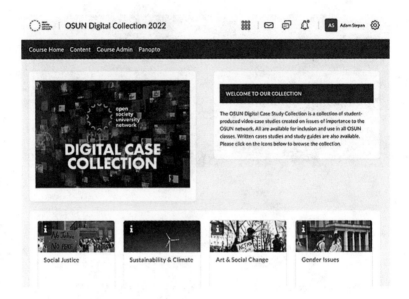

Figure 8.17 OSUN Case Collection

Bangladesh. These assets are part of the growing OSUN Digital Case Collection for use by classes across the network (figure 8.17).

OSUN also invested in creating full case studies for use in the classroom from the student films created in the fall class. This involved hiring especially successful student filmmakers as paid summer interns. Their job is to follow up on the basic student produced film, add additional interviews and materials, and create a written case study. It is part of a tradition we began at Columbia, and it has been key to creating a sustainable program. Having a mixed team of both student filmmakers and professional mentors and teachers creates fantastic cases, and it also trains a new generation of documentary filmmakers and case creators. In addition, it drastically reduces the per case cost of production because many cases are created organically as part of students' research projects. Student case creation also offers students fantastic opportunities to engage in active learning, going out in the world and doing group research and filming.

An example of the integration of student digital case studies into the OSUN curriculum is the Network Collaborative Class titled "Global Citizenship." The course is team taught by a group of professors who meet across the network in campuses that include Bard Berlin, BRAC University in Bangladesh, and AUCA in Bishkek Kyrgyzstan. In the first week of the course, students watch and read digital case studies created by students the previous year. During the class, student research creates the basis for new cases that will be filmed the following summer by student filmmakers as part of a paid summer internship. It's a virtuous cycle of active learning and research.

"Doing is the richest form of learning and demonstrating that learning," explained David Shein (2022) of Bard. "It is bringing theory to practice." Having different student groups collaborate both in the research and then the filming of digital cases is an especially powerful form of this. "The additional value is literally putting a camera in a student's hands and saying, go investigate this, go explore this, go report on this. . . . It's engagement, right?"

Professor Michelle Murray of Bard College, the lead professor in the OSUN "Global Citizenship" collaborative class, believes the use of student-created digital cases in the course also helps support richer interactions in live class sessions. "The virtual elements of these courses provide common experiences that are touchstones," explained Murray. "They can then become an entry point for students to have conversations with each other." The fact that students themselves help make the videos gives them special relevance for other learners. "There is a way my students understand the world that I could never replicate for them . . . they are engaging the material from their own place, from their own perspective, and that opens something up and . . . draws [other] students in."

CREATING A STUDENT-CENTERED CASE PROGRAM

The work of Columbia University, the UNDP, and the many universities of OSUN illustrate the power of digital case studies, and especially student-created cases. We encourage our colleagues at universities across the globe to consider setting up similar programs and sharing the digital cases created. A short video paired with a written case is much simpler, less costly, and more flexible than a MOOC, and it provides an opportunity to share the asset much more widely.

We hope one of the long-term legacies of work in this area will be the continued growth of this international community of digital case creators. We envision the eventual creation of a wider multi-university platform that shares digital cases and other video-based OER materials, similar to what Ted Talks offers to local creators of TEDx talks. We are supporting these efforts with our free-to-the-public Digital Case Method MOOC, offered on the edX, Coursera, and Canvas Commons platforms, along with our ongoing and ever-growing collection of cases and support materials. The Digital Case Method MOOC contains all the materials needed to set up and run a case program at your institution, and users can download and insert videos and readings from the course into an LMS at their own university under the Creative Commons license.

CREATING A DIGITAL CASE PROGRAM CHECKLIST

Here are a few tips for building a case creation program at your institution:

Use Available OER Resources

To jump-start a case study creation program, encourage faculty to use existing digital case studies in their classes. Collections at Columbia and OSUN offer many low- or no-cost options. The Digital Case Method MOOC contains a complete course in digital case creation, which you can download and use in your own local LMS.

Partner with Existing Media Programs

In schools with documentary film programs, student filmmakers are often looking for subjects for their projects. Connecting them with students and researchers who want to document and explore important issues builds fantastic digital case studies. Designing a team-taught course that includes professors both of film and experts in a certain area of inquiry can provide an ideal way to jump-start these connections. Providing some central funding and support for student case creation can help make these collaborations successful.

Fund Student Cases as Summer Jobs

Offering some modest central funding to cover the costs of creating a certain number of new digital cases each year can grow your program, and the per-case cost is only a fraction of 100-percent professionally produced cases. To recruit the best student filmmakers, offer a modest stipend and budget to cover expenses. Treat it as a summer job, demand high-quality results, and only hire students who can create quality content. Connect students with professors who need new cases for their classes.

Partner with Stakeholders

Does your school have special expertise in certain areas? Special connections to certain local industries or local NGOs or government projects? Chances are these partners would love to have a digital case study about their work and would help to arrange access for filming.

Provide Support for Interviews and Video Editing

Depending on the experience of student filmmakers, filming and editing interviews for high-quality documentaries can be a challenge. Consider inviting key stakeholders for interviews on campus, where they can be filmed by students with the technical support and the oversight of your digital education team. Having a small interview studio available for this can be a great time saver and ensures that all interviews meet technical standards. Also, consider a workflow in which students produce rough edits of the planned cases and professional video team staff do final edits. See the MOOC Digital Case Method for more details and suggestions on these collaborations.

Provide Supervision for All Outreach Efforts

Students can create great digital case studies, but they require close faculty or staff support and supervision. They will be acting on behalf of the university, contacting outside stakeholders, and creating a product that represents the institution. A faculty or staff member must oversee this activity as the project's executive producer, with responsibility for managing and overseeing interactions with outside entities.

Create Companion Written Cases

Make sure creation of an eight- to twelve-page written case study is one of the project deliverables for all case study projects. The video case will provide a great introduction to the situation and issues, and the written case can go into more depth. Together they are an impactful package for use in the classroom. Create the written case (at least in draft form) as part of the same project work cycle when the video is made, and when all the key information and research is available and fresh in people's minds. It can always be updated and copyedited later as needed.

Celebrate Successes and Have Fun

Creating digital case studies is demanding work. It is rewarding but requires dedication and focus. A campus film festival offers a great way to celebrate and recognize this work. Make sure to have a master of ceremonies, vote on "best film" for multiple categories, and invite the dean and senior faculty and administrators to deliver prizes. It can be a great way to recognize the value of the student films created and honor the wider community of researchers and professors working on the issues that the films cover.

REFERENCES

Agarwal, Anant. 2021. Interview of CEO, edX, by Adam Stepan. October 19, 2021.

Burton, Katherine. 2020. "George Soros to Start $1 Billion University to Fight Authoritarianism and Climate Change." *Fortune*, January 23, 2020. https://fortune.com/2020/01/23/george-soros-open-society-university-network-davos/.

Butcher, Neil, Asha Kanwar, and Stamenka Uvalic-Trumbic. 2011. *A Basic Guide to Open Educational Resources (OER)—UNESCO Digital Library*. Commonwealth of Learning. https://unesdoc.unesco.org/ark:/48223/pf0000215804.

Cochran, Bill, and David Migliorese. 2021. "Demo of Wiley Platform presented to Adam Stepan. November 16, 2021.

Columbia SIPA. 2019. "Public Policy Case Collection." accessed February 12, 2022. https://www.sipa.columbia.edu/public-policy-case-collection.

Ervin, Jamison. 2021. Interview of Manager of the Nature for Development Global Program, UNDP, by Adam Stepan. November 4, 2021.

Fidelman, Mark. 2012. "Here's Why TED and TEDx Are So Incredibly Appealing" (Infographic). *Forbes*, June 19, 2012. https://www.forbes.com/sites/markfidelman/2012/06/19/heres-why-ted-and-tedx-are-so-incredibly-appealing-infographic/.

Fried, Aaron, Yongjin Lee, Karen Zannini, and Tiffany Koszalka. 2006. "Case Study Method of Instruction." https://web.cortland.edu/frieda/id/IDtheories/43.html.

Genota, Lauraine. 2018. "Why Generation Z Learners Prefer YouTube Lessons Over Printed Books." *Education Week*, September 11, 2018. https://www.edweek.org/teaching-learning/why-generation-z-learners-prefer-youtube-lessons-over-printed-books/2018/09.

Herreid, Clyde, and Nancy Schiller. 2013. "Case Studies and the Flipped Classroom." *Journal of College Science Teaching* 42, no. 5: 62–66.

Hollman, Suzanne. 2019. Interview of Director of the Capstone Workshop Program, School of International and Public Affairs, Columbia University, by Adam Stepan. April 3, 2019.

Hua, Karen. 2015. "Education as Entertainment: YouTube Sensations Teaching the Future." *Forbes*, June 23, 2015. https://www.forbes.com/sites/karenhua/2015/06/23/education-as-entertainment-youtube-sensations-teaching-the-future/.

Jack, Andrew. 2018. "Why Harvard's Case Studies Are Under Fire." *Financial Times*, October 29, 2018. https://www.ft.com/content/0b1aeb22-d765-11e8-a854-33d6f82e62f8.

Jiang, Hao, Craig Ganoe, and John M. Carroll. 2010. "Four Requirements for Digital Case Study Libraries." *Education and Information Technologies* 15, no. 3 (September 2010): 219–36. https://doi.org/10.1007/s10639-009-9108-x.

"Khan Academy Annual Report 2020." n.d. accessed February 12, 2022. https://s3.amazonaws.com/KA-share/2020+Khan+Academy+Inc.+Public+Disclosure+Client.pdf.

Koumi, Jack. 2015. "Learning Outcomes Afforded by Self-Assessed, Segmented Video–Print Combinations." *Cogent Education* 2, no. 1: 1045218. https://doi.org/10.1080/2331186X.2015.1045218.

Lang, James M. 2011. "Teaching Students to Write a Case Study." *Chronicle of Higher Education*, July 5, 2011. https://www.chronicle.com/article/teaching-students-to-write-a-case-study/.

Lundberg, Kirsten. 2015. "Case Method and Case Study Collections." In *International Encyclopedia of the Social & Behavioral Sciences*, 176–82. New York: Elsevier. https://doi.org/10.1016/B978-0-08-097086-8.41003-2.

——. 2017. Interview of founder, Lundburg Case Consortium, by Adam Stepan. December 2, 2017.

Marketing Charts. 2019. "Online Video Use Among Tweens and Teens Surges." *Marketing Charts* (blog). November 11, 2019. https://www.marketingcharts.com/demographics-and-audiences/teens-and-younger-110947.

MIT News. "MIT Launches Online Learning Initiative." 2011. *MIT News*, December 19, 2011. https://news.mit.edu/2011/mitx-education-initiative-1219.

Nazir, Nazreen. 2019. "Dancing to the Tunes of Educational Content." *Entrepreneur*, June 29, 2019.

Scott, Josh. 2021. Interview of Director of Course Strategy, 2U, by Adam Stepan. November 30, 2021.

Shah, Dhawal. 2022. "Khan Academy Tax Returns Analysis (2008–2020): $390M in Revenue, 118M Registered Users." Class Central. *The Report*, January 17, 2022. https://www.classcentral.com/report/khan-academy-tax-returns-analysis/.

Shein, David. 2022. Interview of Associate Vice President for Academic Affairs and Dean of Studies, Bard College, by Adam Stepan. June 17, 2022.

Shimabukuro, Yumi. 2021. Interview of professor of international affairs, School of International and Public Affairs, Columbia University, by Adam Stepan. November 15, 2021.

Stepan, Adam, and William Eimicke. 2016. "Comparing In-Person and Remote Use of Written and Digital Cases." SIPA Study, 2016.

TED. 2012. "TED Reaches Its Billionth Video View!" TED (blog). November 13, 2012. https://blog.ted.com/ted-reaches-its-billionth-video-view/.

9

NETWORKED LEARNING

The social aspects of learning are key, and digital tools can help support and enhance these connections. In this chapter, we explore some of the ways to realize this potential.

SOCIAL LEARNING

Learning materials such as books, case studies, and videos are essential tools for education. But deep learning takes place in relationship between teachers, students, peers, and outside partners. A compelling digital educational experience requires direct person-to-person interactions, whether in person, online, or even asynchronously online. In their zeal to automate learning, companies too often ignore this essential truth.

The challenge of digital education is to combine high-quality digital learning assets (obviously scalable) with personal interaction and mentoring (seemingly unscalable). The revolution in learning will come when we find a way to take advantage of online assets without losing the personal touch. People learn socially; getting feedback quickly, online or in person, is fundamental. Exploring problems with mentors and peers is key. The question is how to scale these activities. To make person-to-person learning scalable, consider the power of networks. We are convinced that the next generation of digital educational tools will be designed around these considerations.

NETWORKED LEARNING 1.0—THE cMOOC

To understand networked learning, consider the case of faith-based communities. In Roman Catholic churches and monasteries and in the Madrasa system of Muslim schools, religious organizations use shared assets, the Bible or the Quran, to learn together and to create deep, engaged local learning communities. Universities use a similar model that incorporates an expanded canon of literature and knowledge. All around the world, local researchers and professors meet and exchange ideas around a generally shared canon of great books and an ever-expanding base of scientific knowledge. For centuries, intellectuals and researchers published books, and a wide community of thinkers would read and comment on them. Within the university, inquiry arose around the major thinkers of the time: from Hobbes to Rousseau, Marx to Darwin, Freud to Foucault. Inspired by these and countless other seminal thinkers, communities of inquiry explored their ideas.

As personal computers emerged in the 1980s, the scale and velocity of the sharing of knowledge and information accelerated. Assets that once required physical form—books, journals, film, archives—were digitized and made available first on floppy disks and CD-ROMs and then on the internet. Within a decade, building on the ARPANET system developed by the U.S. military, computers linked together through the World Wide Web. Electronic mail begat listservs, which begat public repositories of data, which begat the internet. This global network offered new possibilities for collective learning and interaction.

Al Filreis (2022), a literature professor at the University of Pennsylvania, took advantage of early email and listserv discussion boards to teach poetry classes in the early 1990s. In 1994, he decided to use information technology to take a deep dive into the work of Robert Frost, a "poet that students don't care about, but that parents do," said Filreis. He used listserv to "extend the discussion outside of class." His online discussion board brought his students together with "grandparents and siblings, uncles and aunts." Learning was not just a subject in a college catalog; it was a vital community of curious learners on and off campus. "I put the two lists together and we had a hellacious week-long discussion," Filreis remembered years later. "Class would end at three, and then people would run to their terminals and continue to talk all through the weekend until the class met again at one-thirty the next Tuesday."

In retrospect, Filreis created a massive open online course (MOOC) using text-only email. In these online exchanges, a lot of exciting learning took place. After the MOOC boom a decade later, Filreis expanded on the idea. ModPo—an open MOOC on modern poetry—has been running continuously for ten years on the Coursera platform, with more than 63,000 active participants (figure 9.1).

Filreis (2022) calls his course an "xMOOC with the sensibility of a cMOOC" ("c" stands for collaboration). "Our point was to have constant present tense interaction," Filreis remembered. "People collaborate on making the content, not just talking about it."

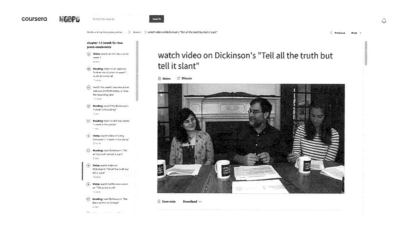

Figure 9.1 Coursera's ModPo

The ModPo community brings together new learners with "expert" members who have been in the course for years. The ten-week course holds live sessions. Each week, participants read and analyze poetry in video recordings, Zoom calls, discussion sections, and rich archives of student-generated content. The course has two thousand objects, two thousand discussions, and access to the "world's largest repository of poets performing their own poetry." "There will be people in the symposium mode this fall who have done it eleven times," explained Filreis, "and there are people just signing up for the first time." Filreis coordinates the course, with the help of eleven TAs, fifty community TAs, and two tech support staff. ModPo is free and open to all and, as Filreis noted, "it's the original MOOC conception."

Erica Kaufman (2022), the director of Bard College's Institute for Writing and Thinking, first joined ModPo as a participant. "It was, in a lot of ways, a better educational experience than I had in a lot of my college courses," she said. "People do things outside of the webcast and talk to each other online and ask questions and that makes up the content of the lecture." Kaufman, who was conducting research on the impacts of technology on writing, was intrigued by Filreis's ability "to create the feeling of a seminar-style course with 30,000 people." When she joined the ModPo team, she began to consider how this experiment in crowdsourced knowledge and learning could be applied to other courses and subjects.

After studying the MOOC phenomenon, Kaufman realized that Filreis's course was radically different from most traditional MOOCs, which generally offered a one-way communication of knowledge, often via recorded video lectures, with little or no peer-to-peer engagement. "The more I began to read and think about the model of the MOOC, the more I realized that what we were doing was quite the opposite," Kaufman (2022) said.

The strength of the ModPo course was its ability to enlist its participants in a sprawling conversation, with everyone contributing to teaching and learning. "If you have 63,000 people, you have 63,000 versions that they can contribute to this giant crowdsourcing that is taking place," explained Filreis (2022). The emphasis on user-generated content followed the model of other social media platforms such as Facebook, Twitter, Instagram, and TikTok. Filreis believes the crowdsourcing of knowledge is the path of the future. For Filreis, peer-to-peer learning is "totally applicable to any field. It's applicable to studying politics. It's applicable to studying art and anthropology. And it's totally applicable to studying math. Even though the outcome is supposed to be constant, the way you get there is the way your mind works around a math problem."

SCALING LIBERAL ARTS—OSUN COLLABORATIVE CLASSES

Another group looking for ways to expand the use of technology and peer-to-peer learning is the Open Society University Network (OSUN), a group of more than forty institutions and institutes around the world that have received support and funding from George Soros's Open Society Foundation. Launched in January 2020, OSUN builds on partnerships forged for years by Bard College, a small liberal arts school in upstate New York. Bard aimed to bring liberal arts education to countries where most universities are focused on technical learning. OSUN worked with partner campuses in Lithuania, Belarus, Bangladesh, and Kyrgyzstan—all working to consolidate democratic institutions with a broadly educated public.

OSUN's liberal arts curriculum offers the "antidote to the traditional Humboldtian model of education in which students are focusing on a narrow disciplinary training," OSUN Vice Chancellor Jonathan Becker (2021) said. "We are dealing with places that are struggling with governance . . . either aspiring to transition to democracy or fighting against growing authoritarianism." The classic liberal arts education, Becker argues, can play a crucial role in this process. "We believe in educating people with depth and breadth," Becker said. "The outcome of that is people who are . . . ready to be engaged citizens and professionals throughout their life, and [adapt] to changing situations." David Shein (2022), Bard's vice president for academic affairs, agrees: "The liberal arts education is distinguished by student-centered learning, by choice, by critical thinking, critical writing, and critical listening."

As Bard and OSUN expanded the liberal arts model, they explored the role of technology. Most traditional Bard classes were built on intense in-person discussion and writing. How could this be translated to digital platforms? For Erica Kaufman (2022) and other OSUN leaders, Filreis's poetry course at Penn hinted at a strategy. "Teaching humanities works particularly well online if one understands the different ways you have to plan for it to happen," Kaufman said. One way to do this was to double down on the use of Bard's writing-based teaching methods and find tools—such as Padlet and Perusall—that allow them to work online.

The other key was to make student-to-student learning a priority. "When I'm teaching in person and a class goes really well, the students forget that I'm there," Shein (2022) explained. "They are talking with one another, and they are engaged . . . that's the magic." This dynamic educational interaction could take place online and be shared across networks. The possibilities are endless, with "a student from Lithuania and a student from Scarsdale talking about how they read a book or responded to a lecture." Done well, this approach would allow OSUN to "replicate a liberal arts classroom on a global scale," said Shein.

But making this work in practice is not easy. One challenge is to design a suite of technology platforms built for interaction rather than for a one-way transmission of knowledge. "Online learning is usually a publishing cycle," stated Philip Fedchin (2022), OSUN's technology strategist. "You have an expert/author, you produce the course as a publication, then you scale it." For OSUN, classes required a fundamentally different "interactive learning process." Collaboration and peer-to-peer work were essential. To start, OSUN worked to get its forty-plus institutions to adopt common technology platforms and to persuade reluctant partners to use new tools. "It doesn't matter what the platform is, it doesn't matter how great it is," Fedchin said. "There always will be a bunch of people at the university who hate it and who will do everything not to use it." The group eventually embraced a technology suite that included

Figure 9.2 OSUN online course on Brightspace

Brightspace as its learning management system (figure 9.2), Zoom for video conferencing, Panopto for video recordings, and Padlet and Perusall for student annotation of reading assignments. To support collaboration, the network has invested heavily in training and support of all kinds.

OSUN classes take many forms, but most combine the intense interactions of in-person seminars with digital tools that make classes available to people across the world. With online discussion boards and Padlet, participants can offer their thoughts in real time. Other networked classes use readings, video lectures, and student-produced digital case studies to connect learners. In OSUN classes, professors customize the course and meet in person or on Zoom.

In the networked collaborative classes, students connect both in person and online. Discussions and projects take place at local institutions: Bard Annandale, Bard Berlin, the American University of Central Asia in Bishkek Kyrgyzstan, and BRAC University in Bangladesh, among others. Students also meet in cohorts online to work on projects, hear guest speakers, or participate in other cross-network events. In all of these courses, peer-to-peer learning and group projects are featured.

Across the world, educators are experimenting with technology to expand the breadth and scope of class discussions—not just with online assets but also with a growing diversity of participants. Online courses, Becker (2021) stated, offer a "unique international experience for people, not all of whom can easily travel, especially on topics where students' experiences in different countries matter to our understanding of the material." Network classes also transform the faculty experience. Discussion and dialogue "lead the faculty to a level of cooperation which is meaningful and rebounds in a variety of ways," Becker explained. Faculty achieve new insights into materials and develop new areas of collaborative research.

OSUN's collaborative remote learning is an ongoing work in progress. "Success is moving from one failure to the other with growing enthusiasm," explained OSUN's Fedchin (2022), citing Winston Churchill's famous wartime quote. "I think it's applicable to this effort especially. You may fail from the point of view of some of the participants, whereas you still move forward in terms of intensifying the collaboration. That's the goal. To keep moving forward with an optimistic approach."

SMALL COHORT LEARNING

OSUN and other innovators have discovered that online learning can be intimate and immediate as well as scalable and diverse. Zoom *lectures* may be underwhelming, but Zoom *discussions* can be riveting. Students can connect online in surprisingly intimate ways. They can see each other just inches away. They need not speak loudly or compete for attention. And they can go deep on analyses of great books and complex modern issues. In many ways, class meetings resemble book clubs. Online students can connect in ways that large public discussions make more difficult. Digital tools allow close intimate interactions and learning in smaller cohorts. The success of small, intimate online learning classes has been largely ignored in the wider public narrative about frustrations over Zoom during the COVID-19 pandemic.

A wide range of websites offer individualized courses for adult learners based on this concept. Maven is one for-profit online platform focused on harnessing the power of small cohort learning. It offers short synchronous courses on subjects that range from "Startup Brand Strategy" to "Hype Free Crypto" to "Financial Planning and Analysis Bootcamp," to "Date Smarter" (see Maven's course catalog). "Learning is Better in Cohorts," Maven's website announces (https://maven.com/courses). "Active Learning, Not Passive Watching—This course is taught live with hands-on projects. Workshops aren't simply lectures, there will be interactivity, breakout rooms, discussions, and Q&A." Peer-to-peer learning is a big pull: "Connect and Learn with a Cohort of Your Peers. . . . Surround yourself with like-minded people who want to learn and grow alongside you." Maven's two- to four-week courses generally cost between $500 and $1,000, with a chance to "learn live from world-class instructors," "grow with a cohort of peer students," and "join a member-only community" (figure 9.3). Many courses require students to apply and be vetted before joining, ensuring cohesiveness and avoiding unprepared students.

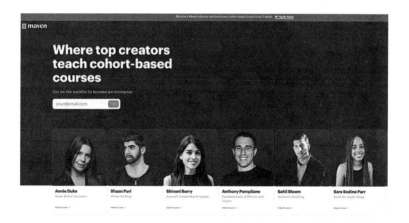

Figure 9.3 Maven website

Figure 9.4 Section4 website

Section4, the brainchild of NYU business professor and serial entrepreneur Scott Galloway, also demonstrates the power of peer-based online learning (figure 9.4). "Intensive, Immersive, Subversive," Section4's website declares (https://www.section4.com/). "Elite Business Education for All." Like Maven, Section4 offers two- to four-week courses for around $1,000. Unlike Maven, Section4 supplements its small cohort live discussion sections with well-produced prerecorded videos and case studies. For an additional $1,000 a year, students enjoy access to all lectures and digital cases across courses. Teaching assistants administer live sessions, with visits from the professor and other keynote speakers (Malcolm Gladwell is one notable to appear). Students meet and network on Slack. Section4 creates an environment of inclusivity as it opens education to a broader pool of learners.

For Nina Huntemann (2021), vice president of learning at edX, the pandemic revealed the power of combining high-quality content with cohort-based learning. "There are a lot of very interesting startups that do this now," Huntemann said. "Whether it's Maven or Section4, you learn asynchronously, but there is also a lot of synchronous activity. You're in a cohort of learners, moving through [the material] together in a condensed period of time." This move toward intimacy, and toward finding ways to adapt MOOCs for use by small local cohorts, Huntemann said, "is probably the most promising and most efficacious next move for MOOCs."

NETWORKED CLASSES AND SPOCS

Armando Fox (2021), at the University of California Berkeley, has been the pioneer of another sort of networked learning that is focused on sharing both content and teaching methods. Fox coined the term SPOC—Small Private Online Class—when creating materials for a computer science course at Berkeley originally created and shared as a MOOC. "We already had large and growing computer science courses," he said. "We needed to find ways to manage student demand other than just trying to hire a ton of additional instructors."

Fox's course materials—videos of lectures, printed readings, online programming labs, auto-grading—had the makings of a self-paced MOOC. But Fox saw the potential for blending the new and the old. Why not teach a small, intimate class, using the digital assets his team had created as a "digital textbook"? This made good sense to Fox (2021) because the collection of digital assets had begun as a textbook project before becoming a full MOOC. "We were putting the book together and thought, 'Here's another experiment that can make the book and the course match each other closely.'"

Fox and his colleagues decided to assemble the course materials and share them in a way that instructors at different universities around the world could download and use, customizing all content to best match their local needs.

Rather than following a one-size-fits-all MOOC model, Fox nurtured a network of university partners around the world who would each customize the class. His experiment became known as the network course model. He managed a network of more than three hundred instructors around the world who customized the course for their own needs, with limited participation by Fox and his Berkeley-based team. Fox used early classes as a beta group to fine-tune his innovation. Fox (2021) explained, "We'd ask them, 'Which of these things did you use from the book? Did you use the videos?' Some of them used everything we provided. Some of them set aside our videos and gave their own lectures. Some of them did a flip." The next

241

Figure 9.5 Armando Fox's website on edX

round of instructors benefited from this early-stage learning. "We put all this into an instructor's manual that said, 'Here's a bunch of ingredients. Here's what we do at Berkeley'" (figure 9.5).

The experiment showed the path to a new model for sharing digital assets—a "course in a box" that can be adapted to meet a wide range of needs. "You have to give them something that just works as a starting point so that they can run it once, get it under their belts, get comfortable, and then they're going to start adding their own customization," Fox (2021) explained. "People love to customize stuff!"

For Fox (2021), the key to educational innovation is to make distinctions between "things that scale" and "things that don't scale." Things that scale—video lectures, digital cases, readings, labs, and exercises—require the highest quality production possible. Things that don't scale include "high-touch" discussion sections and group projects. For Fox, the solution was to break a course into two parts. One part, a four-week course with core teachings, would satisfy the needs of 80 percent of students and could be delivered at scale. The other part, a smaller class run by TAs and other instructors, would involve discussions and small-group projects.

SCALING ONLINE AT GEORGIA TECH

The Georgia Tech computer science program also developed an innovative program designed to combine large-scale enrollments for major core learning with the high-touch qualities of small sections and group projects. Georgia Tech offers a Master's in computer science degree for $7,000, about one-quarter the cost of an equivalent on campus program. The program enrolls 800 to 1,000 students per professor, with a small army of support staff. Classes feature recorded lectures with the lead faculty (figure 9.6), but a big part of learning occurs in cohort-based projects.

Project assignments enable students to do hands-on work and engage with each other. One course combines analytics with computer science and enrolls as many as 1,500 students. The class is broken into small teams who work on projects and presentations with their TAs. Student teams develop a proposal and make a presentation, with regular progress reports and final projects. "These people are all over the world," explained Christie Hayes, the manager of instructional design at Georgia Tech Professional Education. "The faculty does a really great job of helping the students manage themselves" (Bailey et al. 2021).

Figure 9.6 Georgia Tech studio

In a Georgia Tech class on the policy implications of cybersecurity, student teams work on projects based on current legislation on technology. Students analyze legislative bills to determine whether they should be amended. They build models to predict the impact of changes to existing law. These complex projects keep students engaged and ensure a high degree of peer-to-peer learning. "It's designed interaction," says Georgia Tech's Nelson Baker (2021). "That's the key to a team-based approach."

This course model does not fit all subjects. "But where it does work, I think we should do so if it democratizes education and makes it available to more people," Baker (2021) said. The trick is to find the right mix of high-quality content for large-scale learning and also create opportunities for small group interaction. "We all know that the textbook, or any kind of curricular asset, is not the total education," Baker said. "There is something about the experience, the social exchange," that makes learning possible.

MOOCs 2.0

In the brave new world of networked learning, traditional MOOCs have been reborn. Originally seen as a replacement for traditional university courses, they are now understood as complements for a dynamic and demanding approach to education. MOOCs can be used as digital textbooks to support and enhance other types of classes and as low-cost, low-stakes "on ramps" for new learners.

Coursera cofounder Daphne Koller (2021) pinpoints the shift to the 2014 decision by the University of Illinois to open a new online program as a low-cost MOOC. In these programs, students could earn "stackable" credits toward an iMBA certificate or even admission to the university's traditional program. "We convinced them to put the majority of content online as open content via Coursera," Koller said. The credits for subunits of a class could add up to a digital marketing certificate—and, over time, be used toward getting a degree. These stackable credits enable working adults to accumulate credits on their own schedule. "We recognized that stackability is really important for online learners," said Betty Vandenbosch (2021), Coursera's chief content officer.

At the same time, edX and their partners were also developing the stackable credit concept for MOOCs. In 2015, ASU joined forces with edX and announced the gateway concept with Global Freshman Academy. Students could take classes online at a fraction of the cost of traditional courses. Students were required to pay tuition only when they completed their edX courses. "We are open to everyone," the program's welcoming video declared. "There is no application, no transcript, or GPA required.... We have created a learning experience designed to help you ... kick-start your university dreams and get some credit under your belt" (https://vimeo .com/125598584).

The program evolved. In a partnership with Starbucks in 2014, employees could earn credit and eventually earn admission to ASU (Robbins 2014). Students whose GPA and scores once doomed their college chances could now make up for lost ground and get into ASU. The program helped to break down barriers to entry (figure 9.7). ASU ended the distinction between its traditional and online courses. "We are here for one reason, and for one reason only," ASU President Michael Crow (n.d.) said. "That is to

Figure 9.7 Arizona State University and Starbucks partnership

provide access to . . . opportunity at a world-class, discovery-oriented university."

Crow declared elimination of the school's elitist hierarchy. "We don't have a separate faculty doing online," he said. "We have our faculty working on all this." Online learners can earn the same diploma as traditional students. "It's not an ASU Online diploma—it's the ASU diploma. We put our name behind what we are offering and behind your learning experience."

Repositioning MOOCs with credits as a complement to on campus learning helped to revive the online experiment. In 2015, edX and MIT launched their "MicroMasters" concept, which applied the "stackable on ramp" idea of the ASU/edX Global Freshman Academy to a wide variety of master's programs. "We had credit for MOOCs," explained Anant Agarwal (2021), founder and CEO of edX. "It was natural to combine them. And so MicroMasters became a sequence of courses—a program—at the graduate level with a pathway to credit at the end."

In discussions with leaders of graduate programs at NYU, MIT, and the University of Michigan, edX negotiated for students to earn credits before enrolling in the universities' standard programs. "Leading Educational Innovation and Improvement," Michigan's MicroMasters program, is a sequence of five courses over ten months, with a time commitment of two to four hours a week, and a tuition of about $200 per unit (University of Michigan and edX). Graduates receive a MicroMasters Certificate, with twelve credit hours toward a fully online Master's degree at the university's School of Education. In January 2022, 27,370 students enrolled for the first course in the program.

But there is more. Michigan and Rice University now use MOOCs to help traditional on campus students catch up with coursework over the summer so they can earn enough credits to graduate on time (Young 2018). The new MOOC model allows students to use the basic features of a product at no cost, but it charges for advanced features. Free (or audit) versions of classes expand the pool of possible paying customers down the road. edX has added new features to ease the transition from an online MOOC to a course that blends

Zoom meetings with face-to-face sessions with local instructors. "When we launched completely self-paced courses, there was a question of learner engagement," said edX's Agarwal (2021). "So, we have been playing around with this and working on balancing the best of both worlds." By clicking a button in its edX authoring platform, an instructor can change the basic structure of a course from self-paced to instructor-paced.

The website Class Central notes that seventy MOOC-based degree programs are now available, generally at a discount to the cost of the equivalent online degree. Students can participate for free in more than six hundred individual for-credit courses on MOOC platforms. "It is significant that the general public can audit the same courses that paying students are taking for credit," explained Class Central's Dhawal Shah (2021).

NATIONAL MOOC NETWORKS

MOOCs also play a leading role in national and international learning networks. In Israel and India, national learning networks leverage the power of MOOCs to create new sorts of networks—not just between students but between universities. Israel invested $100 million to create IsraelX and Campus-IL in 2018. The government's goal was to create an integrated national educational and training system across all Israeli universities and government agencies. Using the open edX software platform, Israel offers free access throughout the world. "The idea was . . . to democratize education," said Eran Raviv (2021), director of Campus-IL. "Give every person in Israel, who speaks Hebrew or Arabic, free access to education. It's not only higher education. It's also vocational training, general knowledge, professional development."

The project began with requests for proposals to create online courses. As in the United States, some campuses created their own in-house digital education teams, serving as de-facto OPMs for their faculty and partner universities. Course creation costs an average of $100,000. Tel Aviv University created an in-house OPM with

Figure 9.8 Israeli MOOC platform

studios and grants to faculty to develop an innovative pedagogy (Raviv 2021). By 2018, the national platform launched with more than seventy online courses. Israel uses MOOCs to open its network of learners to all its populations (figure 9.8). The Campus-IL version of edX offers instruction in English, Hebrew, and Arabic. In 2021, a course offered on the Campus-IL website by the Al-Qasemi Academic College of Education, located in the Arabic-speaking village of Baqa al-Gharbiyye, was nominated as one of the best digital courses in the world by edX (Dattel 2021).

Campus-IL also took steps toward resolving the issue of credits, which had stalled many national MOOC efforts in other countries. It was resolved that any Israeli university receiving funds from the central Israeli national MOOC agency must offer free university credit at their institution for students completing the MOOCs they create. "All academic courses on Campus-IL give academic credit for the students that are enrolled at the institution that developed the course," explained Raviv (2021). "We have several institutions that offer this credit for outside learners as well." This was a hard-fought concession because most universities around the world maintain tight control over the total number of learners enrolled and credits granted. Universities generally get grants from the government according to the number of students enrolled—which creates competition among universities who do not want to "lose students" to free online MOOC programs and lower their government subsidies. "That is probably why you don't see too many sharing credits," Raviv said, before the government regulations addressed the problem.

Campus-IL has also created a uniform system for civil servants to automatically earn raises for gaining new skills through MOOC programs (Raviv 2021). Such real-world recognition and rewards—college credits and, better yet, raises—are exactly the sorts of incentives that most experts feel are needed to motivate adult learners. It may be that some of Israel's biggest contributions to the digital education movement are to be found in these important management innovations. They hold interesting lessons for other nation's that want to use digital tools to improve adult learning and education.

Another country that has moved aggressively to make MOOCs part of their national learning strategy is India. With a population of 1.37 billion, India is almost 150 times more populous than Israel—and is an even more complex setting for a national education initiative. In addition to using Hindi and English regularly in national affairs, India recognizes twenty-one other regional languages as official. Along with large cultural variations, India faces extreme inequality—the South Asian nation has the world's largest population of the extremely poor and at the same time a rapidly growing middle class and many of the world's super-rich.

India has used MOOCs and digital education to manage these cultural and linguistic differences. In 2017, India launched SWAYAM (Sanskrit for self) as part of the nationwide Digital India initiative of Prime Minister Narendra Modi. The name is an acronym that stands for "Study Webs of Active-Learning for Young Aspiring Minds," explained Professor Anil D. Sahasrabudhe (2021), chairman of the Indian government agency that oversees SWAYAM.

Technology has long been a growth sector for India, with the country hosting huge back-office operations for global IT and financial services firms including IBM, American Express, and India's Aditya Birla Infotech, Tata Consulting Services, and Wipro in Bengaluru, Hyderabad, and Chennai (Friedman 2005; Columbia SIPA 2018).

SWAYAM aimed to extend India's "digital dividend" to education. Built on legacy universities established under British rule, India's public engineering schools are considered some of the best in the world. In 2021, more than 140,000 people across India sat for the dreaded JEE Advanced exam, which grants admission to some of the top engineering colleges in the country. Only 41,862 gained entry, a success rate of less than 30 percent (Indian Express 2021).

With the SWAYAM initiative, India created a national system to finance MOOCs, offering $16,000 to create each course. As in Israel, the powerhouse schools emerged as leaders in content creation. The Indian Institutes of Technology led the way, with courses that featured "rock star" professors.

The SWAYAM project has expanded its network of universities to engage the private sector (figure 9.9). An online portal offers internships for aspiring engineers, data scientists, and marketing students, among others. The universities connect student learners with work-ing engineers and government officials. By 2021, 670,000 students had registered on the portal, seeking a chance for 115,000 internships. "This is also active learning," Sahasrabudhe (2021) explained. "Students will do hands-on work which is actually done in an industry."

All content, licensed under the Creative Commons license, is available for download in all major Indian languages. First-generation students often "cannot afford to pay a high fee for university education," Sahasrabudhe (2021) noted. SWAYAM can level this playing

Figure 9.9 SWAYAM Indian MOOC platform

field. India also distributes MOOCs for use as digital textbooks in regional universities. University courses use the lectures and digital assets from leading Indian Institutes of Technology (IIT) programs to "flip" their own classrooms. To boost participation, SWAYAM provides compensation for professors who create digital assets. "If you teach only in your institution, you reach up to 100 students per class," Sahasrabudhe explained. "But if your quality education can be imparted to 100,000 students, you will feel happier." In 2019, Class Central ranked six SWAYAM courses as part of its global "best courses" list. As in Israel, the national MOOCs are required to grant credit; also as in Israel, local universities have fought against this requirement.

The success of national programs in Israel and India hold many lessons for the United States and other countries struggling to expand adult learning and leverage the power of digital tools to improve education. Many of the innovations that have made the Israeli and Indian programs successful are management innovations. As government run agencies, Campus-IL and SWAYAM are able to use their regulatory and budgeting power to overcome built-in resistance at certain public universities to innovations that expand access. By addressing head-on the concerns of local universities and offering solutions, both agencies opened the doors of learning to an expanded number of students who otherwise would not have had this opportunity.

NGOs AND NETWORKED LEARNING

The other big player in the area of networked learning are the many nongovernmental organizations (NGOs) who help organizations and governments around the world with a wide variety of issues. Groups involved in development issues such as health care, agriculture, education, and environmental protection are almost by definition involved in educational projects that need to be scaled. Digital tools and online or blended classes are often the best way to deliver the training and support that make up much of their work.

Typical of this trend is the United Nations Development Programme (UNDP), the UN's arm for international development operations. With an annual budget of $6,737.92 million, a staff of more than 19,000, and 170 local country offices, it is de facto one of the world's largest international learning organizations. For project manager Jamison Ervin (2021), the move to online education was an obvious decision. "I was managing a project with forty-seven countries . . . and we did fourteen to sixteen in-person trainings a year," explained Ervin. "At a certain point in the second year I said 'This is absolute insanity! Why don't we create something online?'" UNDP's Learning for Nature program now includes more than thirty MOOC-like courses, which it runs on its own MOOC-style platform built to enhance peer-to-peer engagement (figure 9.10). "Within two and half years, we already have 36,000 learners," said Ervin. "We discovered there's just this untapped need for people to access free courses."

The UNDP decided to create its own platform for a variety of reasons. "We wanted a UNDP brand, and this provides a level of trust with learners that this has been vetted by the UN," said Ervin (2021). Ervin also learned that its audience of learners wanted to be able to "engage with the content at their own pace" and come back to previous courses they had taken. They also wanted to "interact and connect with others" working in the same topic area.

Figure 9.10 UNDP's Learning for Nature course portal

Figure 9.11 Acumen Learning Academy for social entrepreneurs

The UNDP team designed special tools to support these peer-to-peer interactions. "We have more than 15,000 peer-to-peer interactions" on the platform, Ervin explained. The platform also borrows ideas from other "network course" models, including the ability to download content and use it to create new local classes. "We host private courses where people can create their own learning groups . . . and connect and learn in a semiprivate environment."

To train specialists often dispersed across geographies, online learning has been a godsend. One example is Acumen, a nonprofit that invests in enterprises with positive social and environmental impacts (figure 9.11). The venture-capital fund has created a learning portal that offers more than twenty-five free online courses on business, finance, and hiring for social enterprises.

Other NGOs have focused on using digital tools and online courses such as MOOCs to bring education to places where traditional schools and universities cannot operate. These include the Germany-based NGO Kiron Open Higher Education, an NGO that operates MOOC-based learning centers in refugee camps in Lebanon and Jordan. OSUN also supports local learning centers for refugees in Kenya, Jordan, and Bangladesh, providing the key local

Figure 9.12 OSUN Hub in Kenya

support needed to access and use online content. These are called OSUN Hubs for Connected Learning Initiatives, and they leverage existing online and OSUN courses and make them available to refugee learners (figure 9.12).

While these NGOs use digital tools to deliver specific classes to specific groups of learners, the World Bank focuses on helping nations integrate digital education into national learning systems. With more than 10,000 employees, operations in 190 countries, and an annual budget of $84.3 billion, the World Bank is both involved in direct investments in local country infrastructure and in training local country teams. Digital education has become central to its mission. It creates and offers a wide range of free classes on its platform, Open Learning Campus, including technical courses on finance, health care management, and telecommunications (figure 9.13).

The bank both creates its own content—generally designed for training local country technical teams—and supports countrywide investments in digital education. Michael Trucano (2021),

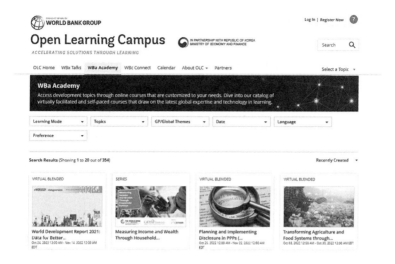

Figure 9.13 World Bank Group's Open Learning Campus

a senior education and technology specialist at the World Bank, said that the bank saw the importance of digital education early in its development. "The first initiatives happened in the late nineties," Trucano said. "There was a big effort called the global distance learning network that provided distance learning infra-structure. . . . The bank was maybe ahead of the curve" in moving in this area.

It soon became clear that any local digital learning efforts needed a great deal of training and support rather than just technology. "Buying a lot of stuff and thinking good things are going to happen because of it, that's the classic sort of magical thinking we've seen repeated over and over again to negligible or negative effects," explained Trucano (2021). Digital tools may play a key role in helping countries improve education, but it will always require dedicated and well-trained local teachers. Trucano rebuts the fear that technology might one day replace teachers: "We see no place in the world where this is . . . likely to happen," he said. Technology will change "the role of teachers and some of what they do . . . over time, teachers who know how to use technology will replace those who do not."

The creation of high-quality content is, for Trucano (2021), just one part of the digital education equation. The other part, and perhaps the most important part, is delivery. Face-to-face learning "gets much less attention and investment than the creation of the content itself," Trucano said, an imbalance that must be corrected. Teachers provide "the connective tissue, the enabling environment around the use of these materials." The bottom line is not the technology or even the course content. "We care about what kids learn," Trucano explained.

Jamie Merisotis (2021), the CEO of Lumina Foundation, agrees that investment in the human side of the digital education equation is key. "Humans learn best in peer-to-peer learning contexts and with guides, with facilitators, with teachers," said Merisotis. The content and tools developed by the giant digital public universities could help to expand access to education but require human support in delivery. "The unbundling and modularization of learning is going to continue," Merisotis said, but it requires pairings with traditional face-to-face education and online training and support. Innovators such as Arizona State University and Southern New Hampshire University succeed because they offer a mix of learning modes. "They are doing wholly online, they're doing hybrid, and they are doing in person," Merisotis said. "They are taking advantage of the human elements . . . and the digital elements to deliver the best quality learning."

For the World Bank's Trucano (2021), the challenge is to find ways to bring equity to local support and delivery. "The delivery of [digital] content scales pretty clearly," but that's not always the case with teaching. Educators must avoid a two-tier system in which the poor get "technology and education" and the affluent get "technology plus people," said Trucano. The need to find the correct balance between investments in creating compelling content and the training and support of excellent local delivery will drive debates on digital learning and public investments in education for years to come.

NETWORKED LEARNING LESSONS

Social Learning Is Key

Professors can offer their lessons and insights live or in recorded lectures. Teaching assistants can play key roles. However they get their lessons delivered, students learn best by working with their peers. Building and planning for these interactions is the key to success.

Networks Provide New Forms of Learning

Technology and networks can expand access, allowing new voices and connections. Networked courses offer opportunities for developing relationships with people from a wide range of different experiences and backgrounds who share their passions and interests.

Make Classes Modular and Customizable

The combination of good learning assets (books, videos, and digital case studies) with passionate and engaged small cohort teaching (on Zoom or in person) is powerful. The key is to design classes to be customized and delivered in different ways.

Support and Celebrate Local Teaching

The best programs invest in the people running course sections and working directly with students. To succeed, faculty need the discretion to customize their classes to the needs of their local student population. No one knows better what works for students than the people who interact with them directly.

Build Lifelong Communities of Practice

Besides learning material on the course syllabus, students also benefit by connecting with people with similar interests. To make learning and development a lifetime process, online courses should keep course websites open, allowing students to access materials and maintain connections with the other learners they have met.

Connect and Celebrate as a Network

It's exciting and empowering to be part of something big. Even if the best discussions and interactions occur in smaller groups, people can expand their imaginations and resources by connecting with cohorts around the world. Short, well-produced group presentations, festivals, and business and idea pitch meetings are great ways to connect with a larger community and purpose.

REFERENCES

Agarwal, Anant. 2021. Interview of CEO, edX, by Adam Stepan. October 19, 2021.

Bailey, John, Troy Courville, Christie Hayes, and Theo McNair. 2021. Demo of Georgia Tech platform presented to Adam Stepan. November 16, 2021.

Baker, Nelson. 2021. Interview of Dean of Professional Education and Professor of Civil and Environmental Engineering, Georgia Tech, by Adam Stepan. October 27, 2021.

Becker, Jonathan. 2021. Interview of Executive Vice President and Vice President for Academic Affairs, Bard College, by Adam Stepan. October 22, 2021.

Columbia SIPA. 2018. *21st Century Digital India*. https://vimeo.com/265236248.

Crow, Michael. n.d. Video for Starbucks ASU Program. accessed February 12, 2022. https://vimeo.com/124063064.

Dattel, Lior. 2021. "It Is One of the Best Open Online Courses. All It Does Is Teach You How to Think." *Haaretz*, November 7, 2021. https://www .haaretz.com/us-news/.premium.HIGHLIGHT.MAGAZINE-small-arab -israeli-college-develops-one-of-2021-s-best-online-courses-1.10347472.

Ervin, Jamison. 2021. Interview of Manager of the Nature for Development Global program, UNDP, by Adam Stepan. November 4, 2021.

Fedchin, Philip. 2022. Interview of Technology Strategist, Bard College Berlin, by Adam Stepan. June 17, 2022.

Filreis, Al. 2022. Interview of Kelly Professor of English, Faculty Director of the Kelly Writers House, and Director of the Center for Programs in Contemporary Writing, University of Pennsylvania, by Adam Stepan. March 1, 2022.

Fox, Armando. 2017. "2. Can MOOCs and SPOCs Help Scale Residential Education While Maintaining High Quality?" In *MOOCs and Their Afterlives: Experiments in Scale and Access in Higher Education*, ed. Elizabeth Losh, 37–50. Chicago: University of Chicago Press. https://doi.org/10.7208/9780226469591-004.

——. 2021. Interview of Associate Dean for Online Education, University of California Berkeley, by Adam Stepan. October 19, 2021.

Friedman, Thomas. 2005. *The World Is Flat: A Brief History of the Twenty-First Century*. New York: Farrar, Straus and Giroux.

Huntemann, Nina. 2021. Interview of Vice President of Learning, edX, by Adam Stepan. October 18, 2021.

Indian Express. 2021. "Over 29% Candidates Clear JEE Advanced 2021." *The Indian Express*, October 17, 2021. https://indianexpress.com/article/education /over-29-candidates-clear-jee-advanced-7574118/.

Kaufman, Erica. 2022. Interview of Director of the Institute for Writing and Thinking, Bard College, by Adam Stepan. February 1, 2022.

Koller, Daphne. 2021. Interview of founder of Coursera/founder and CEO at insitro, by Adam Stepan. October 19, 2021.

Merisotis, Jamie. 2021. Interview of CEO, Lumina Foundation, by Adam Stepan. October 21, 2021.

Raviv, Eran. 2021. Interview of Director, Campus-IL, Israel, by Adam Stepan. November 4, 2021.

Robbins, Lisa. 2014. "Starbucks, ASU Team Up for Employee Education Program." *ASU News*, June 15, 2014. https://news.asu.edu/content/starbucks-asu-team-employee-education-program.

Sahasrabudhe, Anil D. 2021. Interview of Chairman, Buddha Chandrasekhar and Abhishek Kumar, SWAYAM, by Adam Stepan. November 16, 2021.

Shah, Dhawal. 2021. Interview of founder and CEO, Class Central, by Adam Stepan. October 22, 2021.

Shein, David. 2022. Interview of Associate Vice President for Academic Affairs and Dean of Studies, Bard College, by Adam Stepan. June 17, 2022.

Trucano, Michael. 2021. Interview of Senior Education and Technology Policy Specialist, World Bank, by Adam Stepan. October 26, 2021.

University of Michigan and edX. n.d. "Leading Educational Innovation and Improvement MicroMasters® Program." edX. accessed February 12, 2022. https://www.edx.org/micromasters/michiganx-leading-educational-innovation-and-improvement.

Vandenbosch, Betty. 2021. Interview of Chief Content Officer, Coursera, by Adam Stepan. October 22, 2021.

Young, Jeffrey R. 2018. "MOOCs Find a New Audience with On-Campus Students." *EdSurge*, September 27, 2018. https://www.edsurge.com/news/2018-09-27-moocs-find-a-new-audience-with-on-campus-students.

10

THE FUTURE

We began writing this book during a global pandemic that upended traditional teaching and learning. As our book moves to print, we face potential radical change in higher education as AI-driven tools such as ChatGPT and Google's Bard platform present opportunities and threats to our goal of leveling the learning curve. Predicting the future is always difficult, but if we are to lead our educational institutions to deliver better and better learning outcomes for more and more students, predict and plan we must.

This book is about managing technology and people for the good of our students. While specific technology will change and evolve, certain core management issues will remain consistent, and certain trends in technology and innovation seem clear. So we end this book with some of the collective wisdom from the leaders of leveling the learning curve movement and opportunities the coming years may bring.

THE HISTORY OF ED TECH PREDICTIONS

In 2013, Harvard Business School's Clayton Christensen predicted that a quarter of all colleges and universities would disappear in a decade. That has not happened. But with the COVID-19 pandemic, change has accelerated, and an even more powerful process now appears to be underway. Despite the tragic impact of the pandemic, we believe it has triggered an important turning point in the use of digital tools in higher education.

During the pandemic, traditional barriers between online and on campus programs were blurred, perhaps permanently. "It's pretty clear now that this line between residential and online education has completely broken down," Joshua Kim (2021) of Dartmouth observed. "Every class and every program is now a blended program. And we have to accept that. I think it's a good thing. I think that's setting a new standard for all of us." Eric Bullard (2021), UCLA's dean of continuing education, believes "there is no turning back. I think that students and even young faculty . . . expect and demand that we offer hybrid and online courses as we move further into the twenty-first century."

Students now demand greater flexibility in how courses are offered. "Convenience and flexibility are the things that students really love," explained Nina Huntemann (2021) of edX. "Frankly, I don't think that students are going to tolerate that they are going to have to sit their butt in a seat for a particular length of time on a certain day and be lectured at."

Rovy Branon (2021) of the University of Washington points to the petition signed by thousands of students at his campus in September 2021 demanding that all lectures be recorded: "I see us trending toward more choices and options rather than fewer choices and options." Branon also noted that faculty have seen the benefits of including some asynchronous and online components in coursework. Anant Agarwal (2021) of edX agrees: "Any number of survey results are showing that over two-thirds of students on campus want more online teaching." The future will forever blend in-person and online learning. "It's never going back to zero," said Agarwal. "The future is blended, even on campuses." Curtin University in Australia now follows a digital-first strategy, and Rice University has a dual-delivery approach, offering lessons in multiple modalities.

The first-year undergraduate class in the fall of 2022 had almost three years of some form of online learning already, said Paul Krause

(2021) of eCornell; for them, online learning is the new normal. But there's a hitch. Pandemic teaching has "opened eyes [to] the possibilities" of different learning strategies, said Nora Lewis (2021) of UPenn, but most students and faculty have not experienced well-designed, well-executed online courses. University leaders need to show just how powerful online learning can be. "We have to get as many faculty experiencing what truly good online learning is so they can see the differences," explained Kim (2021). University administrators need to show faculty the difference: "This is what you did during the pandemic. This is what we are doing now. Here's how it's different."

The pandemic did not necessarily train most faculty in good online techniques, Matthew Rascoff (2021) of Stanford noted, but it did at least make them more educated consumers of educational technologies. "I see the pandemic as a mass experience of professional development," Rascoff said. Faculty now have greater confidence and can understand and compare different tools, such as the Engageli conference platform or Minvera's Forum. "There are more instructors today [who could] see what is special about it, [a tool like Minerva's Forum], because they have experience with Zoom," Rascoff explained.

Is digital learning here to stay in the postpandemic world? One early indicator suggests that it is. As Israel returned to normalcy, leading the world in vaccinations in 2020 and 2021, enrollment in digital classes on its national MOOC platform continued to remain 30 percent above pre-COVID norms. "The results are amazing," explained Eran Raviv (2021) of Israel's Campus-IL: "Students demand digital learning."

RETHINKING UNIVERSITY MANAGEMENT

Finding our path in this new world will take leadership. Universities need to find new ways to recognize and reward faculty for their digital contributions—not only through financial incentives but also with credit in promotion processes. The University of California Berkeley added the use of digital assets created by faculty to its evaluations for promotions. For this group, the tenure review is based on how well instructors "improve teaching and show that they have had an impact in doing that," noted Armando Fox (2021). James DeVaney (2021) of Michigan is also pushing to make digital scholarship central to all faculty promotions and evaluations. When it happens, he explained, it will be a "major inflection point."

Recognition needs to extend past the "instructors of record" and also include the academic staff who help instructors redesign and deliver their courses. Kim calls such staff members "AltAcs"—alternative academics—who focus on helping other teachers create and deliver digital classes (Kim and Maloney 2020). "We should be creating roles for them," Kim (2021) declared. "They should have equal opportunities for promotion and tenure and status as research faculty."

The University of Washington created new titles including "assistant teaching professor," "associate teaching professor," and "full teaching professor." Washington's Rovy Branon (2021) sees this as an important first step toward acknowledging the work of these professors. "The idea that a small percentage of tenured faculty are sort of ruling over the majority of the teaching workforce," explained Branon, "has become unsustainable."

Indian universities have made digital education training workshops mandatory for all university professors wanting to advance their careers. "We have a massive faculty development program going on," explained Anil Sahasrabudhe (2021), director of SWAYAM, India's national MOOC platform. SWAYAM offers a series of two-day online courses in digital education fundamentals. "They have to pass this course, only then do we give them the certificate," said Sahasrabudhe. "This is mandatory for their promotions, from an assistant to associate to full professor." More than 150,000 Indian faculty received training in 2021; the goal for 2022 is 200,000.

Also ripe for change is the traditional university schedule. As more and more courses are broken down into smaller units of knowledge, universities are moving to modular course delivery, mixing and matching discrete pieces to earn credit. The more flexible the course offerings, the greater the opportunity for adult learners.

"Why is a university course one semester long?" asked Berkeley's Armando Fox (2021). "If you trace the answer back far enough in history, it's because Cambridge did it that way." But this system, which conforms to the seasonal cycles of crop planting and harvesting, makes little sense for most modern learners. "Most U.S. learners are in fact not traditional four-year residential college students at this point," Fox noted. "Fifteen weeks is not a unit of time that makes any sense whatsoever for them."

Digital-first programs have experimented with alternative schedules. UPenn now offers six-week courses for its digital bachelor of applied science program (Lewis 2021). Arizona State University offers seven-week classes in its digital immersion track (Jhaj 2021). With a greater focus on active learning and project-based assignments, many programs have breaks for fieldwork and other projects. For Minerva, the all-online college, the challenge is to create the best sequence for learning activities, alternating intense online interaction with small-group learning and activities. "The key here is the design," said Sharan Singh (2021). "The key is making sure that things are spaced out appropriately, making sure that they're doing a lot of experiential learning on the ground together to build other work online."

Most universities may not abandon the traditional semester system, but more and more will offer shorter modular learning options. Digital short courses will match up with project-based experiential learning opportunities. Students will be able to mix and match stackable digital assets and sequence them with intense traditional and online coursework.

REFORMING TUITION

From 2002 to 2022, tuition in the United States rose from $17,938 to $43,775 at private universities, and rose from $3,738 to $11,631 at public universities (Boyington, Kerr, and Wood 2021).

"How much is instruction alone?" Ubell (2021) asks, and "How much is the 'other stuff' "?

Early student demands for lower tuition for Zoom courses led to little reform. In the fall of 2020, at least 3.6 percent of undergraduate students took "gap years" or deferred starting college (Rodriguez 2021). Most students decided to stay in school and continue their studies, paying full tuition even though courses were fully remote with no access to campus housing and activities. But the genie is out of the bottle for the design of courses. Minerva and others have raised the bar, offering high-quality learning at bargain rates by unbundling services such as housing and campus activities. Students can pay for these benefits as needed.

More students want to access courses remotely but come to campus for events, projects, networking, and socializing. The new mix of in-person and remote learning will shape the physical campus in other ways too. Classrooms must be modernized to capture live class meetings with cameras, monitors, and video systems. Classrooms also must accommodate active learning activities. "Don't build lecture halls, build labs, right?" said Nina Huntemann (2021) of edX. "Don't build auditoriums where people are all facing forward. Build tables with circle chairs."

NEW PLATFORMS FOR LIVE ONLINE AND SHARING CONTENT

Universities can also expect to see new and improved platforms for live class meetings. Online platforms for live seminar-like discussions will play a growing role in the foreseeable future as those platforms evolve and design programs for a wide range of educational and business purposes.

Zoom was designed for business meetings. It did an adequate job keeping schools running during the pandemic, but much more is possible. Already, Minerva's Forum and Engageli offer experiences similar to Zoom but with more support for active learning. Stanford's Rascoff (2021) said: "This, to me, is the frontier." The new

"Class" platform uses Zoom's development kit to create features that turn Zoom into a complete online class solution. With many of the enhanced features of Engageli and Forum, Class allows for the seamless flow in and out of breakout rooms, improved polling, management of speakers, and other functions (Young 2021).

Universities can also expect to see new tools that will support more and more active peer-to-peer sharing, enabling students to create content for other students. "Can we allow students to contribute, create a sort of peer and instructor-vetted system so that courses organically get enriched by the contributions of the students themselves?" asked Frederick T. Wehrle at UC Berkeley (2022).

Easier ways to find good new digital content is one of the greatest demands by teachers and learners everywhere. MIT's OpenCourseWare and other websites are dedicated to sharing open educational resources. But most digital educational content is trapped in the original course learning management system. MOOC platforms edX and Coursera offer courses, and many of them can be audited at no cost. But these videos or digital assets generally cannot be downloaded or shared outside of a specific class on their platform. Canvas allows sharing of assets on Canvas Commons, but few groups use this feature because each school's IT department must enable it. Most don't, citing security concerns. Videos on YouTube, tagged with the Creative Commons license, can be used by others with attribution, but YouTube does not yet offer sophisticated search tools for educational content.

Educators are hungry for better access to free content. Gary Matkin (2021) of the University of California Irvine, whose group both uses and sells digital content, states that poor uploading, cataloging, and searching on YouTube and other sites force many educators to produce lessons that might already be available. "People are not going to spend a lot of time looking for very granular modules unless they really have a line to it," Matkin said. "It seems like a logical thing to do. If there's something great out there and it's free and I can drop it in my course, why don't I use it? But finding it at the exact time you are designing a course is difficult."

Panopto offers video storing and searching, but CEO Eric Burns (2021) acknowledges the need for improvements in both technology and usability. "You're an instructor and you're going to teach a class this semester," Burns explains, so "you should be able to draw on the previous lectures from the same class from a previous semester." Burns hopes to create a searchable library that makes course materials accessible with a simple Google-style search across platforms.

"When I started my career in digital learning in the nineties, we were talking a lot about learning objects and trying to have these shareable assets," recalled Joshua Kim (2021), but this vision was never realized. "We might now be in a place where it is possible," Kim said. "We are creating enough of this. We know much more from learning science about chunking, tagging, and resorting" to pull it off.

MOOCs could lead the way. "edX's or Coursera's library of MOOCs are essentially a huge digital asset library of material on a wide range of subjects," said edX's Nina Huntemann (2021). "What Coursera and edX did was to create digital textbooks. They're asynchronous digital materials that a student can, like a book, pick up and read on their own. What an awesome opportunity to pull pieces out, remix and integrate!"

Daphne Koller (2021), the founder of Coursera, recalled that this idea was one of the early pitches of the MOOC platforms. "We tried to convince universities that it would not be an inferior experience if they were to rely on someone else's digital content, and teach around it." Koller pointed out that "it's not demeaning to use someone else's textbook, even if they don't come from your institution."

That was a hard sell in the early days of MOOCs, but people now seem to be more open to these concepts.

The key for Koller would be to focus new content creation on well-produced shorter modules, designed to work with other materials. "Micro packets of content—a lecture or a few lectures, is really valuable," Koller (2021) explained. The key is to create multiple-platform systems. "One needs to greatly increase the searchability of content and the ability of an instructor to find stuff that works with their curriculum."

For Mark Lester (2023), former Managing Director at UK-based MOOC provider Future Learn, the present moment is perhaps the time for MOOCs to be reimagined and to finally realize their original purpose. "The MOOC movement saw hundreds of universities come together in a learning revolution to help educate humanity. Sadly, it succumbed to commercial interest" explained Lester. "The challenge for the future is to move beyond past orthodoxies that see universities competing on exclusion and content ownership, and instead collaborating on shared platforms to sustain the betterment of humanity."

The obstacles are not technical but institutional. With the leadership of key institutions and players, the dream of wider sharing of digital content can be realized. Paul Krause (2021) of eCornell also sees a future of expanded sharing of assets and the emergence of a universal sharing platform. "I think there will be lots of creativity about how assets are used, both within a department, within a school, within a university, and then across universities."

SIMULATIONS, LABS, AND THE COMING VR REVOLUTION

Another area of clear growth is in digital labs and virtual reality (VR) simulations. Live science labs are expensive, so digital versions would pay for themselves quickly. With online labs, students get a front-row seat to experiments. The savings in damaged equipment can defray the cost of developing online assets. Before introducing digital video labs, Purdue was "breaking $40,000 a year in pipettes," a common lab instrument. With the digital lab, the cost of equipment damage is down to $4,000, explained Purdue's Frank Dooley (2021).

Arizona State, Michigan, Purdue, and other universities are experimenting with new virtual reality labs and simulations. These settings offer 360-degree immersion into worlds once impossible to explore, such as the inside of a human body, the vastness of the solar system, or the lost world of prehistoric species. ASU is investing in Dream-scape, an immersive VR company connected to the university, to create immersive student experiences using 3D headgear. "This can take the form of a virtual field trip, a mission to space, or a deep dive into the human body," said ASU president Michael Crow (2021). Students soon will have access to VR learning experiences that use the experiences of past participants to adapt to student responses and needs. Using advanced computational technology, innovative course developers can build classes around the ever-changing needs and responses of the learner, explained Crow. "These adaptive, open-scale courses allow students to learn at their own speed with the help of computer-based, intelligent tutors."

In the not-too-distant future, students will be able to ask questions of Nobel-caliber experts. Filmed and adapted with artificial-intelligence-powered holography, the experts could be available 24/7 to answer an endless range of questions. "Students could not only hear a lecture recorded ten years ago but actually interact with that professor in a way that they could never do in physical reality," said Luyen Chou (2021) of 2U. "And it doesn't require the professor to actually be there. It's scripted, recorded, and stitched together with AI."

India's SWAYAM initiative has also invested heavily in AI-driven "adaptive learning" solutions. A platform for student evaluation uses AI to match students to content. By understanding the student's level of knowledge, the program can take them on a journey of learning. India provides funding for AI developers to create new experiences, and the developers can sell their products on the SWAYAM-supported platform if they reserve seats for poorer students. "For every four students who buy the product," explained SWAYAM's Anil Sahas-rabudhe (2021), "we are mandated to give one free seat."

THE CHATGPT MOMENT

In November of 2022, ChatGPT, developed by the consortium OpenAI, was released to the public. It dramatically improved AI Chat bot, making it capable of taking written prompts and responding with prose that seem to be written by a human (Grant and Metz 2022). A prompt of "Write a 2500-word examination of the American Civil War's impact on Southern poetry" produces an instant essay, with references and footnotes, that most professors could not distinguish from that done by even their best students.

By December 2022, the full implications for high schools and colleagues were emerging. Initial reaction was fear and panic. If a free tool was available that can allow students to easily complete assignments, what would this mean for teaching and evaluation of students? Some schools blocked access to ChatGPT on their Wi-Fi networks (Roose 2023). Another group launched an app called ZeroGPT, aimed at detecting its use (Grant and Metz 2022). However, even internal efforts by OpenAI to create a tool to detect text created with ChatGPT had success rates of less than 30 percent (*Teaching and ChatGPT Forum* 2023).

Some universities chose to embrace the new tool. They noted that internet search, and Google itself, was initially seen as cheating but soon became an important research and learning tool (Eaton 2022). Perhaps ChatGPT will follow a similar trajectory.

As researchers began to explore the tool, its potential utility became apparent in such fields as law and computer programming. Even for creative writing, a tool to generate suggestions for metaphors and story structure has value (*Teaching and ChatGPT Forum* 2023).

Articles appeared in venues such as the *New York Times*, "Don't Ban ChatGPT in Schools. Teach With It" (Roose 2023). At Columbia University, Victoria Malaney-Brown, Director of Academic Integrity observed, "Artificial intelligence is not going anywhere. In fact, it's only getting better, and we have to work with the technology and not against it" (*Teaching and ChatGPT Forum* 2023).

We believe generative AI programs will play an important role in preparing students for the work place of the future (Roose 2023). Demanding that students ignore these tools is similar to earlier moments when education lagged behind technology change. "When I was in middle and high school in the 1970s and early 1980s, I was told that professional success required good 'penmanship,' and the ability to perform long division by hand," observed UCLA's John Villasenor (2023). "By the time I entered the workforce in the late 1980s, technology advances had rendered these skills obsolete."

One of the most promising frontiers for ChatGPT and similar tools is adaptive learning, used in conjunction with small, bite-sized Open Educational Resources, or OER, such as mini lessons.

As we explored in chapter 8, there is a robust eco-system of high-quality short-form content for K-12 students and teachers. This includes groups such as Khan Academy, Class Central, Ted Talks, and the content provided by sites such as PBS Learning Media and National Geographic. For enterprising high school social studies teachers looking to create an interesting class for their students, a lot of great open and free content is available for placement on their class website.

The biggest barrier to this opportunity is that there is no established platform for finding and sharing this content, nor is there a search engine optimized for this purpose. ChatGPT, Google's Bard, and projects underway at Meta may provide a solution. If ChatGPT and similar platforms become the de facto search platform for finding information, the prompt "Build me an engaging 12-week online class on the history of the American Civil War" may soon be all that it takes to create great experiences for students, especially if the available video lectures and other content was indexed and searchable.

It will then be a short step to something potentially even more powerful—the prompt of "Build me engaging 12-week online class on the history of the Civil War . . . designed to match my level of previous knowledge, and my progress in the course." This could enable adaptive, personalized learning—especially if this search and ordering function can be combined with on-demand mentoring and tutoring, powered by friendly and patient Chatbots. The growth of AI-driven content and learning will challenge long-held ideas about the role of professors and students. For example, is an AI-generated text designed and "curated" by a student his or her original work?

If the future workplace is one where many of the tasks can and will be done by "bots" of various sorts, where should professors and universities look to focus their work and training? What are what Joseph Aoun (2017) calls the "Robot Proof" skills that only humans have, and how can we best refine and cultivate them?

FULFILLING HIGHER EDUCATION'S PUBLIC MISSION

With bots or without them, there is a broad consensus that digital tools already are and will become more central to Universities' public mission. For the University of Michigan's James DeVaney, "Our public values are front and center" in embracing and sharing digital content (2021). "If the University of Michigan, as a great public research university, could deliver a high-quality education at a greater scale without reducing quality, shouldn't we do that?"

UCLA's Eric Bullard (2021) noted that faculty who learned to teach online during the pandemic often want to continue, understanding that digital tools allow them to reach a much wider audience. They realize that teaching in UCLA's new open program enables them to "get their research and scholarship out to audiences that they might not otherwise reach." Offering online courses also reaches learners who otherwise could not attend UCLA. "Many of the individuals that we serve really can't afford to travel to the main campus and participate in in-person classes," explained Bullard. "The flexibility of online and hybrid education is paramount to their success."

UC Berkeley's Frederick T. Wehrle (2022) also sees growth in the number of faculty who want to create digital assets and classes for mission-driven reasons. Wehrle also envisions a future in which the creation of digital classes for mission-driven reasons will offer universities new opportunities for revenue. "If you actually do something good in education that has an impact on people's lives, it will likely work out from the revenue perspective," Wehrle explained.

The mission of Stanford's Digital Education Office is to "reposition digital learning as part of the core of the university, and to link it to the educational mission, the service mission, and also the research mission through partnerships with faculty, students,

alumni, and the community," explained Stanford's new vice provost for digital education, Matthew Rascoff (2021). The office aims
to "connect the digital transformation conversation to the broader
access and equity conversations that are happening across our
education."

The challenge is to reach beyond the Stanford campus. "It's about
remixing and recombining our human and technological capacities
in novel ways," said Rascoff. "Our mission is focused on extending the reach of Stanford and offering educational opportunities to
those who have been underserved." To do this successfully, Rascoff
explained, Stanford needs to collaborate with mission-aligned partners. Especially important is finding partners who "understand the
needs of learners."

The course of the future is "bigger than what we can offer on
campus face-to-face and higher-touch than a MOOC," Rascoff
(2021) said. "There is a largely unexplored middle ground between
the relatively small scale of residential colleges and universities and
the mega-scale of MOOCs." That idea is catching on: eCornell now
offers "embedded" classes in Nigeria and Rwanda, and Columbia
has created similar courses with its Global Center Network and the
Columbia World Projects initiative. In 2019 and 2020, Columbia
partnered with a network of more than twenty NGOs in Africa,
Latin America, and Asia to help them create and deliver their own
online courses, many using cases and assets from Columbia's digital content collections.

New communities of practice connect scholars across the world.
Their collaborations are at the heart of digital education at the
World Bank, the United Nations Development Programme (UNDP),
and the Open Society University Network (OSUN), whose network
collaborative courses are built on the twin ideas of digital sharing
and local focus. As universities expand their work as content creators and consumers, engagement with their larger communities
will evolve.

"It's going to be tough to put the genie back in the bottle," said
Michael Trucano (2021), a senior education and technology specialist at the World Bank, "whether that genie is positive or negative

in all sorts of ways." Universities now need to step up and help steer the course moving forward.

"Big corporations have waded into this with both feet," explained Nora Lewis (2021) of UPenn, noting the initial public offering of Coursera and 2U's $800-million acquisition of edX. "For universities, our challenge is to figure out what's our core mission. What do we do really well? And how should we be playing in this space and representing ourselves?"

Rascoff (2021) echoes these sentiments: "EdTech is at a crossroads—whether it's going to preserve educational values, and amplify them, or bring technological commercialism into education . . . is a real decision, and it's fundamentally a leadership question."

Digital education transforms both learning and research as it becomes a "global learning community that's interdisciplinary, intergenerational, and interprofessional," explained James DeVaney (2021) of Michigan. Nelson Baker (2021) of Georgia Tech adds: "The world in which I operate, the people I talk to, most are very optimistic." Baker believes "this is going to change higher education so that learning is better, more accessible, and reaches more people."

Jamison Ervin (2021), manager of the Nature for Development program at UNDP, sees the answer in simpler tools that enable people to create and share content easily. Ervin envisions a "TikTok for Teachers" that would simplify video creation, especially for those whose voices are often not heard. "There is going to be a revolution in video creation because videos are so powerful," Ervin explained. "You show a few photos you can pull off the web, add some text, and get a video."

For Josh Scott (2021) of 2U, new educational technologies and methods provide the opportunity to make a historic impact. "There are two different models for how you can change the world," Scott said. "You can change the life of one person, or you can do the greatest good for the greatest number of people. I saw the opportunity for us to [make an] impact at scale, and that's what's got me jazzed."

For vice provost Sukhwant Jhaj (2021) of Arizona State University, the pandemic not only increased the rate of change but also revealed dangerous disparities. "This is a moment of rapid innovation," said Jhaj. "Some people are very well positioned to benefit from technology," but others are not. The abilities of students to use these tools varies widely. "Even within a single institution, some students are well-positioned to benefit [but] others need support."

For Jhaj, the pandemic also showed that major change is possible. "Certain inertia, some of it quite negative, that existed in higher ed, it's just blown away," Jhaj said. "It's a very imaginative moment where you can go, 'Oh, that's possible' or 'We must figure that out.'" The pandemic allowed innovation to move "from no to yes rather rapidly on all fronts."

Arizona State University president Michael Crow (2021) embarked on his reinvention of higher education long before the pandemic. Now he has visible support for his mission to make higher education serve both local and global communities and to foster a network of institutions devoted to expanding access to learning. The pandemic "put a spotlight on the gaps between those institutions focused on exclusivity and those committed to broad access and student success," Crow explained. "It reminded us why adherence to a single, outmoded higher education model is problematic, both for the individual and society."

For Jonathan Becker (2021) of OSUN, the new moment offers historic potential. "It gives voice to people from the global majority countries whose voice isn't necessarily heard," Becker said. "It gives an opportunity for students to generate materials and resources that are available and shareable. Getting these insights generated by young people is really empowering—and informative for other students who are observing and witnessing. It's about creating spaces for interactions that provide meaning."

REFERENCES

Agarwal, Anant. 2021. Interview of CEO, edX, by Adam Stepan. October 19, 2021.

Baker, Nelson. 2021. Interview of Dean of Professional Education and Professor of Civil and Environmental Engineering, Georgia Tech, by Adam Stepan. October 27, 2021.

Becker, Jonathan. 2021. Interview of Executive Vice President and Vice President for Academic Affairs, Bard College, by Adam Stepan. October 22, 2021.

Boyington, Briana, Emma Kerr, and Sarah Wood. 2021. "20 Years of Tuition Growth at National Universities." *U.S. News & World Report*, September 17, 2021. //www.usnews.com/education/best-colleges/paying-for-college/articles/2017-09-20/see-20-years-of-tuition-growth-at-national-universities.

Branon, Rovy. 2021. Interview of Vice Provost for Continuum College, University of Washington, by Adam Stepan. November 30, 2021.

Bullard, Eric. 2021. Interview of Dean of Continuing Education and UCLA Extension, UCLA, by Adam Stepan. November 22, 2021.

Burns, Eric. 2021. Interview of Dean of Continuing Education and UCLA Extension, UCLA, by Adam Stepan. October 18, 2021.

Chou, Luyen. 2021. Interview of Chief Learning Officer, 2U, by Adam Stepan. October 27, 2021.

Crow, Michael. 2021. Interview of President, Arizona State University, by Adam Stepan. November 23, 2021.

DeVaney, James. 2021. Interview of Associate Vice Provost for Academic Innovation and Founding Executive Director of the Center for Academic Innovation, University of Michigan, by Adam Stepan. October 29, 2021.

Dooley, Frank. 2021. Interview of Chancellor, Purdue Global, by Adam Stepan. October 25, 2021.

Ervin, Jamison. 2021. Interview of Manager of the Nature for Development Global Program, UNDP, by Adam Stepan. November 4, 2021.

Fox, Armando. 2021. Interview of Associate Dean for Online Education, University of California Berkeley, by Adam Stepan. October 19, 2021.

Huntemann, Nina. 2021. Interview of Vice President of Learning, edX, by Adam Stepan. October 18, 2021.

Jhaj, Sukhwant. 2021. Interview of Vice Provost for Academic Innovation and Student Achievement, ASU, by Adam Stepan. November 1, 2021.

Kim, Joshua. 2021. Interview of Director of Online Programs and Strategy at Dartmouth College, Senior Scholar, Georgetown University, by Adam Stepan. October 21, 2021.

Kim, Joshua, and Edward J. Maloney. 2020. *Learning Innovation and the Future of Higher Education*. Baltimore, MD: JHU Press.

Koller, Daphne. 2021. Interview of founder of Coursera/founder and CEO at insitro, by Adam Stepan. October 19, 2021.

Krause, Paul. 2021. Interview of Vice Provost of External Education, Cornell University, and Executive Director, eCornell, by Adam Stepan. October 22, 2021.

Lester, Mark. 2023. Interview of former Managing Director at Future Learn, by Adam Stepan. February 8, 2023.

Lewis, Nora. 2021. Interview of Vice Dean for Professional and Liberal Education, School of Arts and Sciences, University of Pennsylvania, by Adam Stepan. October 26, 2021.

Matkin, Gary. 2021. Interview of Dean of Continuing Education and Vice Provost for Career Pathways, University of California Irvine, by Adam Stepan. October 19, 2021.

Rascoff, Matthew. 2021. Interview of Vice Provost for Digital Education, Stanford University, by Adam Stepan. October 29, 2021.

Raviv, Eran. 2021. Interview of Director, Campus-IL Israel, by Adam Stepan. November 4, 2021.

Rodriguez, Christian. 2021. "College Interrupted: Many Students Chose to Take Time Off Instead of Remote Learning During the Coronavirus Pandemic." CNBC, June 9, 2021. https://www.cnbc.com/2021/06/09/many-college-students-chose-time-off-over-remote-learning-during-covid.html.

Sahasrabudhe, Anil D. 2021. Interview of Chairman, Buddha Chandrasekhar and Abhishek Kumar, SWAYAM, by Adam Stepan. November 16, 2021.

Scott, Josh. 2021. Interview of Director of Course Strategy, 2U, by Adam Stepan. November 30, 2021.

Singh, Sharan. 2021. Interview of Senior Managing Director of Strategic Partnerships, Minerva Project, by Adam Stepan. November 2, 2021.

Trucano, Michael. 2021. Interview of Senior Education and Technology Policy Specialist, World Bank, by Adam Stepan. October 26, 2021.

Ubell, Robert. 2021. Staying Online: How to Navigate Digital Higher Education. New York: Routledge. https://doi.org/10.4324/9781003036326.

Wehrle, Frederick T. 2022. Interview of Associate Dean, Academic Affairs, UC Berkeley Extension, by Adam Stepan. June 20, 2022.

Young, Jeffrey. 2021. "Startup Class Technologies Bets Big on the Future of Online Learning (and Zoom)." EdSurge, September 24, 2021. https://www.edsurge.com/news/2021-09-24-startup-class-technologies-bets-big-on-the-future-of-online-learning-and-zoom.

11

BETTER WAYS TO TEACH AND LEARN

We believe the COVID-19 pandemic forced those of us in higher education to improve our practice of teaching and learning. Using active learning strategies and better instructional design, we can enhance learning. By leveraging technology, we can make our courses more interesting, effective, accessible, and interactive. To get better, we need to make an active effort to explore pedagogical innovations and the next wave of educational technology and strategy.

There are clear steps we can take as we continue on this journey. Take the time to meet leaders in the scholarship of teaching and learning and the digital education fields. Take an online or digital class. Invite OPMs to demonstrate what they can do. Ask to see actual course websites, educational videos, and digital cases. You might start with our free Blended Learning Toolkit—a MOOC on the platforms of edX and Coursera—which includes many examples of actual courses and activities from the programs cited in this book.

Once our courses are rebuilt with new pedagogies and digital tools, it will be easier for students to learn from their instructor and each other and more rewarding for instructors to teach. These new models also create new revenue streams to reinvest in new programs for learners of all kinds. Creating high-quality digital learning experiences requires time and financial resources. Make this investment to set up your organization to reap long-term benefits.

Both course creation and teaching digitally require support. We need to give teaching assistants greater support and authority. Set high standards, demand quality, and provide financial incentives for work well done. Consider digital asset creation in performance evaluations and promotions. Encourage faculty to create and share short-form digital lectures, and oversee the creation of digital case studies. Celebrate this work in public events and conferences, and make digital case studies available on university websites.

Recruit, train, and hire student employees to be part of the course redesign and digital case study teams. Students can be excellent web designers, video editors, writers, and editors. Pair them with instructors to create compelling digital assets that can be used for years to come. Engage students in co-creating digital assets; in the process, you will create a new generation of digital education leaders.

Digital courses open new avenues for universities to connect with their communities. Digital case studies offer a great way to engage with local and global stakeholders. Create accurate, honest case studies and allow partners to use them in a variety of ways.

The pandemic forced higher education to change many things very quickly. We had a grand experiment in online learning and got many things right. Let's not get back to normal. Let's agree to create an even better educational system for the future.

ACKNOWLEDGMENTS

This book was truly a team effort in more ways than one. It was conceived and written during a global pandemic, when huge strains were put on personal and work lives. It was only possible with the help and dedication of family and colleagues who supported us in these efforts, enabling us to complete this work during this most difficult period.

This book was also a team effort because it is built on the collective work of the many digital education leaders who so kindly shared their insights, workflows, and suggestions. If there are helpful insights in this book, it is largely due to their wisdom and generosity. The shortcomings and errors that may be found here are all our own.

WILLIAM EIMICKE

Thank you most to Adam Stepan and Soulaymane Kachani who taught me so much and worked without pause to make this book happen. I thank all my students who teach me much more than I teach them. Thank you to all my SIPA colleagues who strive to keep me informed about innovations and best practices in teaching and research. Thank you to our Picker family who help make the world of our students better every day. And a special thanks to our SIPA family members who are doing so much to help others every day, particularly New York state Attorney General Tish James, Jersey City Mayor Steven Fulop, and Tom Trebat, Lisa Hines Johnson, Richard Greenwald, Tiffane Wang, and my dear friend Steven Cohen.

SOULAYMANE KACHANI

Many thanks to my amazing coauthors Bill Eimicke and Adam Stepan for this wonderful partnership that started during the early days of the pandemic. I would like to express my sincere thanks to my colleagues, mentors, and friends: Mary Boyce, John Coatsworth, Ira Katznelson, Shih-Fu Chang, Garud Iyengar, Costis Maglaras, Dennis Mitchell, Jay Sethuraman, Georgia Perakis, Sandesh Tuladhar, Merrell Norden, Marina Zamalin, Ann Thornton, Kris Kavanaugh, Carlos Alonso, Sarah Jubinski, Dan Driscoll, Linda Mischel Eisner, Carrie Marlin, Catherine Ross, Amanda Irvin, Adina Brooks, Justin Pearlman, Gerry Rosberg, Anne Sullivan, Julie Kornfeld, Troy Eggers, Melissa Begg, Eugenia Lean, Jeannette Wing, Keren Yarhi-Milo, Amy Hungerford, Gillian Lester, Maneesha Aggarwal, Gaspare LoDuca, Maurice Matiz, Mark Phillipson, Laura Nicholas, Suzanna Klaf, Mark Hawkins, Barry Kane, Sean Wiggins, Steve Blomgren, Helen Lu, Barclay Morrison, Theresa McKenzie, Neil McClure, Jenny Mak, Gabby Gannon, Jeanine D'Armiento, Letty Moss-Salentijn, Greg Freyer, Geraldine McAllister, Tom Matthewson, Jane Booth, Felice Rosan, Donna Fenn, Jess Fenton, Patrice Le Melle, Beryl Abrams, Tian Zheng, Emmanuel Kattan, Caroline Stern, Christine Venezia, Anna Spinner, Jessica Fertinel, Tania Velimirovici, Liz Strauss, Alexis Moore, Andy Chae, Esther Schwartz, Keely Henderson, Carmen Ng, Shi Yee Lee, David Park, Nancy Chung, Camilo Galvis, Nadir Elbied, Ali Sadighian, Attakrit Asvanunt, Cyril Shmatov, Irene Song, and Vadim Krisyan.

I also want to thank my many colleagues and friends from across the world of digital education who agreed to be part of this book and provided our team with interviews, demos, advice, and suggestions.

Many of you have also been kind enough to join us here at Columbia as part of our Provost Conversations on Online Learning talk series. Others have been kind enough to receive us at their institutions or joined us remotely as part of this research project.

All have been incredibly generous with their time. These include my colleagues from partner universities: Nora Lewis, Jacqueline Candido, Angelina Conti, and Zach Humenik from UPenn; Paul Krause and Sally Berkowitz from eCornell; Catherine Zabriskie of Brown University; Joshua Kim and Sarah Cloud from Dartmouth; Matthew Rascoff of Stanford; Caroline Levander of Rice University; James DeVaney, and Lauren Budde, Ben Hayward, and Jeremy Nelson of the University of Michigan; Rovy Branon of the University of Washington; Gary Matkin, Camille Funk, and Kris Velasquez of the University of California Irvine; Eric Bullard of UCLA; Frederick Wehrle and Armando Fox of the University of California Berkeley; Frank Dooley and Chantel Levesque-Bristol from Purdue Global; Nelson Baker, John Bailey, Troy Courville, Christie Hayes, and Theo McNair of Georgia Tech; Jonathan Becker of the Open Society University Network; and Michael Crow, Sukhwant Jhaj, Philip Regier, and Justin Harding of Arizona State University.

This book also benefited hugely from interviews with many of the leaders of the private companies in the EdTech, OPM, and MOOC sectors, who have been partners in much of the innovation discussed here. I would also like to thank the many CEOs and senior leaders for taking the time to meet with us and share their insights. These include Anant Agarwal, founder and CEO of edX; Daphne Koller, founder of Coursera; Betty Vandenbosch, Chief Content Officer of Coursera; John Baker, CEO of D2L; Ashwin Damera, CEO of Emeritus; Dan Avida, CEO of Engagli; Furqan Nazeeri, CEO of Extension Engine; Ben Nelson, CEO of Minerva; Eric Burns, CEO of Panopto; Andrew Hermalyn, Luyen Chou, and Josh Scott of 2U; Todd Zipper, Bill Cochran, and David Migliorese of Wiley Educational Services; and Dhawal Shah, CEO of Class Central.

I want to also thank those friends from the world of philanthropy and development who generously met with us and shared their important perspectives: Jamie Merisotis, CEO of the Lumina

Foundation; Michael Trucano of the World Bank; and Jamison Ervin of the United Nations Development Programme. Finally, we were honored to speak with the leaders of national digital education programs of India and Israel, and I thank Chairman Anil D. Shasrabudhe, director of India's impressive SWAYAM program and Eran Raviv of Campus-IL in Israel.

Finally, I would like to thank my late father and my mother who have been a great inspiration for me, as well as my two sisters and brothers-in-law, and niece and nephews. I am indebted to my wife Houda and our two wonderful children Ryan and Sarah for their love and support.

ADAM STEPAN

First and foremost I thank my coauthors Bill Eimicke and Soulaymane Kachani, who are friends as well as colleagues. Working on this project with you has been one of the most rewarding experiences of my life. Bill and Soulaymane are rare leaders who combine great insight into the nuance of complex issues with the ability to decide on and enact practical solutions. It has been fantastic to work together on many projects in the last ten years, and it has been a special treat to work together on this project, documenting our own hits and misses and learning from such a fantastic group of colleagues around the globe.

I also thank the more than fifty digital education leaders Soulaymane and Bill have listed who agreed to do interviews and demos for the project. The months Spent in Zoom calls and discussions with them were some of the most rewarding moments of my professional life. It was fantastic to meet so many brilliant and dedicated people working on similar problems in different places. Thanks to you all for your time and patience and for challenging us to think more widely about how these tools can be used for the better good and how to overcome the many challenges that remain.

I would like to thank my fantastic colleagues, both at Columbia's School of International and Public Affairs (SIPA) and across other

Columbia schools. These include professors and colleagues at SIPA, Glenn Denning, Andre Correa D'Almeida, Yumi Shimabukuro, Joann Baney, Suzanne Hollman, and Anya Schiffrin. I want especially to thank my colleagues at the Picker Center for Executive Education: Arvid Laukauskas, Valerie Zimmer, Jeremy Ceballo, Cecilia Barcellos-Raible, Monica Wiles, and Bismark Diaz, and my Picker Center Digital Education Group colleague Bernhard Fasenfest. A noted documentary film editor and programmer, Bernhard combines deep technical know-how with a commitment to the people on our team and the students who will use the courses and learning assets. Many of the innovations documented in this book, including creation of the Canvas Coursebuilder, and many key elements of our digital case method are Bernhard's creations.

I also express a special thank-you to Sandesh Tuladhar, Columbia's Associate Provost for Online Education. Sandesh and I have been colleagues and friends since 2013 when I first came to Columbia. He has been integral to this book project and has had a huge role in the success of many of the projects described here. I also thank my friends and colleagues at Columbia's Center for Teaching and Learning; they have been central partners in our work and in the creation of the Blended Learning Toolkit and Digital Case Method MOOCs. Thanks especially to Maurice Matiz, Amanda Irvin, and Mark Phillipson for their help on these projects.

I would also like to thank the fantastic team of video makers, writers, graphic designers, and programmers with whom I have worked. These include cinematographers Adam Morrell and Brian Miller, graphic designer Siah Singh, and producer Chris Andersen of Nevessa Production. I include a special thanks to case writer and author Charlie Euchner, who helped research and copyedit key elements of this book and who has written many fantastic case studies and video scripts for our center over the years.

I also thank my colleagues at the many partner institutions where I have had the honor of working, including those at the Open Society University Network (OSUN) and the National School of Public Administration (ENAP) in Brazil. Visiting with you in New York, Annandale, Germany, Bangladesh, and Brazil, and the many other locations where we have worked has been special. I would like to thank especially Jonathan Becker, OSUN Vice Chancellor, for your leadership and support. Creating and launching OSUN was one of the most challenging and successful endeavors in which I have participated. Thank you for letting us have a front-row seat in this adventure and for embracing new ways to put OSUN's students in contact with each other and the world. I would also like to thank my OSUN colleagues for their many fantastic contributions both to this book and to digital learning innovation more widely: Daniel Calingaert, Erica Kaufman, Philip Fedchin, David Shein, Roger Berkowitz, Ramona Mosse, Michelle Murray, Bonnie Goad, Seamus Heady, and Anita Tarnai. At ENAP in Brazil, I would like to thank our colleagues Bruna Santos and Diogo Godinho Ramos Costa.

At all of these institutions, I have had the special honor of working with young student filmmakers, many of whom have gone on to exciting careers in digital education. A special thanks to those who worked multiple years with the Picker Center helping to create great cases and many of the innovations shared here. I would like especially to thank those who were instrumental in our team's early development and growth: Ruby Lee Simon, Nora Johnson, Constance Nuttall, Julie Tumasz, Daniel Aho, Elijah Zulu, Sean Steinberg, and Marino Bubba, who helped compile much of the data in this book.

Three people who deserve special thanks in this project are Tom Trebat, Director of Columbia's Global Center in Rio, Luiz Valente, a friend and mentor from Brown, and Peter Kingstone, my thesis advisor at Kings College in London. All were instrumental in the intellectual and professional journey that has led to this book.

I would also like to thank my parents and extended family. My late father Alfred Stepan was one of the most inspiring people anyone could know. He was a scholar who always kept real-world impacts and people front and center. Our many conversations on the differences and overlaps between the worlds of academia and journalism and media sowed the seeds for many of the themes that have driven my work and this book. My mother, Professor Nancy Leys Stepan, is also a huge inspiration. A renowned scholar and author, her life-long appetite for knowledge and learning have sparked action in thousands of students and readers, not to mention her two children and seven beloved grandchildren! My sister Tanya has been the best sister anyone could imagine. A noted poet and mother of five amazing children, she has always had the time and energy to help keep us all on track.

Finally, I would like to thank my wife Raquel and my daughters Elle and Heloisa. Elle and Heloisa were high school students during the writing of this book (now at college!) and gave me a window into how things appeared from a young student's perspective. They also have often served as the "quality control committee," evaluating and rating (generally poorly!) our efforts at making engaging websites and classes. Thank you!

My wife Raquel is my muse and partner, who continues to inspire me every day. She has always believed in this book and in me, and helps me remember what is really important.

We all express our appreciation for the team at Columbia University Press, especially Brian Smith and Myles Thompson for their wisdom and support. And we are deeply grateful to senior leaders at Columbia University who have guided and supported our efforts to enhance teaching, learning, and educational innovation at Columbia and beyond.

APPENDIX

INTERVIEWS AND DEMOS CONDUCTED

(Note: All positions and titles listed are those held at time of interview.)

Arizona State University

Michael Crow, President

Sukhwant Jhaj, Vice Provost for Academic Innovation and Student Achievement

Philip Regier, CEO and Dean for Special Initiatives, EdPlus

Justin Harding, Senior Director for Instructional Design and New Media, EdPlus

Bard College

Jonathan Becker, Executive Vice President and Vice President for Academic Affairs, Vice Chancellor OSUN

Erica Kaufman, Director of the Institute for Writing and Thinking

Michelle Murray, Professor of Political Science

David Shein, Associate Vice President for Academic Affairs and Dean of Studies

Brown University

Catherine Zabriskie, Senior Director of Digital Learning and Design

Campus-IL Israel

Eran Raviv, Director

Class Central

Dhawal Shah, founder and CEO

Columbia University

Glenn Denning, Professor of Professional Practice in International and Public Affairs and Director of the Master of Public Administration in Development Practice

Jason Healey, Senior Research Scholar in the Faculty of International and Public Affairs and Adjunct Professor of International Affairs

Yumi Shimabukuro, Professor of International Affairs at Columbia's School of International and Public Affairs

Cornell University

Paul Krause, Vice Provost of External Education and Executive Director of eCornell

Sally Berkowitz, Senior Director of Product Development

Coursera

Daphne Koller, cofounder of Coursera
Betty Vandenbosch, Chief Content Officer

Dartmouth College

Joshua Kim, Director of Online Programs and Strategy
Sarah Cloud, Assistant Director for Online Learning and Innovation

D2L

John Baker, CEO

edX

Anant Agarwal, CEO
Nina Huntemann, Vice President of Learning

Emeritus

Ashwin Damera, CEO
Lisa Brem, Director for Short Form Certificate Programs
Lars Mackenzie, Senior Design Manager
Karen Mahon, Director for Long Form Programs on U.S. Design Team

Engageli

Dan Avida, CEO
Adam Spivak, Leader of Partnerships

Extension Engine

Furqan Nazeeri, CEO

Forth Rev

Mark Lester, Chief Partnerships Officer

Georgia Institute of Technology

Nelson Baker, Dean of Professional Education and Professor of Civil and
Environmental Engineering
John Bailey, Instructional Online Media Manager
Troy Courville, Director of Learning Design Analytics
Christie Hayes, Manager of Instructional Design
Theo McNair, Leading Producer of Instructional Design

Lumina Foundation

Jamie Merisotis, CEO

Minerva Project

Ben Nelson, CEO and founder
Sharan Singh, Senior Managing Director of Strategic Partnerships

Panopto

Eric Burns, CEO

Purdue

Frank Dooley, Chancellor of Purdue Global
Chantal Levesque-Bristol, Executive Director of the Center for
    Instructional Excellence at Purdue Impact

Rice University

Caroline Levander, Vice President of Global and Digital Strategy

Stanford University

Matthew Rascoff, Vice Provost for Digital Education

SWAYAM

Anil D. Sahasrabudhe, Chairman and Professor
Buddha Chandrasekhar, Chief Coordinating Officer

2U

Andrew Hermalyn, President of Partnerships
Josh Scott, Director of Course Strategy
Luyen Chou, Chief Learning Officer

United Nations Development Programme

Jamison Ervin, Manager of the Nature for Development Global Program

University of California, Berkeley

Armando Fox, Associate Dean for Online Education
Frederick T. Wehrle, Assistant Dean for Academic Design and Innovation
at UC Berkeley Extension

University of California, Irvine

Gary Matkin, Dean of Continuing Education and Vice Provost for Career
Pathways
Camille Funk, Director of Learning Innovation and Instructional Design
Kris Velasquez, Assistant Director of Media

University of California, Los Angeles

Eric Bullard, Dean of Continuing Education and UCLA Extension

University of Michigan

James DeVaney, Associate Vice Provost for Academic Innovation and
Founding Executive Director of the Center for Academic Innovation
Lauren Atkins Budde, Director of Open Learning Initiatives at the Center
for Academic Innovation
Ben Hayward, Director for Educational Technology at the Center for
Academic Innovation
Jeremy Nelson, Director of the Extended Reality Initiative at the Center
for Academic Innovation

University of Pennsylvania

Nora Lewis, Vice Dean for Professional and Liberal Education at the
School of Arts and Sciences
Jacqueline P. Candido, Senior Director of Online Learning and Program
Design
Angelina Conti, Director of Digital Learning
Al Filreis, Kelly Family Professor of English and Director, Center for
Programs in Contemporary Writing
Zachary Humenik, Associate Director for the Online Learning Studio

University of Washington

Rovy Branon, Vice Provost for Continuum College

Wiley Education Services

Todd Zipper, President
Bill Cochran, Associate Director of Instructional Media
David Migliorese, Vice President of Academic Services

World Bank

Michael Trucano, Senior Education and Technology Policy Specialist

INDEX

Page numbers in *italics* indicate figures or tables.